In the
Great Green Room

In the
Great Green Room

The Brilliant and Bold Life of
Margaret Wise Brown

Amy Gary

FLATIRON
BOOKS
NEW YORK

www.flatironbooks.com

Designed by Kathryn Parise

THE LIBRARY OF CONGRESS CATALOGING-IN-PUBLICATION DATA
IS AVAILABLE UPON REQUEST.

ISBN 978-1-250-06536-0 (hardcover)
ISBN 978-1-250-06537-7 (e-book)

Our books may be purchased in bulk for promotional, educational, or business use.
Please contact your local bookseller or the Macmillan Corporate and Premium Sales
Department at 1-800-221-7945, extension 5442, or by e-mail at
MacmillanSpecialMarkets@macmillan.com.

First Edition: January 2017

10 9 8 7 6 5 4 3 2 1

For Nap,

with gratitude for a life of love and laughter

Contents

Foreword

by James Stillman Rockefeller Jr.

I met Margaret on Cumberland Island, Georgia. This magical place, a step back in time, belonged to my mother's family and is now a national park. The year was 1952. Margaret was there as a guest of my cousin, and I was there outfitting my boat, an old Friendship sloop, prior to setting out for the South Pacific.

Our eyes first met in my Kentucky cousins' 1892 mansion with four towering Corinthian columns that rose from a broad lawn studded with giant live oaks. Tall cedars lined the curving oyster-shell road leading to the front steps that ascended to a *Gone with the Wind* porch and a huge front door framed with bronze sconces.

In a room smelling of gun oil and bourbon, she stood next to the gun rack. She looked at me from under her straw-colored hair, with blue-gray eyes that studied me, went through me, while absorbing everything in sight. I knew instantly this was a turning point in my young life. We moved toward each other, the rest of the room faded, and the next morning, shortly after dawn, we were walking on the high dunes overlooking the beach, hand in hand.

With the sunrise, she told how she wrote children's books. Seventy-two to date. The latest was called *The Noon Balloon*. And she told how the Queen Mother of England kept *Little Fur Family* by her bedside. The image of such a regal person keeping something so small and fuzzy so close amused Margaret.

She contemplated the rolling surf and said, "I hope to write something serious one day as soon as I have something to say. But I am stuck in my childhood, and that raises the devil when one wants to move on."

In the days to come, I saw how she walked in her own sunrise and sunset, cloaked in the mists of her art that hid the petty daily doings from sight until she was forced to face them. I remember her saying, "Evening is like morning to me—full of change and renewal and excitement. My low time is from eleven to lunch. At noon, the light is all glaring and blatant, and some of the magic seems gone from the day."

She left Cumberland for her publishing world all too soon. We wrote each other most every day. I told her about Diana, the pet deer, who hung around the house with her offspring. She was in the process of writing a book for Osa Johnson about Osa's African adventures. She wrote back, "The first time I ever held a baby lion cub in my arms it was just like a living toy or a child, a dream come true. And that warm clean smell of that little armful of something I couldn't believe was real, and the tenderness of that small great beast will always fill me with wonder. Love, Tim." Margaret had many nicknames: Tim, the Bunny, and the Bunny-no-good. I called her my bunny, and she called me her warlock, as I looked so fierce in my dark beard.

When she returned to Cumberland for her second visit, I

worked on the boat, while she explored the island with all its wildlife. She soon had stories about all of them. Listening to her, one wasn't sure whether people acted like animals or animals like people. Mr. and Mrs. Toad would come out every evening as we sat sipping wine on the steps of my grandfather's house. She asked them what they did in their spare time and if they didn't get tired sleeping on their tummies, especially if they were full of juicy bugs. I wondered how many books would come out of Cumberland.

A day before she left, we sat in the cupola of the original family mansion, now long deserted. Looking out over the marsh, thinking about the month we had just spent together growing ever closer, it was impossible to foresee a life without her. It was then she said, as much to herself as me, "You can never in this world love anyone you love enough."

We talked of a future together, how I would sail the boat to Panama and she would go to Europe and then meet me in Panama. We would get married, sail the Pacific, and move on to further horizons.

After Cumberland that summer, we spent idyllic days at the Only House, her Maine island paradise. She called it the Only House because "you could see no other light at night." The Gothic little building with its steeply pitched roof and weathered clapboards nestles in a tiny meadow of wildflowers. At the front of the house, a granite wharf juts into the small bay with its little islands, while at the back, a spruce forest forms a curtain to hold the outside world at bay. The only access is by water.

Margaret had written to me about the place. "The song sparrow is singing and a clowning gull is trying to crow like a rooster, cluck like a hen and laugh like a gentle maniac, all at the same time. The house is a boat. Only the weathers and the fog and the times of day and night sail by the house instead of the house sailing away."

During those halcyon days spent with her there, she showed me the fairy ballroom, a weathered rock clearing high above Hurricane Sound, where the little people danced at midnight. Then there was the magic mouse and his house down a hole beside the path. Of an evening, we would stand in the ballroom and watch the dusk enfold the sound. Often those eyes of hers would go far away where none but she could go. One evening, she turned suddenly and said, "We are born alone. We go through life alone. And we go out alone."

I will never forget that moment, painful as the words were. She saw herself in a frame where human beings were but one component of a larger whole. To me, walking in the pastures of her imagination was like strolling through an enchanted forest. I saw her as an island in a limitless sea, radiating light farther than any lighthouse.

It has been sixty years since those days, but over a half century later, her light is burning ever brighter.

A Note from the Author

For over twenty-five years, I've tried to live inside the wildly imaginative mind of Margaret Wise Brown. In 1990, I co-owned a small publishing company, and we worked with Margaret's sister, Roberta, to reprint four of Margaret's out-of-print and mostly forgotten books. Children's publishing was again on the rise, and librarians still treasured Margaret's works. We hoped to bring many more of her titles back to market, so one afternoon I found myself sitting on the floor of Roberta's house in Jamaica, Vermont, looking through the bookshelf that was filled with Margaret's books.

I had become friends with Roberta over the years as we worked together. We both had horses and collie dogs; we both had strong ties to Hollins University. Margaret graduated from that school, as did her mother. Almost all the women in my husband's family were Hollins alumnae—in fact, his great-grandmother had attended Hollins at the same time as Margaret and Roberta's mother.

Riffling through that shelf of books that day in Vermont, it suddenly struck me that I should ask Roberta if Margaret had left behind any unpublished manuscripts. Margaret had been prolific, and she died very suddenly. That meant there was a strong possibility that quite a few manuscripts had been left unpublished or unfinished. I hesitated before asking because Margaret is considered one of the foremost writers of children's literature; educational programs at universities study her writing techniques. *Goodnight Moon* is a perennial bestseller, and many of the books she wrote for Golden still hold spots on their spinner racks in bookstores, drugstores, and department stores around the world. I figured that if Margaret had left a manuscript behind, surely another publisher would have discovered it long before I.

I was surprised by Roberta's answer that yes, Margaret had been working on a large collection of poetry when she died. She'd called it *The Green Wind*. Unfortunately, that manuscript was in storage in the attic of Roberta's barn; she would have to get the neighbor boy to bring down the heavy trunk.

Almost six months passed before Roberta called to invite me to come look at the manuscript. I arrived on a cold winter's day in January, driving along snowy roads to get to her lovely farm at the base of the Green Mountains. When I walked in, Roberta was filling out sweepstakes coupons, the sort that had Ed McMahon as their spokesperson. I felt sorry for this divorced woman who lived alone in the woods of Vermont, hoping for a financial bonanza to arrive at her door.

Roberta opened the trunk. Inside were thin papers stacked end to end. She pointed to one end and said that *The Green Wind* manuscript was there. All the other papers in the trunk were unpublished, too. At first, I didn't believe her. There were hundreds of papers in that trunk! Songs, music scores, stories, and poems. I thought surely I had misunderstood, or maybe Roberta was mistaken. It seemed unlikely that even someone as prolific as Margaret could have left behind all these manuscripts.

I took a stack of the papers back to my hotel that night. Their musty smell was too much to bear in the small room, so I opened a window to let the frigid Vermont air in as I read over each of the works. I didn't recognize a single one of them.

Now that these gems had been uncovered, I was terrified they might disappear. I spent the next three days copying every piece of paper in that trunk, making a circuit between Roberta's house, the bank to get quarters, and the local library, where the only copying machine in town was located.

The trunk held manuscripts and ideas for books that were years ahead of their time. Books with flaps and die cuts. Books that emerged from balls and toy barns. Stories written for the backs of cereal boxes. And songs, lots of songs. I hadn't known Margaret loved music and was hoping to write popular songs that made it onto jukeboxes.

From that day to this, I have spent the better portion of my career working with Margaret's papers, and it is a pleasure to work in her rarefied air. I have studied her contracts, read her diaries and letters, talked with her friends and loved ones. She gave me an education on how to work with illustrators and how to negotiate a contract. More important, she showed me how to live with awe and to love with abandon. For that, I am especially grateful.

Prologue
1950

First cry
Of the first hound.
And then other cries
Till it's all one cry
Across the fields.
First spring
I have ankles and hinged feet.
An old body
Rises up in the new
And leans forward into the wind.

"RUNNING TO HOUNDS"
White Freesias

On a crisp, cold morning in January of 1950, a crowd of almost seventy people, clad in tweeds and corduroys, knee-
high boots, and warm jackets, gathered at the stables of the large
estate on the north shore of Long Island waiting for the call from
the hunt master. The day's hunt was to be a course of more than
ten miles extending across neighboring estates. The direction of the

expedition would ultimately be determined by the hounds' chase of the hares. The rain from the previous evening had softened the ground, making for steadier downhill running for the hunters. On hard ground, it was easy to slip. The rains also removed all traces of lingering snow, which held the scent of hares long gone.

Some of the beagling clubs had resorted to hunting cottontails instead of the imported jacks as these hunts grew less and less successful. Sprawling country estates were being divided by creeping suburbanization. An Austrian jackrabbit was spotted the day before almost a mile northwest, so the field would travel in that direction.

The hunt master readied his horn and blew for the hunt to begin. The crowd followed the hounds at a rapid clip across the road and onto a newly plowed field. The beagles were of the shorter variety, only fourteen inches at their withers, so runners could keep up. They ran far behind the dogs to avoid contaminating the trail. They picked their way around bushes, fences, and thick forests, hoping to be the first to the site of the kill and earn the trophy from that day's hunt—a coveted mask or pad of the rabbit. The group followed the dogs over a hill and into a valley.

Margaret Wise Brown drove up in her yellow convertible after the field had crested the horizon. She liked to arrive late and knew she would have no trouble catching up to the group. This one day of the week away from the city and her busy life of telephone calls and deadlines was her favorite time. She might walk alone, or run behind the group in silence. Most of the time, though, she found herself chatting effortlessly for six or seven miles with someone who owned a stable of Thoroughbred racehorses—or the person who mucked the stalls of those same horses. A shared desire to run with the hounds was the common bond.

She parked her car near the kennel and walked down the road. A man near a barn pointed, and she took off running in that direction. She soon heard the crooning release of the hounds as they spotted a hare and the cry of "Tallyho!" to her right. They were beyond the woods, past a furrowed field. She adjusted her course to intersect with the dogs, leaping over the small, even rises of dark dirt that were littered with frozen pink and white turnips too small to harvest. She liked the popping sound they made under her sneakers and timed her pace to land on the little bulbs as she made her way to the trees.

Her stamina and agility often placed her at the front of the throng. She was known to plunge fearlessly through a thicket rather than around it, as most of the hunters opted to do. Those scratchy shortcuts won her more than a few rabbits' feet. As she approached the woods, she realized she would have to skirt this patch of trees. Horse brier vines covered the ground, and even she was no match for their fierce stickers. She passed the woods and looked for a path in the valley beyond. A trail would eventually appear, she was sure. It always did.

She ran lightly, pulling herself up by her shoulders as she sprinted through the green and red grasses of the valley. The past few months had taken a toll on her body and spirit. She desperately wanted to lose the twenty pounds she had gained since her lover had left her. Most evenings, wine seemed a better remedy for her loneliness than exercise.

Running in these fields, though, Margaret once again felt young. She had grown up here, and she had spent many afternoons of her youth riding her horse through these same pastures. She had swum in the nearby ocean and built houses of sticks and leaves in these forests.

She saw a trail of trampled grass and broken sticks and instantly knew it was a path the dogs had made. She followed it up the hill and on the next rise saw one of the whips coaxing a dog back on course with the snap of his whip while at a full run, something she had yet to conquer. She caught up to him as the pack circled a dead hare in the grass. The dogs were particularly excited; they hadn't hunted for a few days, and it would be hard to pull them back. The master called the dogs down and then reached in to grasp the body of the bunny. He held it high above his head, an indication to the dogs that this prize was no longer theirs. The pack reluctantly obeyed.

It was clear this rabbit was dead before the dogs had found it, shot by a frustrated farmer, no doubt. As the rest of the runners drew close, two gunshots were fired in the distance. Margaret quipped that two more rabbits had just been killed, which drew a round of chuckles from the field. In reality, she always felt sorry for the death of the rabbit, especially if it were one that had escaped before.

Suddenly, there was a stir among the hounds. Then they went still. Their quickening sniffs meant another hare was close by. The master shouted to the field to hold hard, and all the hunters froze, allowing the dogs to pick up the new scent. The dogs flushed a hare from a patch of grass, and once again the hunt was on. The jack bounded across the field, then darted sideways. Margaret knew the poor bunnies often circled back in desperation. Sometimes this tactic worked, but if the rabbit ran straight, the hounds could seldom keep pace. Sooner or later, though, it would run for home or cover, and the attempted escape often sent the bunny straight into people or hounds instead of an open field.

This one, though, burst onto a grassy road and sped away from the dogs and humans. He held his ears high and straight as he bounced out of sight. That, Margaret thought, was a beautiful thing to see.

One

1910–1914

> *Once upon a summertime*
> *A bug was crawling on a vine*
> *A butterfly lit on a daisy*
> *While a little bee*
> *Buzzed himself crazy in a wild pink rose*
> *And a child ran through the wet green grass*
> *In his bare feet and wiggled his toes*
>
> *"ONCE UPON A SUMMERTIME"*
> *The Unpublished Works of Margaret Wise Brown*

The moon and sky over Brooklyn, New York, was bathed in the golden hue of an aurora borealis in the early morning hours of May 23. Sheet lightning to the south and east illuminated the shifting rays in a staccato dance of light. As the rising sun diminished the auroral lights, panic rose in the house of Bruce and Maude Brown. The baby they had been expecting more than two weeks earlier was now arriving in a rush. But the doctor was nowhere to be found.

Bruce was seriously ill with malaria contracted on a recent business trip and could be of little help. His nurse and Maude's mother prepared, as best they could, to deliver the baby. Anna, their stern Irish nanny, paced the downstairs entry with the Brown's two-year-old son, Gratz, waiting for the doctor to arrive. Maude's screams in the final throes of labor were heard throughout the house and out the open door as the doctor dashed in. He bounded up the stairs, rolling his shirtsleeves as he climbed, reaching the bedside just in time to deliver the baby girl. He held her up for her mother to see, his cuff links still dangling from his sleeves.

That night, the sky was again ablaze with gold, green, and blue of the borealis that illuminated another celestial phenomenon. The earth's shadow slowly stole the light of the full moon in a total lunar eclipse. It seemed as if the heavens were putting on a show to welcome the little girl Maude named Margaret Wise Brown.

Four years later, Maude Brown pressed Bruce for them to move from Brooklyn to Long Island. She found the walls of their neighborhood claustrophobic and believed the abundant nature Long Island offered would be good for their children. Bruce was reluctant to leave their formidable home on a hill. From there he could see the East River, and their house was a short walk to the docks and American Manufacturing Company's warehouse, where he worked.

It was his job to travel to distant lands to purchase hemp and jute that were loaded onto massive cargo ships like the ones that streamed up and down the East River. Day and night, tiny tugs twirled about in the river, leading those large boats into port or out to sea. The whistles of the ships often drifted up the hill to the open windows of the Browns' home. Transients from the docks, too, sometimes wandered into their neighborhood. The brick walls and wrought iron fences that lined the yards and streets silently declared that those people weren't welcome. Even the cathedral at the end of their road appeared hostile instead of hospitable. Its imposing red doors cast a fortresslike air over the neighborhood.

The day Margaret and Gratz came home with a stranger, Bruce changed his mind about moving. The children were playing in their neighborhood park when they saw the man lying on the grass, looking up at the sky. They asked him what he was doing. He said that the sky's shade of deep blue reminded him of his beloved homeland, Ireland. They delightedly told him that they, too, were Irish, so he shared captivating tales of the land he had left behind. The children invited him home for lunch, certain that their parents, who were quite proud of their Irish heritage, would want to meet this fellow countryman. Maude was gracious to the obviously impoverished man who sheepishly joined them at the table. Margaret and Gratz were not chastised for bringing the stranger home, but it wasn't long before the Browns bought a sprawling home in Beechhurst on Long Island.

On the day of their move, Margaret sat in the back of the family's open-air car with her grandmother as her father drove out of Brooklyn toward their new home on Long Island. She was named after this grandmother, a jolly Welsh woman with a beautiful singing voice. Margaret adored her and her lovely, lilting accent that sounded like music. She was much kinder than Margaret's nanny, Anna, who dunked the little girl's head under cold water every time she held her breath until she turned blue or threw a temper tantrum. Anna's treatment had no lasting effect on Margaret's innate stubborn streak. She liked the feeling of cold water on her face.

As the Browns left Brooklyn, they drove past the skyscrapers of New York City. When the veil on her grandmother's hat billowed like a streamer behind their car, Margaret felt like they were in a parade. Once they reached Long Island, they rolled slowly past opulent mansions lining the coast and then rode inland toward fields and hills topped by towering trees. Bruce turned the car into the long dirt driveway of their new home. On either side of the car, tall green grass stretched out as far as Margaret could see. It looked like they were in the middle of a bright green ocean. When the car stopped in front of the newly built house, Margaret leaped from the car and ran straight into the meadow. The grass was higher than her head, and it felt like she were running through a wild green forest. It was the freest, happiest moment of her life.

Two
1917–1923

Cecily Cerisian powders her nose
For a powder puff uses a rose
Her nose gets yellow and off she goes
Up to a mirror she stands on her toes
And dusts it off where she can see
What kind of lady will Cecily be?

Pretty Poll has a little doll
Dresses it up in folderol
Makes it dresses to go to a Ball
And dresses for winter and summer and fall
By her patterns you can see
The kind of a lady Miss Polly will be.

Mary Madorn climbs in trees
Scratches her arms
And scratches her knees
Isn't afraid of dogs or bees
Swims in crashing cold green seas
It's a little hard at this time to see
What kind of lady brave Mary will be?

WHAT WILL THEY BE?
Unpublished

Seven-year-old Margaret and her younger sister, Roberta, sat in their child-size rocking chairs, facing the lit fireplace. The hearth was decorated with tiles depicting characters from nursery rhymes. In dark blue lines against white tiles were Little Boy Blue, Mother Goose, from "Hey Diddle, Diddle" the Cow Jumping over the Moon, and other nursery rhyme characters in dark blue lines. Their spacious room was painted a soothing robin's egg blue, and in the middle sat a large rocking horse, worn from years of loving attention. Margaret's very first memory was of stuffing long cotton strands into the horse's nostrils and around its neck to give it fluffy white reins. Currently, the horse's mane and tail were adorned with colorful ribbons the girls braided into its hair. On the far wall, a built-in bookcase was lined with dozens of books. Ornate scrolls and letters were stamped in gold onto most of the spines, including a set of books, bound in burgundy leather, called *The Book of Knowledge*. These childhood encyclopedias contained a vast array of information and were Margaret's favorite. She had a knack for memorization and was able to recite dozens of works from those pages. Every page was illustrated in color or with photographs and filled with fascinating facts, stories, poems, and songs. On Margaret's lap was a book of fairy tales from that collection. She read the story of Hansel and Gretel aloud to Roberta, who hadn't yet learned to read.

The little girls looked nothing like sisters. Margaret had long, golden waves of hair and Roberta a short mop of bright red strands. Margaret's delicate face, full lips, and bright gray-blue eyes were accentuated by her little sister's plain looks. It wasn't unusual for their mother to be stopped on the street by strangers who remarked on the fair-haired girl's remarkable beauty. They rarely noticed the little red-haired girl standing next to her dressed in identical clothes.

Roberta listened attentively as her sister read, although Margaret didn't relay the story verbatim. She added an extra character, as she often did during their story time. In Margaret's version, Hansel and Gretel had a little sister with red hair. The heroines in Margaret's twisted tales usually had blond hair and blue eyes. Just as often, something terrible befell the red-haired little sister. This time, she was gobbled up by the cannibalistic witch. Courageous Gretel, though, saved herself and her brother by outwitting the witch and shoving her into an oven. They took the witch's treasure and then returned home to live happily ever after with their father.

Gullible Roberta was eager to hear the story again, but Margaret snapped the book shut. She proclaimed it to be time to go to sleep and crawled into her bed. Her sister reluctantly followed. It was their ritual to say good night to their toys, rocking horse, chairs, books, and pictures on their walls. Margaret first, then Roberta. Before long, their door opened, and Anna whispered good night to the two little girls, then turned off their light.

A light snowfall swirled around nine-year-old Margaret and her father as they walked along the bustling port of the East River. Aromas of coffee, tar, and sea met them as they passed cargo being loaded into vast warehouses along the docks. They stepped into the largest building, the American Manufacturing Company, where the scent of hemp and jute permeated the air. Workers stood beside row after row of tables piled high with fibers they twisted into ropes and bags. Margaret followed her father past the tables and up the stairs into his office. It was common for the little girl to come here with her father when he wasn't traveling to a far-flung land. She preferred to be by his side whenever he was home.

In the office, she took her usual perch on a stool next to the window and looked out on the river. Below, squat tugboats moved slowly because layers of ice had formed in the river. Frozen white chunks bobbed and tumbled in the dark green water of the river. She loved the way each season changed the port's tempo, sights, and sounds. It seemed she had always known the language of the tugs' captains, spoken in blasts from their horns as they pushed and pulled enormous ships past each other on the waterway.

The Great War had ended that year. The unrest that enveloped the world over the last six years only increased Bruce's business, and the Brown family remained comfortably situated in their new home. Long Island suited Margaret far better than Brooklyn. She played in the woods and fields whenever possible, and their home was rural enough for the children to have dozens of pets, including rabbits, squirrels, dogs, and horses. When one of Margaret's pet rabbits died, she skinned it and proudly displayed the pelt to her family. Her father, who taught her how to hunt, fish, and sail, was no doubt amused by this antic, unlike her mother, who tried to counter the girl's roughness by enrolling her in ballet and refinement classes.

Margaret cared nothing for the typical society girl parlor niceties. She shared her father's love of the outdoors and adventure. When her father was home, he and Margaret spent weekends sailing, golfing, and fishing. Bruce was raised in a family that expected as much, if not more, from the daughters as the sons. There were many accomplished men in his family, but their success was attributed to their matriarch, Elizabeth Preston, the brains of the dynasty. It was the boast of each consecutive generation that every male in the line had a sister with greater intellect and stronger character. At a time when high society dictated a path for little girls that favored polite conversations and needlework, Bruce encouraged Margaret's athleticism and independence.

She stared out of her father's office window, and tears filled her eyes. Her father would board a ship docked on the other side of Manhattan later that day. Those boats were so large they often needed three or four tugs to escort them safely out to sea, and once there, they kept going, carrying people to far-off lands. Margaret was always eager to hear stories of her father's exotic travels, but she hated to see him leave. Every time he boarded a boat, she was convinced she would never see him again, so her tears soon turned to sobs. The father held his daughter in his arms and, as he dried her tears, told her she shouldn't worry about him, he would always return.

Margaret grew used to her father being away. She also grew used to solitude. For much of the year, her brother, Gratz, and most of the neighborhood children were away at boarding schools. On walks to and from school, she often stopped to watch the comings and goings of bugs, birds, and butterflies. Roberta had no patience for her sister's dawdling or cloud watching—another favorite pastime of Margaret's. Roberta preferred to be inside reading with their mother.

When summer came, Margaret's domineering personality, quick

wit, and endless imagination made her an unquestionable leader of the neighborhood band of children. She led daylong expeditions through the forests or fields and relished being able to outwit her companions. She once convinced them that she alone owned the woods. Anyone who wanted to enter had to pay her an entrance fee, which, not surprisingly, they paid.

In the summers when they went to visit their cousins in Virginia and Kentucky, it was common for the children to sleep on huge screened porches designed to capture cooling night breezes. It was routine for Margaret to be the center of attention on those nights. She stood on her cot, one in a long line crowded onto the porch, and crooned to her cousins. As they fell asleep, she told stories—some from memory, others from imagination. She could make up a story about almost anything they asked her to. She knew a great deal about a great many things and enjoyed spouting trivia on a variety of topics. If anyone doubted her, she told them she knew it to be so because she had read it in *The Book of Knowledge*.

Margaret's best friend, Jayne Thurston, had a father who was a famous magician. Playing at their house was always an adventure because he liked to test his latest illusions on the neighborhood children before performing in front of a paying public. It wasn't unusual for his crew to parade giraffes, monkeys, and elephants up and down the streets. Teatime there once included a fake cobra that slithered across the table and poured their tea, and the girls often dressed up in glitzy stage clothes in the warehouse where theatrical props were stored. Deadly pets also were kept there, including a lion. Margaret was astonished by its sheer size as he paced in his cage. She had seen a lion in the zoo, but this enormous beast was close enough to touch. Jayne's father also let them hold a lion cub, and that moment filled Margaret with awe. The warm tenderness and soft fur of the small beast was like holding a living toy.

One day, Margaret, Roberta, and Jayne found a dead bird at the edge of the forest, and it was Margaret who decided they should hold a funeral for the unfortunate creature. She dispatched Roberta to gather the other neighborhood children while she and Jayne headed to the Brown house to collect a Bible and shovel.

Margaret held the oversized Bible as she led the children back to the edge of the woods. None of them had ever been to a funeral, but Margaret instinctively knew what to do. They dug a small hole and then lined it with ferns from the woods. They wrapped the bird in leaves and placed it into the ground. Margaret read a passage from the Bible, and another child said a prayer. They sang a sad song, then covered the grave. On top, they placed flowers collected from the field, and Margaret spoke for the group. She promised they would return every day, bring new flowers, and always remember the poor little creature. And for a few days, they did, until the warm days of summer made them forget.

Three
1924–1927

Up in a cherry tree in the sun
The cherries ripened one by one.
Big red cherries, there they hung
And I ate them in the sun.
Some were yellow, some were red
And birds were singing round my head.
On their stems they hung
And I ate them one by one.
Spring was late, I couldn't wait.

"RED CHERRIES"
Mouse of My Heart

When Margaret turned fourteen, her father's work required that he move to India for two years. Maude would live with Bruce, and they would send their girls to Château Brillantmont, an exclusive boarding school in Lausanne, Switzerland, that catered to upper-class families from around the world. Placing Margaret and Roberta in Europe would make it easier for Maude to visit on school breaks and for the three of them to tour different countries over those two years.

Maude and her daughters bought matching hats for their passport photos and planned an excursion for the weeks preceding the start of school. They would shop and dine in Paris. In Italy, they would see museums in Florence and the Vatican in Rome. Their house was sold, and the possessions Margaret held so dear were placed into storage along with the family's furniture. It seemed a good trade-off for the adventures that lay ahead. Margaret wanted to see more of the world.

Her parents showed her a catalog from Brillantmont that featured photographs of smiling girls hiking the Alps and skiing on the nearby slopes. It promised trips to foreign cities and museums. Classes were taught solely in French, which thrilled Margaret. It was her best subject. Cooking classes in haute cuisine and pâtisserie baking were offered in a state-of-the-art kitchen.

This was supposed to have been a grand adventure. Within days, though, Margaret was miserable. She missed her parents and was unaccustomed to the discipline of the school. The adventures promised in the school's brochure were mostly for older girls. At fourteen and twelve years old, respectively, Margaret and Roberta were relegated to the section of the school for younger students. Almost every moment of their lives was chaperoned, regulated, and demanding. This suited the studious Roberta, but Margaret longed for her days of freedom on Long Island.

On daily walks along Lake Geneva, Margaret had to keep pace with the girl in front. Their teacher insisted they stay in a straight line. Like the other students at Brillantmont, Margaret wore a pleated plaid skirt and a white blouse accented by a small scarf. These outdoor trips should have been the bright spot in her day, but instead they felt like torture. On this outing, they walked from the main château-style hall of the school, past terraced gardens overflowing with flowers. Wild cherry trees burst into bloom on the hillside, and as they neared the water's edge, the calls of crew masters to their rowing teams broke the silence that enveloped the girls. Not once did the teacher stop and invite her students to take in the wonder around them. Rigid order was far more important. Margaret knew that if she lagged or stepped out of line, she would be forced to sit alone in the front hall after evening classes again. The swinging pendulum of the antique clock on the wall would be her only entertainment as its hands counted down her punishment with a constant ticktock.

Margaret joined the ski and field hockey teams in order to be outside as much as possible. She also found freedom in the library and music salon. Through books and records, she escaped the school's walls and embarked on adventures in stories and song. She read volume after volume in English and French and made a game of memorizing poems by singing them to her favorite tunes. She sat beside the phonograph, singing along to emotional French ballads in her thin, wavering voice. The passion of the songs moved her, especially one called "The Time of the Cherries," a ballad written during the Parisian Commune Revolution in 1871. It was a symbolic anthem to the blood spilled during the uprising, as well as to remorse for life unappreciated and nature's wonder unnoticed.

Margaret was fascinated by the story that inspired the song. It was dedicated to a young ambulance nurse shot during the rebellion. Her white uniform, stained with bright red blood, reminded the songwriter of the splashes of red cherry juice on the streets of

Paris. The season of the cherries, typically cherished and celebrated, had come and gone as barricades were built and battles fought. By the time the revolt was over, cherries had blossomed, ripened, and fallen to the ground.

Most likely the song touched Margaret so deeply because she keenly felt the loss of everything she cherished. She had taken her freedom on Long Island for granted. She missed roaming the fields, riding her horse, and playing in the woods. Most of all, she missed her home and family. Their life may not have been perfect; her mother was prone to depression and nagging; her father was away far too frequently. But Margaret missed the times that once seemed so ordinary—evenings around the piano when her mother felt well enough to play and sing, vacations on the coast of Maine, adventures in the woods, and cool mornings spent walking on the golf course with her dog beside her.

Those moments were gone. Now Margaret had to carefully measure the space between her feet and the heels of the shoes marching in front of her. Looking around at the lake or landscape distracted her, and she wanted to go to the library instead of sitting still in the hall and listening to that incessant clock.

By the time Maude came to retrieve the girls two years later, Roberta had closed the educational gap between herself and her older sister. Margaret read voraciously but had little interest in other studies. She now, however, harbored a secret desire to be a writer of great literature.

Bruce stayed on in India for another seven months while Maude oversaw the building of the family's new house in Great Neck on

Long Island. Margaret and Roberta attended a private school in the neighborhood until they were able to enter Dana Hall, a boarding school in Wellesley, Massachusetts, about fifteen miles from Boston. To Margaret, the close-knit community of the school felt like a second home. The twelve small cottages and the main building on its campus were bordered by fields of buttercups, timothy, and white violets. The courses, lectures, and assigned readings were challenging, but Margaret enjoyed learning new philosophies and discussing them with friends and teachers. She joined the equestrian team and a sorority and for the first time developed an intimate circle of friends. She grew close to her roommate, Katherine Carpenter, and they gave each other nicknames. Because Margaret's hair was the same color as the timothy grasses surrounding the school, she was called Tim. Katherine was dubbed Kitty.

Having spent the last two years studying abroad, Margaret had missed many of the rites of passage other girls at Dana Hall participated in, such as coming-out parties. Nevertheless, the effervescent Margaret made friends quickly and pledged a sorority. She was thrilled to have those girls as her sisters, but in order to belong, the strong-willed Margaret had to submit to the older members. Pledges were required to run errands for the seniors and to refer to themselves as "It." Margaret made their beds, delivered their packages, saved seats for them in chapel, and even tried to sew stripes onto the pants of one senior. She failed miserably at keeping the stripes straight, and after staying up all night trying to correct her handiwork, she was demoted to sewing buttons onto another girl's coat. Even though she was a failure with a needle, in May, a group of girls blindfolded Margaret and led her to a ceremony where she was welcomed to the sorority.

That same month, Margaret's mother and father met her in Boston for her birthday. At dinner, they gave her a brown leather diary with her name stamped on the front. On its pages she wove literary allusions, poetry, and quotes that inspired her.

To calm her racing mind or when she became overwhelmed by an experience, she took mental notes of her senses—what she was seeing, tasting, feeling. It seemed to slow time down and let her remember those moments clearly so she could record the details in her diary that night. Without fail, she noted a portion of her day and at the top of each page filled in the designated spaces for documenting the weather and the phase of the moon.

As her first year at Dana Hall was complete, Margaret returned to Long Island, but her stay there was brief. Her mother had been hospitalized with high blood pressure and depression after Margaret's birthday dinner in Boston. When the girls came home to Long Island for their summer break, Bruce decided it would be better for Maude's recuperation if he sent Margaret and Roberta to spend three weeks with his family in Kentucky. Although Margaret loved being back on Long Island, where she could swim in the ocean, ride her bike, or walk for miles on the golf course next to their new home, this trip was a welcome respite from the pressure cooker inside the house. After returning from India, Maude had joined the Theosophical Society and frequently attended lectures and séances. She had lost both her sister and father unexpectedly within a year of each other, and this religion strongly appealed to Maude in her grief. Despite her newfound faith, Maude's bouts of depression had become more severe. She frequently shut herself away in her room for days, shouting commands to her husband and children from the doorway of her room. She demanded that they drop whatever they were doing and immediately attend to her often petty needs. She complained about her husband and constantly corrected her children. This angered Bruce and exhausted Margaret. Rather than divorce Maude, Bruce bought a large boat and docked it nearby. If he needed to escape their circular quarrels, he stayed on board his boat.

Bruce's family knew his marriage was troubled and wanted to make certain his girls enjoyed their time in Kentucky. When Margaret and Roberta arrived at the train station, the conductor knew who they were and who they were coming to visit. This amused Margaret. She loved the friendly people and slower pace of life in the South.

For seventeen-year-old Margaret, the trip was a dream come true. Her Kentucky relatives were adventurous, well connected in local society, and part of the Thoroughbred horse racing community. To entertain the Brown girls, they planned a variety of activities, including luncheons, horseback riding, swimming, aquaplaning, and sailing. Every day was a new adventure. At night, they sang around bonfires, stargazed, and made wishes on the unseen new moon, then talked together on the sleeping porch until the early morning hours.

One relative took her up in his open-cockpit plane. When she put her hands in the air, the wind was so strong she thought her arms might blow away. When her aunt took them on a tour of the stables, Margaret got to pet the legendary racehorse Man o' War. At an uncle's house, she fell asleep with her legs dangling out an open window. The sounds of sheep lowing in his misty, moonlit fields was sweet summer music.

Margaret and Roberta spent most of their time with their cousin Dr. Marius Johnston and his family at Montrose, their farm near Lexington. Dr. Johnston was a kind, respected physician and was married to Nancy Carnegie, a daughter of the steel magnate Thomas Carnegie. They had one son together, Junior, and Nancy had four children from her previous marriage—Coley, Retta, Lucy, and Morrie—whom Marius adopted.

On the night of Margaret and Roberta's arrival, the Johnstons took the girls to a dance at their country club. Margaret had never met so many boys. Her all-girls schools kept boys at bay. In Kentucky, young men buzzed around the blond beauty with the quick wit and smile. Her dance card was filled right away, and she accepted three dates for the following week. She danced until midnight and then played parlor games until dawn at the Johnstons'. She went to bed as the morning sky turned a pale green and birds began to sing. It was the first time she had ever felt popular, and she pressed the corsage she wore on the night of that first dance into her diary to keep the memory alive.

The Johnstons took the girls to visit other relatives at Liberty Hall, the home her great-great-grandfather built. There Margaret heard stories about their ancestors whose portraits surrounded the room. She recognized many of those faces. Similar paintings hung in the guest room of her family's house, where she was always relocated when sick. Their stoic visages and unsympathetic stares would bear down on her as she recovered from colds, influenzas, measles, and a broken leg. Three members of their family had been vice presidential candidates. Her redheaded grandfather, Benjamin Gratz Brown, who was known as the Kentucky Cardinal, had led the fight against the expansion of slavery into Missouri. John Brown, the man who had built the Kentucky house where Margaret was staying, had served in the Continental Congress with his good friend Thomas Jefferson. Monticello was undergoing a renovation around the same time, and Jefferson had given construction advice to Brown. Years later, Brown's beautiful widow was visited by Marquis de Lafayette, and it was reported that Lafayette had held the widow's hand for far longer than was appropriate. The teacup Lafayette had used stood on display in the china cabinet next to the table, which Margaret eyed with wonder during supper.

Margaret's relatives shared story after story, and before her first dinner at Liberty Hall was complete, she had come to see those faces on the wall differently. Margaret felt a surge of pride that she was part of this interesting and courageous family. Other hilarious stories about their father growing up flowed from her aunts and uncles as they retired from the dining room to the breezy porch.

Margaret was about to go to bed when she heard the story of the ghost, the Gray Lady, who was said to have haunted this house and its grounds for more than a hundred years. Margaret was immediately intrigued and desperate to see the ghost, but was too afraid to search for it alone. She convinced her cousins and reluctant sister to follow her to the most logical place she could think to look—the bedroom where the Gray Lady had died. It was in that room where the ghost was first seen by Margaret's grandmother on her wedding day.

Margaret crept up the stairs toward the room. Her sister and cousins were behind her as she climbed the creaky stairs. As Margaret arrived at the bedroom door, she turned around to find that she was alone. The others were watching from a safe distance on the landing below and motioned her to go in. She would have to do this by herself. She paused to gather her courage, then turned the door-knob and pushed. It didn't budge. Relief that the door was locked flooded through her. She ran back down the stairs, and the giggling group stumbled to the porch and out into the moonlit garden.

Kitty, Margaret's roommate from Dana Hall, also lived nearby. She held a dinner for the Brown girls and the Johnston children, then they all went to see the famous John Barrymore in the movie *The Beloved Rogue*. Afterward, they danced for hours at the country club. Morrie was immediately smitten with Kitty, and Margaret was happy for her friend even though she, too, had become enamored of her cousin. Morrie was a charming rascal who made common moments into exciting escapades. Conversation with Morrie was easy for Margaret; they talked for hours as they rode horses or sat on the riverbank, watching the moonlit reflection of the trees on the water. Margaret was thrilled his boarding school, Middlesex, was close enough that they could see each other when school be-gan in the fall.

At the beginning of their senior year, Margaret, Kitty, and their mothers took the train to Boston for several days of shopping be-fore settling in at Dana Hall. Kitty continued to date Morrie, who introduced Margaret to his classmate Bryan Lyseck. The four went on regular outings to the Massachusetts countryside or met in Boston on special occasions. Bryan quickly was besotted with Margaret. After their first date, he sent her a bouquet of roses and, soon afterward, a pair of diamond earrings. Margaret held them up to the moonlight, and the reflections created a beautiful spiderweb of refracted light. Bryan was handsome and charming, but Margaret warmed to the relationship slowly. She swore to herself that she would never allow her emotions to be swayed by jewelry.

On Thanksgiving, the foursome had lunch at a nearby hotel. After the lunch, Margaret went with Morrie to his cousin's house for dinner. The cousin was expecting her first child, and in that visit, Margaret got a glimpse of the life she hoped to have. It wasn't envy she felt, simply excitement for this same future she believed was to be her own. The problem was she felt like a satellite orbiting around Kitty and Morrie. For the sake of their friendships, Margaret kept her attraction to Morrie to herself. She liked Bryan, but try as she might, she couldn't muster the same feelings for him that she had for Morrie and Kitty. She loved them both dearly.

When she returned home to Great Neck for the Christmas holidays, it was the first time she had spent a long amount of time at the new house. All the family's belongings that had been in storage were now in place. It felt like home—finally. Even her parents seemed happy to be together.

On Christmas Eve, the family sang carols as her mother played the piano. Margaret took eggnog to her room that night and made resolutions for the new year. She was so happy to have been reunited with her belongings and furniture that she was often too excited to sleep during the holiday break. She read until the early hours of the morning, occasionally looking up from the pages to admire her little haven, decorated with all the girlhood possessions she loved.

For the new year, she resolved to keep a regular diet of fifteen hundred calories a day until she was 120 pounds, or else in perfect form. She also vowed to give up cigarettes entirely. She made a final wish for love and laughter.

Four
1928

Eyes like emeralds in the road
Tell the presence of the toad
Eyes like rubies in the dark
Catch the alligator's spark
And tiger's, tiger's burning bright
In the stillness of the night

Unpublished

The early winter of 1928 in Massachusetts was particularly harsh. Back in school at Dana Hall, Margaret soon fell into a listless gloom. The cold winter days compounded her blues, brought on by her parents' constant squabbles. Margaret dreaded phone calls from home because the conversation often turned into verbal jousting between her parents, seemingly fought to win Margaret's approval and affection. She also couldn't break her attraction to Morrie but cared too much for Kitty to act on her desires.

Her spirits were lifted when the Johnstons invited her and Roberta to join them on Cumberland Island, the family's private retreat off the coast of Georgia, for spring break. Margaret was thrilled, but a shopping trip to Boston with her mother soured her mood. Maude angrily recounted Bruce's recent failings and then berated Margaret for having gained weight. Margaret couldn't understand why her mother couldn't simply enjoy the good moments instead of picking apart the people who loved her.

For two weeks, Margaret exercised strenuously. By the time she stepped foot on Cumberland Island, she was ten pounds lighter and certain her new wardrobe would fit. The girls had to take a train and a ferry to reach the island, but the most enchanting ride was from the dock to Plum Orchard, the Johnstons' home on the island. The Johnstons' car was electric, perfect for the low-speed, bumpy drive along the sand-and-crushed-oyster-shell road. Gnarled branches of water oaks on either side of the road arched above them to form a darkened tunnel, and staccato rays of sunlight danced in the twisted limbs. Every so often, the wheels of the car sank a little too deeply into the soft, deep valleys of sand and swung the back end of the car to the edge of the narrow road. There the tires once again found traction and pitched the car back into the middle of the road. This exotic island was more magical than she could possibly have imagined.

Cumberland was larger than Manhattan and was a carefully preserved paradise. The island hosted over a hundred species of migrating birds and was home to dozens more. Along its primitive shores and throughout its dunes dwelled bears, alligators, turkeys, eagles, and boars. Over a hundred horses freely roamed the island—descendants of a herd left in the 1500s by Spanish sailors.

Plum Orchard was a Classical Revival–style mansion that had been built for Mrs. Johnston's older brother, George Carnegie, and his wife, an expert gardener. Flower and vegetable gardens bordered the extensive grass lawn that led up to graceful steps and soaring columns of the twenty-room home. Stables, a paddock, and a riding ring accommodated fifteen horses. After George died, his widow married a French count who came to Cumberland with no expectation of staying. The couple shipped every item of value in Plum Orchard off to a New York auction house. Furniture, first-edition books, and chandeliers disappeared before George's mother, Lucy "Mama" Carnegie, sent the newlyweds packing, as well. She held the deed to the house and gave it to her daughter Nancy, who renovated the house. Modern features, including a sauna and an air-cooling system that drafted air from the basement out through vents in the roof, were added. The bathroom was fitted with towel heaters, shampoo dispensers attached to bath faucets, and elegantly styled wall fixtures that held flint stones and matches. Hand-painted wallpapers were hung throughout the house. One of deep red was repeatedly embossed in gold with the Carnegie family crest. Another wallpaper that Margaret particularly admired hung in the game room; it was painted in bright blues, greens, and yellows to resemble the pond lilies that grew along the banks of the marshes behind the house.

Evenings were often spent in that room. Sedate hours were passed playing parlor games or listening to Morrie play the piano and Coley, the violin. Margaret particularly liked a game called "Coffeepot," in which a person had to guess what noun or verb had been substituted by the word *coffeepot*—Do you coffeepot alone? A more raucous indoor game they called "Watch on the Threshold" involved dividing into teams with the intent of capturing members of the opposite side. Lights were turned off throughout the house, and players quickly hid or searched through closets and nooks and behind furniture. Quiet skulking gave way to giggles and delighted screams as hiding places were uncovered. The Johnstons were competitive, but it was cloaked in an air of good humor that inspired Margaret. Roberta, though, turned glummer as the days went on. At first, Margaret attempted to cheer her sister, but saw that, like their mother, Roberta relished layering a foul mood over happy occasions.

Margaret spent most of the vacation rushing from adventure to adventure. She was determined to enjoy everything the island had to offer. There was so much to see and do that she only had time to jot down cryptic notes in her diary. She ate tannis pudding, sat in a gumbo limbo tree, and made friends with an Australian Cattle Dog her cousins said was called a *Wemba Womba* hound. She joined a crew of men on an alligator hunt, watching with fascination as they lured the beast close, then shoved a knife in its head.

She and her cousins sailed, fished, galloped horses in the surf, and paddled around the island for hours. They held friendly competitions and acrobatic displays on the shore or in the giant sand dunes of Lake Whitney, where the ever-athletic Margaret recorded an impressive seventeen-foot broad jump. She and Lucy picked shells as they walked along the shore. The coquille shells were so colorful and plentiful the sand looked like it was dotted with flowers.

It was customary for her cousins to swim "as is" when no adults were around. Those times were rare, though. Dr. Johnston usually accompanied them to the beach and sat on the roof of his car with his rifle in hand. Years before, he had been bitten on the leg by a hammerhead shark while surf fishing with his mother-in-law, Mama Carnegie. The feisty and fast-thinking woman saved her son-in-law's life by applying a tourniquet and racing him to her mansion, Dungeness, to get medical assistance. If a dorsal fin appeared while his children and their guests frolicked in the surf, Dr. Johnston, an excellent marksman, was prepared. Once, on an arctic expedition, he killed a polar bear, and on safari in Africa, a lion. The many trophies from his hunts were on display in the game room of Plum Orchard, although he only occasionally showed off his greatest souvenir—an unused ticket for the ill-fated ocean liner *Titanic*. He had been too sick to travel on the day the ship set sail.

On the last day of their trip, Margaret sat in the front seat of the open-air car as her older cousin Retta drove along the straight, sandy road. Lucy was in the backseat and, like Margaret, scouted the marshes and woods for human forms. A hunter had gone missing from the Cumberland Island Hunting Club at the north end of the island. Roberta, who had left earlier that morning to look for him, also seemed to have vanished into the wilds. Patches of dense foliage that dotted the island made it easy to get lost in day or night. Margaret was frustrated with her sister for heading out on her own to look for the hunter because they needed to take the afternoon boat to the mainland to catch their train back to Boston and Dana Hall. Besides, thought Margaret, a naval crew from the battleship anchored off the island and the members of the hunting club had organized a search and were certainly better prepared than her little sister to find the lost man. Morrie had joked that the hunter probably shot one of his family's cows by mistake and was busy burying the evidence; everyone seemed sure the man would eventually make his way back to the lodge.

Retta eased the car onto a grassy road that led into the woods, mindful that at any moment a startled deer or one of the island's feral horses might bolt into their path. It was best to keep a safe distance from these large and unpredictable beasts, especially the foals. They were constantly watched by their protective mothers, who were known to attack cars, wagons, and people who posed a threat.

The car's tires slowed as the vegetation gave way to rolling sand dunes on either side of the road. Wooden planks kept the car from sinking into the sand as the car crested a hill and the Atlantic Ocean sparkled in front of them. The girls looked north and south but saw no one.

Retta turned the car north, and Margaret could hear the sound of shells crunching under the car's wheels as the car cruised along on the firmest part of the shore. Margaret first learned of the dangers of driving the car close to the water one evening as the tide came in. A crew of men had come to her rescue and saved the car before the waves washed over its wheels. Margaret had been shaken up, but the Johnstons were unfazed. This happened at least once a year, they assured their cousin.

Margaret looked out over the horizon as Retta steered the car. A storm was building over the ocean. It was common for a brief shower to appear in the afternoon, but this one looked more threatening than the average short downpour. The girls decided to head back to Plum Orchard. It was lunchtime, and they could continue their search later on.

Lunches on Cumberland were almost always sumptuous picnics,

allowing every opportune moment to be enjoyed outside. But the disappearance of the hunter—and of Roberta—had made today's lunch anything but normal. Mrs. Johnston's servants had prepared a buffet for the naval officers and members of the hunting lodge. Turkey, cranberry sauce, eggplant, sweet potatoes, corn pones, beaten biscuits, freshly churned butter, strawberry ice, and coconut cake were elegantly displayed in silver dishes for the guests. No one had located the missing hunter, but a few of the luncheon guests had found Roberta and had returned her to Plum Orchard.

Much of the food came from the island. Trees bore exotic fruits, such as kumquats and bananas. Cattle, chickens, and pigs were farmed, while deer and boar were hunted to add to the family larder. Bountiful dinners revolved among the different families at the smattering of homes on the island. The grandest meals were served at Stafford, another Carnegie family home that belonged to Nancy's brother Andrew. Formal dress was required for dinners at his home, a tone that had been set long ago by Mama Carnegie at Dungeness. Tables were candlelit and set with ornate silver, gold-rimmed china, and crystal glasses embedded with gold lace. Margaret loved the formality of those occasions. Even though life with her parents was strained, she was very grateful for their generosity. She loved the clothes her mother bought her, especially her dresses.

After dinners, the adventures always continued. The cousins would drive around the island in the electric car or take nighttime strolls with flashlights in hand. On one ramble, the sweet aroma of cake meandered through the air as they passed Greyfield, another Carnegie family home. Morrie couldn't resist creeping over to the open window to snatch a cooling cake. He was such a charming scamp. When someone placed shadow crabs in their room, the girls knew who to blame.

One night, their group was making its way through the darkest part of the forest, where entwined tree limbs formed a thick canopy, when Margaret turned her flashlight into the woods. The beam caught the red eyes of a whip-poor-will and then the yellow eyes of a toad. Another sweep of the light illuminated the fearsome glare of a large, unknown animal at the edge of the woods. The scare had sent the group scurrying for the safety of the car.

Margaret filled her plate at the sumptuous buffet on the lawn of Plum Orchard and then sat with some of the officers at a table and chatted—they were quite amiable for military men. During the search, the men had worn huge cloaks as a defense against the thorny bushes and poison ivy—native to the island—and as a safeguard against the potential rain. Margaret borrowed one officer's cloak and swooped around the yard, enveloping anyone who came in her path.

After lunch, the girls piled back into the convertible and headed toward the beach for one last walk before boarding the boat back to the mainland. They stopped at Stafford to play with the Johnstons' younger cousins on the front lawn. Margaret noticed how drawn the children seemed to Retta. Her cheerful smile and pleasant manner were infectious. All the Carnegies were so inspiring. They were an exemplary family, remarkable in every way, Margaret thought.

Why couldn't her own family be more like them? Each Brown family gathering ended in arguments or alienation. Margaret was grateful she would soon go off to college but hated to leave behind the friends she had made at Dana Hall. She feared losing touch with the people who meant the most to her, including Lucy, who was getting married later that summer. Margaret knew Lucy's marriage would distance them; it had happened with other friends. When girls got married, they disappeared completely into their new lives, and Margaret couldn't help but feel left behind.

As she and Roberta boarded the boat that afternoon, there were tears in Margaret's eyes as she said good-bye to Lucy. Changes, she decided, were an inevitable part of life, and she must accept them. She could choose to wrap herself in disappointment and anger like her mother or she could choose to live with the same fervor, adventure, and love of life as the Johnstons and Carnegies. She vowed to rise above her parents' petty arguments; she would refuse to side with either of them in their marital war. She had to save herself, Margaret realized, otherwise she, too, would drown in their sorrow.

A month later, Margaret awoke while it was still dark in her dorm room at Dana Hall. She wanted a cigarette, but didn't want to disturb Kitty's slumber. She sneaked out of the room and stepped quietly to the end of the hall. She lifted the large window and crawled out onto the fire escape. She was fire marshal for her floor and well aware that this was against the school's rules. She would graduate in two weeks, so she didn't think the headmistress would impose a serious penalty for this minor infraction. The punishment they gave her when she was caught breaking curfew was to send her to the library after dinner for a week. That was like throwing Joel Chandler Harris's rabbit into the briar patch. The library was exactly where she preferred to be.

She sat on the metal slats of the fire escape and looked out on the small school that felt like home to her. The moon illuminated a layer of fog over the fields that surrounded the school. Her life at Dana Hall was so comfortable she considered remaining on the school's campus to attend their postsecondary school, Pine Manor. They offered a certification for teaching, but Margaret couldn't overcome the feeling that she would make a terrible teacher. She hated sitting still in class and studying. Also, she had little patience for children. It would probably be best for her to attend her mother's alma mater, Hollins College.

Many of Margaret's classmates had already decided where they would attend college. Roberta was going to Vassar. Margaret's uncertainty about where she would be the next year weighed on her. She also wasn't sure how she would survive without the friends she had made, especially Kitty.

As she thought about all the things she would miss at Dana Hall, she developed an intense craving for a toasted cheese sandwich and milkshake from a local café. Likely, the craving was intensified by nostalgia and fear of the future, but before she could remind herself of the school's strict rules, Margaret had devised a plan. She saw how easy it would be to slip down the fire escape and to walk to the café. She could get to town, eat, and be back before her first class began. It would be an adventure!

She went back inside and tried to convince Kitty to come with her. Leaving the campus without permission was a serious school infraction. Girls had been expelled for less. Kitty wisely declined, but Margaret was undeterred. She succeeded in convincing two sorority sisters to accompany her. One was valedictorian, a position of almost assured immunity if they were caught.

It took a great deal of enthusiasm and charisma to keep the other

girls walking for almost four miles in the dark. When they finally
arrived at the café, it was daybreak, but the restaurant was closed.
If they waited for it to open, they would surely be late to their first
class and their crime would definitely be discovered. They had no
choice but to turn around and walk back to Dana Hall. The other
girls were furious with Margaret for leading them on such a foolish
venture. When they arrived back on campus, their housemother
and the headmistress of the school were waiting for them. Their
escapade had been found out when a school administrator drove past
the girls on the road. She recognized them because they had been
wearing their school uniforms.

For days, it was uncertain if the girls would be allowed to graduate. Margaret was sincerely remorseful. This caper had almost
cost their housemother her job and could mean the end of school
for Margaret. She scolded herself for acting so impulsively and swore
to herself that in the future she would consider the consequences
of her actions more carefully.

It hadn't been easy to convince her father to pay for her college
education. He believed Maude's schooling in the liberal arts at
Hollins had been a waste of money. He had gone to work instead of
attending a prestigious university like his brothers and sisters, yet he
was the only financial success in the family. He still sent monthly sti-
pends to two of his well-educated sisters, but he expected more out
of his own daughters. He agreed to pay for Margaret's college, but
stipulated that she had to earn a degree or certification in something
that would lead to gainful employment.

Roberta planned to teach. Gratz was an engineering student at
Massachusetts Institute of Technology and already shared a patent on
an air-cleaning system for automobiles. As Margaret waited to learn

her fate, she decided that she wanted to go to her mother's alma mater, Hollins. She knew better than to confess her desire to be a writer to her father, though, so she promised to become a landscape gardener.

Bruce was rightly worried about Margaret's lackluster performance in school. It was clear she was smart, but she habitually did the least amount of schoolwork required to pass. He wanted to inspire her to greater heights and to turn the competitive nature she showed in sports toward her education. During one of Margaret's visits home, her father had brought out his family scrapbook to show her the many accomplishments of her ancestors, especially the women in the family. He read his daughter an article her great-aunt had written, which traced their ancestors' journey from a farm in Ireland to the upper echelons of Washington politics and society.

It had the desired impact on Margaret. She wanted to live up to her family's colorful and influential history. Most of all, she wanted to make her father proud. By the time she graduated from Dana Hall, Margaret had added her middle name, Wise, to her signature to remind herself of her ancestry.

If Margaret had acted alone on her walk to town for a toasted cheese sandwich, she would have surely been dismissed from the school. But the presence of the class valedictorian made things more complicated for the school administrators; indeed, the headmistress was reluctant to eject their best student, who was bound for great things, and allowed the girls to graduate with their class.

That summer, the family went on vacation in Maine. Margaret was disappointed that the trip to Paris they had originally planned had been canceled because of Maude's elevated blood pressure. Margaret's parents spent more and more time apart, and on the Maine vacation, they saw very little of each other. When they were together, it seemed they were always arguing.

Bruce took Margaret and Gratz on overnight excursions on a fishing boat. Roberta had no desire to go with them. Margaret loved being with her father on the sea. Prohibition was still in force, but Margaret and Gratz had found the bootlegger that skirted the shore along the northern tip of Long Island before they left. The trio drank and talked into the late-night hours. Bruce took his children to where the phosphorescent fish swam, and together they studied the stars. Margaret and Gratz had seen little of each other over the past few years, and they enjoyed the time together. Margaret hoped she and her brother would never grow so distant again.

Although the Browns had visited Maine before, Margaret was struck, for the first time, by the beauty of its rocky coast and lush, green forests. She tried to recapture her days on Cumberland, taking picnics with her to island hop or walk in the woods. On one excursion, she fell asleep while lying in the woods, listening to the rustlings around her. That night, Margaret had found her way home in the deep darkness of the moonless night. She picked blueberries and went on starlit sails. She took long, exploratory drives, once returning with an entire carful of honeysuckles.

Her mother spent most days with Theosophical Society friends in Rockport, and on rainy days, Margaret went with her. She sat with her mother's friends as they held talks and séances. She attended a lecture on the meditation techniques of Yogananda and one on Celtic spirituality, the belief of her ancestors. This religion held that nature was sacred and God is present in every living creature and plant. These beliefs resonated with Margaret far more than the traditional religious teachings that had been handed down to her in chapel at Dana Hall. But Margaret was not entirely convinced about reincarnation, the topic of another lecture her mother brought her to. If she had been reincarnated, she teased, then she must have been a fish in her former life because she never wanted to get out of the cold, invigorating water of Maine.

On her way back from the family vacation, Margaret camped in upstate New York with a group of friends that included Bryan and Morrie. They rafted down the rapids of West Canada Creek and fished for their dinner. Some sang and others played instruments, with Margaret on the mandolin. When night came, the group listened to rustlings in the forest with a bit of fear and wide-eyed alertness, assuming the noises might be rummaging bears. The next day, Morrie invited the group to stay in the barn of a home his family owned nearby. Margaret was very happy to see Dr. and Mrs. Johnston and relieved to be sleeping in the safer quarters of the hayloft.

At the end of the getaway, Margaret waved good-bye to Bryan and was certain this was the last time they would see each other. They were headed off to different schools, miles and miles away from each other. She felt more relief than sadness. This vacation confirmed that she hadn't conquered her attraction to Morrie.

Margaret's last days of summer were spent alone in the family's Long Island home. Her mother was with Roberta at Vassar and her father with Gratz at MIT. Margaret had a few days alone to prepare for her departure for the Blue Ridge Mountains of Roanoke, Virginia, where she would be attending Hollins College.

This was the start of a new world for her. Margaret vowed to control her racing mind and lazy body. She believed everyone should develop their God-given talents, and since she was doomed to be an athlete, she refused to be a poor one. She felt sluggish and bothered by the ten pounds she had gained over the summer, so she bicycled, swam, and walked for miles, determined to be fit and healthy by the time she left for school.

She used the quiet hours to read in the family's large library. The Kelly green of the golf course outside its windows blended smoothly into the same shade of green on the walls in the calm, quiet room. She read a memoir of a nurse in the Great War and wondered if she would have been as courageous in the same circumstances. She also read a biography of Robert E. Lee, then letters of her ancestors who fought with him. She found wrenching letters from her grandfather, who fought on the side of the Union in the Civil War, to his brother, a Confederate officer. She studied the family scrapbooks and read her grandparents' journals. There was a streak of boldness that coursed through her family's blood. Rules, one ancestor said, were made for people too afraid to bust them. This inspired Margaret. She, too, had a sweeping style, and conventional thoughts weren't for her, she decided. She wanted to make her own mark on the world. She was headed to the state her ancestors once called home, and she was going to make herself worthy of her distinguished family.

On her last night at home, Margaret took a stroll along the shore and watched the moon rise as the stars slowly appeared in the night sky. Earlier that year, her astronomy teacher had lectured on the formation of the galaxy. His talk had disturbed Margaret deeply. The joy of observing the stars through telescopes, memorizing their names, and spotting the major constellations vanished when the professor gave a visual demonstration of how minute the earth was in comparison to the known universe. Margaret had suddenly felt insignificant. If the earth was a mere drop of water in the vast ocean of the cosmos, then her life must be of little matter, she had thought. She desperately tried to make sense of her place in this unfathomably large world. She became obsessed with looking at the stars. One night, it occurred to her that the stars seemed to have individual personality traits. Some were slow to appear, some emitted a bright steady light, while others twinkled in apparent excitement. Eventually, Margaret stopped calling the stars by their proper names and instead renamed them after people she knew who exhibited those same characteristics.

As she left the beach and returned home on her last night in Long Island, she wasn't ready to leave summer behind quite yet. She climbed onto her balcony and slept in the light of the moon, underneath the blanket of her friends, the stars.

Five
1929–1932

Rush

Knees

Part of a horse

Own body gone now

Part of the horse

Air comes upward

Up from the chest

Into the wings

Part of the horse

Breath suspended

Part of the horse

Gather

Sail away

Over

Unpublished

In her junior year at Hollins, Margaret was chosen for the coveted role of Mary in the annual Christmas pageant. It was commonly known that being chosen to play the Madonna was akin to a beauty contest at the school. The casting was turned over to the whole student body, who could vote for any girl to fill the part of Mary whether or not she was part of the drama club. Margaret was an active member of that club, though, so she felt confident stepping onto the stage as the pregnant Mary. The play was written by another student and the role of Joseph assigned to a fellow classmate. At the all-girls' school, it was common for girls to play the male roles onstage and even at the spring cotillion at which many of the girls dressed in men's tuxedos and donned fake mustaches. Others dressed in formal gowns and were escorted by their "dates" to the dance.

As Mary, Margaret wore a shapeless white dress. Her locks of blond hair were left loose, and a silky blue scarf was pinned at the top of her head. In the play, a young girl happens into conversation with Mary outside the walls of Bethlehem as Joseph seeks shelter for them for the night. The girl is in despair and seeks meaning in life. Mary consoles her, and in exchange, the girl offers her stable as a place for the expectant couple to rest. With her fair complexion, Margaret resembled the Virgin Mary only in pious expression, but her performance was very well received.

Margaret thrived on the social scene at Hollins. In addition to the drama club, she was a student government representative, wing on the hockey team, and charter member of the riding club. On her first visit to Hollins, she had seen some run-down stables on the far side of campus. She convinced the headmistress that an equestrian team, like the one she had belonged to at Dana Hall, would be a desirable addition to the school. Her mother's sway as an alumna and her father's checkbook had helped turn the shabby shack into a line of stalls reminiscent of those she'd seen at a Kentucky racetrack.

The Hollins campus suited Margaret's desire to be physically active in the outdoors. The school's buildings were nestled into rolling hills against beautiful mountains. Carvin Creek ran alongside the campus, and a stream meandered through ancient willows and oak trees. Margaret loved how each season brought changes to the valley. Colorful fall leaves gave way to quiet blankets of snow. Spring brought flocks of robins, bursts of cherry blossoms, and luminous greens of new leaves. She waded in the creeks, noted the arrival of different birds to the campus, and could watch the sun set on the shimmering trees of Tinker Mountain from her dorm window.

She loved the school's many traditions and that her mother often came to campus to share them with her. The school was initially a coeducational seminary but in 1852 became the first chartered school for girls in Virginia. Charles Lewis Cocke was principal of the seminary and, when faced with overcrowding, saw a golden opportunity. He had long believed in the importance of educating women even though many believed that to be futile, if not dangerous. Charles thought a better society could only be attained through providing young women the same academic opportunities as young men—and holding them to the same high standards of achievement. He was considered a forward thinker, even if grace and refinement were part of the school's stated educational requirements when Margaret's mother was a student in the School of Elocution and Physical Culture. By the time Margaret arrived at Hollins, they offered a variety of degrees in the sciences and arts. Her science grades were too low for her to receive certification as a landscape gardener, so in her junior year, she entered the English literature and psychology programs.

Margaret had come to Hollins with every intention of being an excellent student, but her enthusiasm faded after her first semester, when she failed freshman English. She was an avid reader, and she loved to write, but having learned punctuation in the minimalist French style, she received low grades from her English professor. He had refused to accept her French-based education as an excuse for poor grammar, punctuation, or spelling. She took that class again the next year and learned to follow his rules for writing. Proper spelling still eluded her, but she made passing grades.

At the end of her junior year, Margaret's inability to balance her schoolwork and social life almost brought her college days to an end when she failed chemistry. As was proper, she wrote a letter to the dean withdrawing from the school. Margaret got lucky, though. The Depression had taken a toll on the school's attendance, so the dean was more lenient than she might have been in previous years. Margaret was assured that her academic issues could be corrected if she took chemistry again in her senior year. The dean urged her to direct her attention to her schoolwork instead of sports. She suggested Margaret seek assistance from her teachers if her grades slipped again. Most of the professors were eager to help the bubbly girl, even if she valued her popularity more than her grade point average. One professor in particular recognized Margaret's creative potential. Dr. Marguerite Hearsey, another English professor, encouraged Margaret to polish her writing skills. She assured Margaret that her depth of literary knowledge and vivid imagination could take her far as a writer, but she needed to be more disciplined with her grammar. Dr. Hearsey assigned Margaret articles to write for the yearbook and alumnae quarterly—tasks the young student relished. Margaret loved seeing her words in print. She never gave up field hockey or the riding club, but she did learn to work more efficiently, and her grades improved.

She spent most of the summer between her junior and senior years in Kentucky. She'd gone there hoping to see Morrie. He and Kitty had broken up years before, and in Margaret's sophomore year, he enrolled at nearby University of Virginia. She took the train to Charlottesville a few times to see him, and by Christmas, she considered him to be her boyfriend. By the new year, though, he had suddenly ceased all communication with her, and she had no idea why. When she arrived at the Johnstons' home in Kentucky, she found out he was engaged to be married to another girl. She was crushed but kept her spirits up through the summer party circuit. Her dance card was always quickly filled with eligible young men, and she soon met George Armistead. His family, like Margaret's, was an early arrival to Virginia. George's namesake was a relative who commissioned a garrison flag that could be seen from great distances at Baltimore's Fort McHenry during the War of 1812. When the fort was attacked, he successfully commanded the defense of the fort through the British assault. As the British ships retreated, Major Armistead ordered the massive flag raised. Eight miles away, Francis Scott Key saw the flag and knew that the fort and Baltimore, and thus the nation, had been saved. The sight inspired Key to write a poem depicting that moment, "The Star-Spangled Banner."

George Armistead was dashingly handsome. With his blond hair and bright blue eyes, he and Margaret made a striking couple. He went to college in Texas, but they had plans to meet at school breaks.

In between, letters sufficed, and by the new year, they were engaged.

A formal engagement party was planned in Kentucky over their spring breaks. Margaret's family traveled from New York and George's from Texas to toast the couple. However, soon after arriving in Kentucky, Margaret told George that she could never marry him. She told him she loved him, but she longed for something more than being a cattle rancher's wife. She didn't tell him that she knew he was exactly the kind of man her father wanted her to marry and that she had overheard the two of them sharing a laugh over how to control her. She had thought George would stand up to her father instead of colluding with him. That moment showed her who George really was. When she returned to Hollins, she burned all his letters.

The week of her graduation from Hollins, Margaret competed in the school's final equestrian event of the year, hoping to impress her mother and sister who were part of the nearly one hundred spectators. The crowd was larger than normal due to the upcoming commencement. Some spectators sat on the hoods of their parked cars, while others leaned against the fence.

Margaret sat erect in the saddle, heels down in the stirrups and hands poised. A press of her legs was all it took to urge her horse through the open gate and into the riding ring. The larger pieces of charcoal in the ashy ring crunched underneath her horse's hooves as she led him around the rail to prepare for the first jump.

Margaret was the most experienced rider on the Hollins equestrian team. She also had designed her school's flashy riding jackets. Their coats of white silk with bright blue felt letters sewn onto the back stood out against the prominent brown tweeds or black velvet customarily worn by the other teams. Margaret had known her design would catch the judges' eyes. She also knew that the best way for her to be noticed was to remove her hat as she entered their view, allowing her hair to fall free. This trick, along with her considerable talent, had earned the golden-haired beauty on the golden palomino many ribbons over her four years at the school.

Margaret was glad her mother was there, but it felt odd to have Roberta at Hollins. The sisters had grown apart these last four years. The little time they spent together on Christmas break or on vacation in Maine only seemed to emphasize their differences. Hollins was something Margaret alone had shared with her mother. Her sister felt like an interloper.

The graduation horse show was going far better than the previous year's event, when a car had startled one of the horses. At the time, the riding ring's fence was only partly finished, and the small pine trees they had used to outline the oval couldn't contain the frightened mare when it bolted. The runaway horse didn't stop until it reached Carvin Creek, where it dumped its rider into the water with an abrupt halt. It had been the first competition for several of the girls, and more than a few had fallen from their horses. The ashes the equestrian team shoveled into the ring fortunately softened their spills.

Margaret's first jump was effortless, and she kept her horse at an easy canter as they flew over the next fence. She loved the feel of the horse as it lifted itself off the ground. It was up to the rider to position and pace a horse and then relinquish control to the horse as it carried them into the air and over the gate. It wasn't the horse's ability to leap over the jumps that was in question but the rider's ability to become one with the horse at just the right moment. Margaret loved that moment.

Lately, worry had wrapped itself around her. She was leaving college with no certifications that would earn her a respectable job. She hadn't applied to graduate schools because of her engagement to George. Margaret wondered what was wrong with her. Why couldn't she be like most of her friends who were happily preparing for marriage? She wanted, more than anything, to be a writer, but that seemed entirely unlikely. She felt like a candle burned at both ends. Her only option was to move home and look for work.

Margaret and her horse faced the last two jumps. This was the last time she would compete in this ring she had helped to build. She was going to miss this school, her friends, and her teachers. Hollins felt more like home than the big house on Long Island. She desperately wished she could stay on there instead of returning home. Barely a single civil word passed between her mother and father anymore. Bruce's de facto home was his large boat anchored close to the Brown house in Great Neck. Margaret would have no such escape available to her when she moved back. Perhaps she had given up the fairy-tale wedding because she was afraid of repeating her parents' miserable marriage.

Margaret refused to let her friends or family know how much she feared failing as a writer, nor would she let them see the waves of regret that flooded over her every time she thought about George Armistead. Humor, she decided, was the best way to deflect doubt and fear. She laughed off her broken engagement in front of her friends but was angry with herself for being the oddity instead of the norm.

Of course, there were moments when that strategy failed and her heart ached. But she didn't want to think too deeply about that now. She settled herself in the saddle and sped the horse forward. They cleared the last jumps with ease. Their performance was certainly worthy of a ribbon, if not the trophy. Margaret looked toward her mother and sister along the rail, then slowed her horse to a walk as she led him slowly out of the gate.

Six
1934–1935

Black and yellow
Little fur bee
Buzzing away
In the timothy
Drowsy
Browsy
Lump of a bee
Rumbly
Tumbly
Bumbly bee.
Where are you taking
Your golden plunder
Humming along
Like baby thunder?
Over the clover
And over the hay
Then over the apple trees
Zoom away

BUMBLE BEE

Every seat in the auditorium was taken, but people continued to file in. Gertrude Stein had requested that only five hundred tickets be sold to the lecture, but it appeared the struggling Brooklyn Academy of Music was reluctant to turn patrons away. Chairs lined the aisles, and people perched where they could in the slivers of space that remained.

The audience was primarily comprised of women, although Stein's arrival in America had been widely heralded to all. Newspaper headlines and an electric sign in Times Square welcomed the famous author home from her self-imposed exile in France. The academy was her first stop on a thirty-seven-city lecture tour. A radio interview, the only one she had ever given, had been broadcast two weeks earlier from NBC's studio. Margaret and another Hollins alumna listened to the broadcast at Margaret's Greenwich Village apartment. They shared an admiration for Stein's work while at Hollins, unlike most of the girls at the school who found the writer's work perplexing. Stein's repetitious style was meant to evoke clarity, but her use of minimal punctuation frustrated many American readers. In the interview, Stein claimed that punctuation crippled deep understanding of the written word. Margaret wanted to take colored chalk and write that theory all over the blackboard of the professor who had made her repeat freshman English.

Both of the girls were living in New York and attempting to write for a living. Neither was succeeding. Her friend had sold only one poem, and Margaret hadn't sold a single piece. Her work as a nanny and shopgirl didn't cover her living expenses, but an allowance from her father gave her a comfortable enough life. Her apartment didn't have hot water, but she always had enough money to dine out, see plays, and attend lectures like the three that Stein was to give at the academy.

Newspaper reporters took pleasure in taunting Stein's style in their pun-riddled copy, but the author's celebrity status and carefully orchestrated interviews drew enormous crowds to her events. Her first lecture was about her most recent book, *The Making of Americans*. In the semiautobiographical novel, Stein chronicled three generations of a family. She described how the characters' personalities were formed by their choice to repeat the actions of their parents. Those repetitions shaped their own lives and the lives of their children. Like wave after wave, each generation was formed by the previous generation, which created a collective family culture. The next generation had the choice to carry on the family's culture or break away. Breaking away was difficult because it fragmented the family.

Margaret had been deeply moved by Stein's book. It clarified for her why her own family was so broken. Her parents' individual personalities had been formed long before they met and were influenced by their very different families. They once loved each other enough to overlook those differences, but now her father lived on his boat and her mother was alone in the house on Long Island. There were no plans for family gatherings on Thanksgiving or Christmas. Even so, Margaret missed the structure of holiday breaks that had been a part of her college life. She also missed her friends from Hollins. The summer after she graduated, she served as a bridesmaid in four weddings, but as each friend left the church on the arm of her new husband, Margaret knew the couple was walking off into a life that eventually left her behind. The things she and her now married girlfriends once had in common would erode, especially when children came along. Before long, Margaret knew the letters that bridged her and her friends' distance would cease and they would lose touch completely.

She tried not to think too hard about the future and kept herself busy. There was always something to do in the city. She visited museums and took classes at The Art Students League of New York. Her instructor had her paint only color with no shape or intention so she could understand the moods colors could evoke. Then she molded forms with clay to get a feel for dimension. After days of that, she painted still lifes and nude model after nude model. This soon bored her. She decided to save money by quitting the class and painting her own pile of fruits and vegetables.

After that, she took a short story course at Columbia University, where Basil Rauch, her new brother-in-law, was earning his doctorate in history. Basil was far too serious for Margaret's taste, but he suited her docile sister. Basil and Roberta lived close by, and the sisters had become closer in recent months. Margaret teased Basil about his somber dark brown tweed suits, and he considered it an amusing challenge to find interesting dinner companions for Margaret. A parade of professors, writers, and editors were served at his and Roberta's table, but Margaret found most of them too gentle and dreary. She had no trouble finding good-looking young men with more money than intellect to accompany her to plays, movies, and restaurants around the city. Inevitably, though, she would cast them off, too. They were fun but unable to hold a decent conversation.

She loved living in the city. At night, she lay in her bed and listened to the city grow so quiet she could hear the click of heels on sidewalks and the shutter of the traffic lights as they changed from red to green. She woke early to write and watch the city come to life. When she walked through her Greenwich Village neighborhood, she chatted with street vendors and shopkeepers around Washington Square Park. She helped the French baker around the corner with his English, and he gave her lessons on the French horn in return. Every week, she bought a bouquet of flowers to liven her tiny apartment. She loved how almost anything could be found in the city. In the depths of winter, she discovered white narcissus for sale in the subway, and for a few cents, she bought the memory of spring.

The Great Depression still gripped most of the nation, but the Browns saw no changes in their lifestyles due to the economic downturn. Margaret continued to receive a healthy allowance, and the Browns went on vacations across the country and to Europe. On a family skiing vacation in Lausanne, Switzerland, Margaret met the pretender to the defunct Spanish crown, Infante Juan, count of Barcelona. They dined and skied, and although their relationship wasn't serious, it was often mentioned by her family that she once dated the prince of Spain.

Margaret's father had grown tired of waiting for her to marry or find permanent work. He threatened to cut off her allowance and force her to move home if she didn't find a full-time job or a husband soon.

Margaret was desperate to stay in the city. She confessed her hopes and exasperation in letters to her former English professor Marguerite Hearsey. In one, Margaret shared her dream to write great literature and in the next was resigned that she might as well give up and marry a good man. Dr. Hearsey encouraged Margaret to continue to write—her talent and literary foundation would eventually open the necessary doors.

Margaret wasn't so sure. A year after graduating, she had convinced her father to pay for her to take a couple of graduate courses at the University of Virginia. There she rented a charming house from Stringfellow Barr, a lauded history professor who allowed Margaret to sit in on his renowned literary salon. She made many editorial connections through Stringfellow and pressed her new friends to consider her short stories for publication. No one, though, wanted to buy, and she wasn't quite sure why.

As Margaret sat in Stein's lecture, listening to the famous author discuss repetition in writing as a way to reinforce understanding, Margaret felt inspired. The author had stepped onto the stage in heavy, low-heeled shoes. She wore her signature long tweed skirt topped by a white collared shirt and black vest and approached the lectern without looking at the crowded auditorium. She launched into her speech and kept her eyes on the papers in front of her. After several minutes, she lifted her gaze and asked the audience if they understood what she was saying. Polite nods assured her they did.

This was particularly true for Margaret, who listened to Stein speak and instantly recognized the simple beauty of the great author's style. Stein's reliable rhythms created a cadence that bound the reader to the page. Repetition allowed readers to grasp a basic premise, and then, by turning phrases over and over, successive layers of understanding were peeled away.

Margaret realized that everything she respected about Stein's style was lacking in her own muddled work. Her short stories and articles were obtuse and elitist. She used her own privileged life as the basis for everything she wrote, while Stein's easygoing verse sprang from universal themes. Stein's language was clear and concise, but behind those unpretentious words lay complex meanings. Meanwhile, Margaret's writing was overblown and haughty.

Before this moment, Margaret had believed that formality was what literature required, but now she saw how a simple approach was possible and even respected by critics. She grasped the mechanics and the deep emotional well of Stein's style and was electrified. She saw the same things in Stein's verse that she'd come to understand in nature and art. There was always something new to discover in both because our lives and perspectives were always changing. The same type of daisy she had picked and admired as a child was certainly similar to one she might pick today; what changed was the way she saw the flower. This was true of great literature like Stein's. It endured because it opened the door for a reader to embark on an ever-changing road of self-discovery.

For a long time, Margaret had felt like uncooked green peas whirling about in a pot, hoping to become a properly prepared dish. Now she was ready to write in a whole new style. She walked out of the lecture hall more determined than ever to become a writer of importance.

Margaret continued to write and hone her style, but by the beginning of 1935, she hadn't sold a manuscript. At her father's insistence, she moved back home to live with her mother. Margaret distracted herself by joining with a group of fellow Long Islanders to start the Buckram Beagles, a hunting club. Its members and their guests gathered each weekend in the fall and spring to run for hours through the island's vast estates behind the hounds. Their prey was imported Austrian hares, a long-legged jackrabbit traditionally used in the sport. The hunt was capped by a dinner or tea on one of the estates, and Margaret was grateful for the opportunity to chat with these new friends even though the topic always seemed to be the habits of rabbits. At the teas and dinners that followed the hunts, the conversations were engaging, and Margaret met the most interesting people. She befriended a woman who had been the head of the Red Cross in France during the Great War and the man who was heir to the Singer sewing machine fortune. He preferred to bend the rules of the sport by following the runners on horseback, but no one complained because they often hunted on his land. Whenever possible, Margaret traveled with the club as it competed against other kennels in field trials around Long Island and as far away as South Carolina. She hated being at home with her mother, who was skilled at finding inane errands for Margaret to run.

That next spring, Margaret escaped Long Island by finding work as a live-in tutor through one of her beagling friends. Her charge was Dorothy "Dot" Wagstaff, a twelve-year-old girl who had been sick and had fallen behind at her private school in Manhattan. Margaret's primary job was to make certain Dot caught up with her class and passed her end-of-year exams.

Dot reminded Margaret of herself at that age. The young girl had a keen mind, but like Margaret, hated sitting still to do her schoolwork. She would rather be playing with her dog or at the stables with her horse whenever possible. She didn't work efficiently and watched the clock instead of paying attention to what she had to learn. Margaret enjoyed finding ways to interest Dot in her studies. She also developed a reward system that encouraged Dot to focus her efforts intensely so they could go to museums, movies, or horseback riding.

When they rode horses together, Margaret sang hunting songs, show tunes, and ballads. A song titled "Abdul Abulbul Amir" was one of Margaret's favorites. It told the mournful tale of two men who fight to the death in a battle of outrageous pride. Her recall of lyrics was impressive, and she amused Dot with her performances while in the saddle.

When Margaret discovered that Dot was an exceptional artist, Margaret taught her the techniques she had learned at the Art Students League. Dot preferred to paint her horse and dogs instead of landscapes or people, but her knowledge of the animals' muscles and movements shone through in her art. At the end of the school year, Dot passed all her exams, and Margaret was thrilled. Teaching could be exciting, and most surprising of all, Margaret was really good at it.

Another of Margaret's beagling friends had recently earned her teaching certification through the Bureau of Educational Experiments, or Bank Street, as it was commonly called due to its location. The friend praised the vitality and creativity of the school's progressive program, so Margaret filled out an application. She was accepted into the teaching college for their fall term and hired on the spot as a teacher's aide for a class of eight-year-olds at one of Bank Street's associated schools.

Bank Street's founder was Lucy Sprague Mitchell, a brilliant, fast-talking, chain-smoking educator who had previously been the dean of women at the University of California in Berkeley. While at Berkeley, Lucy had grown frustrated that the only jobs available to her graduate students were as teachers or nurses, even with their advanced degrees. In 1919, when Lucy left the highest realms of education to start Bank Street, the courses being offered at women's schools were clearly inferior to the ones offered to men. Lucy believed that those less rigorous undergraduate classes kept women from meeting requirements to enter many graduate programs and thus advance in their careers. Until girls were held to the same demanding educational standards as boys, their vocational options would remain limited.

Moving women out of their standard career roles and prescribed subservience in marriage would take time. Girls had to see themselves as equals, and it had to begin at the early levels of education. Boys also had to see girls as true peers, and teaching methods needed to be reformed for this revolution to take hold.

Lucy had studied theories on education and had been deeply influenced by John Dewey's groundbreaking ideas. He believed education should be a cooperative adventure between teachers and students and that collaboration would naturally foster equal-minded children. Dewey held that children learned better through a hands-on approach and proposed a less regimented curriculum that didn't force children to memorize mountains of information. Instead, a teacher was to be a facilitator instead of an instructor. They were to guide and encourage children as they learned. All children, he believed, were explorers on the greatest journey of their lives—that of childhood.

Lucy admired Dewey's philosophies but felt his methods required testing on a broad basis. Fortunately, Lucy received a generous inheritance and used it to fund a school laboratory—thus Bank Street was born. Bank Street began as a center where psychologists and educators could test and share new approaches for teaching.

It wasn't long, though, before Lucy realized that math and science easily conformed to a fair-minded classroom. What challenged her was finding children's literature that didn't subjugate women. Fairy tales often positioned marriage as the ultimate goal for a girl. Moreover, the violence and questionable morality of the characters in those stories were not appropriate for children. She needed literature that reflected children's lives in an evenhanded way.

The curriculum Lucy needed to support their classrooms simply didn't exist, so she created it. By the time Margaret arrived at the school's front door, Lucy's textbook, a thick collection of stories and rhymes, had been used for more than a dozen years in progressive schools. Lucy labeled her book and the literature movement behind it the Here-and-Now philosophy. Her writings met children at their own stages of development—where they were emotionally and psychologically at that moment. Children became more aware of the larger world as they grew. Two-year-olds' perceptions and interests differed vastly from six-year-olds'. Stories about Mother, Father, bed, and breakfast were fascinating subjects for a toddler. By the age of six, they were more interested in the outside world. They were not only curious about vehicles and buildings but how they were made.

Margaret walked into Bank Street at the most opportune moment. Lucy had been hired to write another large collection of stories and poems in the Here-and-Now style for her publisher, Dutton. The last book had consumed an inordinate amount of her time, and she knew she needed help to meet the publisher's deadline. She was looking to hire an editor and author for their new publications staff. Margaret's graduate writing courses coupled with the psychology classes at Hollins qualified her for an interview. Lucy was impressed with the pretty blond girl's quick mind and spunk. On a hunch, Lucy hired her, and although it was only a part-time position, Margaret's writing career was finally about to take flight.

Margaret was thrilled to be earning money as a writer, even if it was for a children's textbook. Her days were packed. She woke early in the morning to write, then reported to her classroom of eight-year-olds at the Little Red Schoolhouse. There, Margaret read manuscripts to her class and others. She kept extensive notes on what captured the children's attention and what bored them. The children, too, shared stories, songs, and poems with Margaret so she could home in on the words they used at each age level. Margaret hurriedly wrote down what the children said and then created lists of age-appropriate words. She listened to the way they described the world around them, and in their words, Margaret recognized flashes of true poetry. She was in awe of how naturally the children expressed themselves.

Afternoons were spent at Bank Street, where Margaret took courses necessary for teacher certification or chased behind Lucy, sharing her notes on which manuscripts did or didn't work in front of the young audiences. It was soon clear to Margaret that her own stories lacked a certain spark. Her writing was stilted; not at all as effortless as a child's own language. It took a while for Margaret to understand what felt false in her simple lines, but one day she realized she was talking down to children in her writing. She was handing them a version of their world filtered through her words, emotions, and eyes. Somewhere along the way, she, like most adults, had forgotten how it felt to be a child.

Books and music had helped Margaret escape the walls of her boarding school; stories and songs had lifted her from her own troubles and transported her into a carefree world. That was what she wanted to do in her own writing, but adulthood had dulled those memories. Her senses, once so keen as a child's, had a blanket over them. Even in recalling those days, Margaret was revisiting them as a grown woman with a different perspective. If she were ever to write honestly for children, she'd need to be able to see the world as they saw it. Margaret became convinced that she needed to recapture the pleasures and frustrations of childhood.

She returned to the fields and woods of Long Island and physically positioned herself to see things from a child's point of view. She picked daisies, watched bugs crawl, and gazed at clouds floating by. But it was going to take more than seeing the world from a child's physical vantage point to capture those moments clearly. She had to experience it as a child would, with a sense of awe and wonder. That was the real key to writing for children. She had to love, really love, what they loved.

When writing about a certain topic, Margaret would spend days studying the subject. When writing about farms, she drove to the north end of Long Island and picked potatoes in the hot summer sun. To write about boats, she spent days at the Hudson and East River docks, watching ships come and go, learning sailors' songs, and talking to the tugboat captains. She even paddled a canoe around Manhattan. She recalled her childhood days of walking on these same docks and the way the cargo and rivers changed with the seasons. She struggled to remember what it felt like as a young girl to watch her father sail away; she tried to recall her overwhelming fear that he would never return and also her joy when he came home with gifts from exotic lands.

After studying every aspect of boats, sailors, and the sea that she could, she led a group of students that varied in ages to the same docks. She noted what impressed them, what generated questions, and what language they used to describe what they saw. On any given day, they might visit a skyscraper or she might lead an expedition to the zoo to watch the seals swim. The day after she wrote a poem on bees, she and the students buzzed around the classroom together, pretending to be bees.

Once Margaret realized she needed to be writing about the world from the perspective of a child, ideas for stories and poems seemed to simply flow out of her. She often woke with a headful of them and had to scribble them down before they left her head again. When she completed her manuscripts, she immediately brought them to the classroom to be tested. Children were ready and honest critics if they weren't concerned with pleasing the adult who was reading to them, so she never told them she was the author. She knew they would pretend to like it to spare her feelings. If given the chance, children were quite capable of detecting minute flaws in a manuscript and pinpointing where a story went astray. Margaret soon learned that if she watched their eyes and looked for their jaws to go slack, it meant she had succeeded. In their imagination, they were no longer in the classroom, but had stepped into the world of the story.

It wasn't serious literature, but Margaret's talent impressed Lucy, who offered her coauthorship on the Dutton reader. Lucy found that all she needed to do was steer Margaret toward a subject and she could write about it. Lucy may have created the Here-and-Now style of writing, but this young girl gave it wings.

Seven
1936–1937

Ahead of a boat
Across the sea
There is always another land.
There is land for a boat to come from.
There is land where a boat will go.
The ocean is empty
And the ocean is wide,
But still the sailors know
On the other side
Is the land where the boat will go.
There is always a land to come from
And a land where the boat will go.

"BOATS"
Story Parade

The job at Bank Street allowed Margaret to move back to the city. She shared an apartment with a friend in a town house on West Tenth Street in Greenwich Village—across the street from where Mark Twain once lived. On weekends, she hunted with the

Buckram Beagles if weather allowed. A friend that lived across the hall was a fellow beagler and a Spanish socialite. She helped smooth some of Margaret's brusque social tendencies. Margaret's mind raced, and she frequently forgot much of what someone had just said to her. Margaret dedicated herself to giving all her attention over to listening when someone else was talking.

She was dating Charles Cocke, the grandson of the founder of Hollins, and brought him to dinners at her sister's home. Even Basil approved of the gentle, kind man. He was an engaging conversationalist and, like Margaret, enjoyed everything the city had to offer. They went to plays, museums, and restaurants. She envisioned how her life would be if they were married and living in Virginia. She thought he might make her happy, but she worried about what living so far away from New York would mean for her writing career.

In her desk drawer, Margaret kept a collection of notes and ideas for picture books or stories and poems that wouldn't fit in the reader that she and Lucy were writing. Before the end of the year, Margaret had drafted manuscripts for almost a dozen books in various stages of polish. Before leaving on a beagling trip to Virginia, she impulsively stuffed a couple into an envelope and sent them off to an editor she had recently met who worked at Harper & Brothers.

Since 1917, the national beagle field trials had been held in Aldie, Virginia. On the five-hundred-acre farm, the Buckram Beagles' hounds competed to improve their club's standing and the breeding value of their beagles. Footraces for the hunters also were held. The Buckram's beagles didn't bring home any titles, but Margaret won her race, earning her the title of the fastest female runner in the sport.

After the field trials, Margaret went to Richmond and ran into a fellow Hollins alumna. The girls took an impromptu trip to their old school to attend Sunday chapel. Once on the Hollins campus, they also went wading in Carvin Creek, picked dandelions, and saw the first robins of the spring. Margaret was tickled to run into a former professor, who feigned alarm at seeing his ex-students, nicknaming them Bad and Worse. It delighted Margaret that she was labeled only the Bad.

The visit to Hollins invigorated Margaret and renewed her soul. She was happy enough with her life. She had become close friends with the other teachers and writers at Bank Street, who had nicknamed her "Brownie." She was especially close to Edith "Posey" Thacher, another teacher, and Rosie Bliven, a Bank Street volunteer. Rosie and her erudite son, Bruce, regularly invited Margaret to their literary gatherings in their apartment. Rosie was well connected in New York society, and Bruce was a remarkably talented writer. He and his friends were some of the most prestigious young writers in Manhattan. Margaret sometimes joined jazz revelries, playing with more passion than talent, but her band members didn't care. It was all in fun. Margaret's life in the city was full and interesting, but being in Virginia away from the city's hectic pace reminded her that New York wasn't the only place she could live.

She wondered if settling down somewhere like Virginia would doom her chances of being a writer. Stepping back into a place you loved didn't necessarily mean you weren't moving forward. And she really did like Charles. Maybe she could be happy being married and living near Hollins. Margaret's vacation came to an end with these questions swirling around in her head.

Despite her doubts about her future, the young teacher returned to work at Bank Street feeling strong and invigorated. The vacation had renewed her, and she was quite proud of her national championship as a runner. Another triumph was soon hers, too. While she was away, the Harper editor had read her manuscripts and had loved her writing. Waiting on Margaret's desk upon her return was a letter offering to publish one of her stories as a picture book. Best of all, the editor asked to see other stories Margaret had written.

Before long, Margaret held her first advance check in her hand. She headed for the bank, glancing at this little piece of paper that made it official: she was an actual author. She had been writing poems and stories for the Dutton reader, *Another Here and Now Storybook,* but that was part of her job at Bank Street. It wasn't a separate book that earned royalties and would be illustrated in full color. This book would have her name printed on the cover.

Margaret stopped at the flower cart near her apartment for her weekly bouquet. The apartment's living room walls were painted the same bright green as the library in her family's home but lacked the luxuries of that house—it was old and cold. There was no hot water for a bath, but Margaret liked being on her own again.

Seeing the profusion of color and scents on the flower cart thrilled her. It was spring in the city once again. She looked down at the check in her hand and then up at the flowers. She was now a real writer. She hoped there would be many more book advances in her future, but there would only be this one first advance, and she wanted to make it memorable. She wanted to celebrate! She decided she'd throw a party unlike any other and convinced the vendor to take the check in exchange for delivering the entire cart of flowers to her apartment.

By the end of the year, Margaret had a book advance from another publisher for a collection of stories and poems. It was enough to pay for a trip she'd long wanted to make to Ireland. She was eager to see the land of her ancestors, but her father had refused to let her go alone. She coaxed Roberta into coming along by arranging for her to receive an advance as the illustrator of the book. Most likely because Basil would join them, her father approved of the trip.

Margaret planned to write and visit art museums in London for two weeks prior to meeting Roberta and Basil in Paris. Her plan went astray on the ocean liner as it crossed the Atlantic. On the boat, Margaret met a charming group of young men who asked her to join them on a bicycle trip along the coastline of Cornwall. It was the best way to really see the land, they promised the adventurous Margaret.

She bought a bike when the boat docked and followed the boys. They stayed with farmers and fishermen along the way and found pubs in every hamlet. Their haphazard planning didn't always assure comfort. One night, Margaret's makeshift bed was a bathtub. She woke with a very sore neck and vowed to plan her travels more carefully. It was, though, a glorious trip—much better than traveling alone or with another girl.

If her father had known his daughter was traipsing unchaperoned through the English countryside with a gaggle of boys, he would have been horrified. It certainly defied convention, but anyone of literary merit wouldn't have turned down an adventure like this.

Nor would he or she have stayed away from the pubs, where cider and conversation with the local villagers made for colorful evenings. This was the England she had pictured. Kind farm people, dark pubs, fields of heather and stone that disappeared into the sea and fog. This felt like a pilgrimage and she like a real author.

On her last evening on the coast, she walked through a fine rain as it drifted over the granite-topped hills of Dartmoor in North Bovey. Dusk was setting in. She was alone on the rocks except for the occasional bunny or sheep that materialized out of the waves of mist blowing over the heathery land. The farmhouse where she was staying wasn't far; she would be there before dark.

Over the past few days, she had grown close to the couple who rented her a room at their small country house. They shared warm dinners and hours of conversation with their American guest. Margaret was delighted each time their orphaned pet calf mooed at the back door for milk. Kittens, dogs, and geese wandered the farm, too. It was a most relaxing place, and Margaret hoped to stay there for three more days, writing and painting. As she walked along the moors, she wondered about her future as a writer.

Just thinking about her deadline sent a twinge of anxiety down Margaret's spine. She really should have finished the book by now. Snippets of poems were coming to her, but they were far from sonnets; they were merely ideas without solid purpose or form. She still wanted to write something serious, something literary. Margaret thought that perhaps a course in playwriting could help her step out of the children's literature world. Learning a new way to write might unlock her ability to write for adults. But as the English mist swept around her, she reconsidered. The problem wasn't her style of writing, she realized; it was that she couldn't think up anything of importance to write about. Maybe she should stop writing altogether and just grow up. She wasn't sure how to do that, though. Growing up seemed to be something that happened rather than something that was done.

Margaret headed back toward the farmhouse. The bicycle trip had been impulsive, but it had led her on a wonderful journey. She felt stronger than she had in years, and she wanted to ride her bike around Ireland. Maybe she would ride it to Paris to meet Roberta. She didn't know where she would stay between here and there, but she had faith that the winds that blew her to this corner of England would see her safely south.

After meeting Roberta and Basil in Paris, they went to the International Exposition of Arts and Technology in Modern Life, which was being held near the Eiffel Tower. Countries from around the world displayed their latest inventions and art in pavilions built especially for this world's fair. The swastika of Hitler's political party marked Germany's exposition, but its menacing shadow had only begun to cast darkness over Europe.

Margaret was fascinated by the modern art she saw on display in the French pavilion. Long ago, she'd learned that art was a window into every era. As she visited medieval castles in these ancient lands, she scribbled notes on scraps of papers. Try as she might, she couldn't separate her modern view to imagine life inside those walls centuries ago. She promised herself to visit art galleries more often on her return to America. Perhaps by seeing the changing world through artists' eyes, she could better understand history and her own place in this world.

. . .

When Margaret came back to work at Bank Street, she found that Lucy Mitchell had been busy starting a writers' collective called the Writers Laboratory. As a member of the publications staff, Margaret was automatically a part of the group. The other members had been handpicked by Lucy to write for Bank Street's publication division. Its members met each Wednesday to review works in progress and to discuss the results of manuscripts that had been tested in front of children. Lucy was a good-humored and enthusiastic coach who helped the writers tailor their words to the interests and language levels of their desired readers. She critiqued their work through plumes of cigarette smoke while sitting on a worn green couch. All the members considered these productive sessions a rich reward for having survived Lucy's courses on grammar.

Lucy also found Margaret another new part-time job. Lucy had convinced Bill Scott, the parent of a Bank Street student, to start a publishing company to produce books based on the school's literary principles. Lucy provided office space in the Bank Street building and suggested that Scott hire Margaret as his editor and principal writer.

Scott's aim was to produce unique children's literature that did not copy what had been done before. Exploring new ways to make books appealed to Margaret's sense of adventure, too. She saw so many opportunities in this field that, even though she desperately wanted to write something more serious, she considered it her duty to make certain juvenile literature was set on the right course. She settled in as editor at William R. Scott Inc. and was proud enough of the letterhead that bore her name and title that she pasted multiple versions of it into her scrapbook.

Eight
1938

They fished and they fished
Way down in the sea,
Down in the sea a mile;
They fished among all the fish in the sea
For the fish with the deep sea smile.

<small>FROM *THE FISH WITH THE DEEP SEA SMILE*</small>

B ill Scott's mostly family-run operation published five books in 1938. His wife, Ethel, wrote one of the books, and her brother John McCullough acted as the company's editor in chief. The small publishing company pushed the boundaries of the standard book—adding textiles and textures, writing from unique perspectives, and inviting accomplished fine artists to try their hands at illustrating for children. Margaret had learned a great deal about editing and publishing during her time at Bank Street, and she brought everything she knew to Scott. Her mind was always searching for new ways to engage children through books, and fortunately for her, Bill was bold enough to try most anything she dreamed up.

One of their first books was written by Margaret's friend and Bank Street alum Posey Thacher. Margaret wrote another two of Scott's first books, edited all of them, and found illustrators willing to work for low fees. It was standard for publishers to pay artists a flat fee for their work, and the fledgling company was on a tight budget. For *Bumble Bugs and Elephants,* one of Margaret's books, she found an excellent artist through her friend Montgomery "Monty" Hare. Monty had attended college with an artist named Clement Hurd, whose work Margaret saw hanging in Monty's bathroom. She loved Hurd's style and wanted to call him right away, but Monty knew he had no phone. Instead, Monty and Margaret headed over to his apartment in a run-down Greenwich Village building. One wall was crumbling and made the place feel like a war zone. Margaret was fairly sure from his living conditions that she could afford to hire him, and she was right. The next day, she was training him to illustrate for children.

That summer, Bill and Ethel Scott invited their staff, illustrators, and writers to join them at their Vermont farm to brainstorm ideas for their next list. Dogs roamed around as their owners reclined in chairs, on hammocks, or on the soft green ground. Margaret had an idea but didn't want to appear too eager. She had recently heard a broadcast of Gertrude Stein comparing the nursery rhyme "A Tisket a Tasket" to one of her own writings. It dawned on Margaret that Stein might be interested in writing for children. She proposed they contact Stein.

Everyone agreed her idea had merit. Being able to list a literary giant as one of their authors would be a coup for any children's publishing house, especially a small one like Scott. Other authors whose styles might work for children were suggested. They also wanted to contact Ernest Hemingway and John Steinbeck, whose descriptive but simple writing styles would easily adapt to children's literature.

At Bank Street, Margaret led workshops for writers and teachers on how to write for children. She was certain she could coach established writers how to tailor their work successfully. Margaret was sure that if a Stein or Steinbeck stepped from adult books to children's, the questionable designation of their Here-and-Now books as literature would disintegrate. Those hard-to-please critics and self-important librarians who showed such disdain for their work would not dare dismiss a children's book by Stein or Hemingway as pabulum.

Fortunately, most librarians, book buyers, and reviewers were impressed with Scott's first list of books, and sales were brisk. Even so, Bill was worried about his company's future. While the library market did not return books, it was customary for bookstores to return unsold copies to a publisher. The Scotts' barn served as their book warehouse, and some of those returns were making their way back to Vermont. No one was sure how many more copies would end up back in the barn.

Returns were not something the fledgling company had accounted for, so Bill needed to reset the estimated earnings and reduce expenses on further publications if they were to survive. As a favor, Bill asked Margaret to agree to a reduced royalty on the books she wrote. She loved working with Scott and believed they were changing the landscape of children's literature. These were her friends, so she agreed. In a small operation like Scott's, everyone had to pitch in any way they could. One of their first books, *Cottontails,* had been printed on cloth with cottontails sewn onto the illustrated bunnies. But the tails on the bunnies weren't attached firmly enough, and they soon began falling out of the books. Margaret had not been able to sew straight stripes on a sorority sister's pants, but she was handy enough with a needle and thread to tack the cotton onto the bunnies' tails alongside the rest of the staff.

Margaret was delighted that Bill liked her idea to contact established writers. She longed to meet Stein. How marvelous it would be to work with her literary hero and tell her how instrumental her words had been in shaping Margaret's style. Bill, though, tasked John with approaching each of the authors. If the writers responded, then Bill himself would work directly with the authors. Margaret was crushed, but she agreed to help craft the letters.

John told Margaret this was a fruitless venture. He bet her a set of box seats at the Metropolitan Opera that none of the authors would respond. Margaret felt certain they would at least hear from Stein; she took him up on his bet.

Margaret also spent part of the summer off the coast of Camden, Maine, with fellow Bank Street staff members Jessica Gamble and Tony McCormick. Tony brought her two sons and piano along to the spacious old house on Vinalhaven Island. The rambling cabin, Sunshine Cottage, was rustic, but that didn't bother the merry band from Lucy Mitchell's ranks. Even the bats that occasionally made their way into the upstairs bedroom and bath couldn't spoil the mood. A rowboat and a sailboat came with the rental of the house, and Margaret and her friends explored the series of islands dotting the shoreline off Long Cove, the slough where the house was situated. They had a marvelous time getting to know the locals, exploring the forests and islands, and picnicking anywhere that struck their fancy.

Margaret's book *The Fish with the Deep Sea Smile* had been published earlier that year by Dutton, and dozens of glowing reviews were sent her way. *The Streamlined Pig* was about to be published by Harper & Brothers, who asked her to think of a suitable nom de plume for her books with them. She was already published by Dutton and had been contracted by her friend Al Leventhal at Simon & Schuster to write a series of Disney books. It was suggested she use a different pen name with each publisher, and Margaret liked the idea of having unique names for her different writing styles or age-specific works. She hoped to come up with pen names that had hidden meanings, like Mark Twain, and was considering Darnel as a last name because it was one of the grasses used by Shakespeare's King Lear to create his own worthless crown when he went mad. Like timothy grass, it also turned gold at harvest time—the same shade of gold as Margaret's hair.

One afternoon, the trio found themselves in a predicament. Jessica had experienced a panic attack as they were rowing back to their rented house and insisted they pull the boat to shore. She hopped out and peered back at Tony and Margaret from behind a spruce tree, convinced that if she got back into the little rowboat she would die of a heart attack. The situation was growing dire because the sun was setting, and walking through the thick forest back to their rented house would be treacherous over land dotted with granite quarries. Margaret and Tony tried to appease their terrified friend, saying that they would row along the shoreline, but to no avail.

Fortunately, a large boat was cruising by and came to their rescue. At the helm was Big Bill Gaston, a handsome man with a ruddy face. He looked at the women. He felt no urgency to speak, and Margaret was suddenly self-conscious about her appearance. She was wearing a torn sweater and blue jeans. She typically took pride in her worn clothes and even had a name for them—boops—but under this man's gaze, she found herself wishing that she had worn something more attractive for the day's adventures.

Bill introduced himself, although Margaret already knew who he was. The tragic suicide of his wife, Rosamond Pinchot, earlier that year had made front-page news. Many of the reporters placed the blame on Bill, whom they described as a womanizer.

Bill offered to give Margaret and her friends a lift and to tow their boat. It took a great deal of persuading to get Jessica off dry land, but they boarded the boat, and Bill fixed them rum and Coca-Colas. Margaret watched him as he moved about the boat and talked with her friends. He appeared gracious and amiable, not at all the callous philanderer that the reporters had made him out to be. She liked his directness. She desperately wanted to make an impression on him, and when they discovered they had a friend in common, Margaret nervously chatted on about the fellow. She immediately regretted placing more importance on that friendship than it warranted. But there was something in Bill's eyes that excited and aroused her; she wanted him to like her.

. . .

Bill came by the next day to take Jessica and Margaret sailing. He moored his boat, and they swam to a small island with a white pebbled shore. Lying near the great expanse of sea, they talked openly about their lives. The pretenses of adulthood were wiped away, and it felt like they were teenagers again. They played a game of telling secrets, pretending they were talking of someone else, but really sharing stories about their own lives, hopes, and dreams. Jessica confessed that she had dated a New Yorker once who was so wealthy that policemen stopped traffic when he drove her downtown; they had been able to speed straight through all the red lights. Margaret told them about a man who threatened to shoot himself if she didn't marry him, but then didn't. Bill wished life was just one long prom, with boys in tuxedos and girls who never grew older.

As the days passed, Bill served as their local guide. Maine had long been his family's summer residence. After the death of his wife, it served as a haven for himself and his boys and their nanny. He had a comfortable home situated prominently above the water on a private island in the middle of the slough where Margaret and her friends were staying. For years, a steady stream of celebrities, politicians, and friends flocked there to swim in the calm waters around his island and dance under the stars on his outdoor ballroom floor. That summer, only a few of his friends came to visit, so he often sought time with Margaret alone. He made dinner for her at his home and took her for cruises on his luxurious boat to gaze at the stars.

Tony was not fond of Bill. Once Bill invited the three of them over for lunch and had promised to pick them up at their dock at one o'clock. They dressed and sat waiting for over an hour, but he never showed. Tony said Bill drank too much and was wrong for Margaret. But it didn't matter what she said because Margaret was already too much in love to listen.

When Margaret returned to New York, Bill called her every day, begging her to come back to Maine. At the end of the summer, she hopped on a train to Rockport to go see him, but when she arrived, he was nowhere to be found. On the platform, there were groups of people kissing hellos or directing their chauffeurs to their luggage, but Margaret stood waiting, unsure of what to do. A cab driver saw her anxiety and offered to help with her bags. She declined. Bill would be there soon, she hoped.

She thought she saw Bill slouching her way but was mistaken. Had she gotten the day or time wrong? She looked up and down the platform again. The cab driver was waiting to see this final desperate sweep of her eyes. He sidled in, gripping one of her bags firmly, and asked where she needed to go. She told him to take her to the docks.

As the cab crested the hill, Margaret saw Bill tying off the stern of his boat. Relief washed over her. He hadn't forgotten, after all. The cab driver unloaded her bags and walked them to the boat. Margaret barely noticed. When she faced Bill, the rest of the world disappeared. It was as if they were the only two people on an island. She loved how he looked in his casual summer clothes with his sun-browned skin. She could tell he was excited to see her, too, by the way he smiled up at her every so often as he tied ropes and placed bumpers around the boat.

They walked from the docks toward town and into a store that

sold canned goods, meats, and an assortment of homegrown vegetables. It smelled of stale crackers. Old women from town shuffled around the store, and over Margaret's head hung flypaper strips,
too full to be of any more use. The place charmed her.

As they walked back to the boat, Margaret felt the gaze of the
small town's gossips upon them, but she didn't care. She breathed
in the mingled scent of kelp and salt water. She loved that smell.
She and Bill untied the boat and set out to sea.

Margaret stood on the boat, watching the water and land around
her. A bell buoy clanged on a distant wave, and a fish hawk wheeled
above her. She saw its nest of sticks nearby in the top of an old
dead tree. Moss hung from the tree's branches, reminding her of
the trees on Cumberland Island. She told Bill it looked like a tropi-
cal island. He promised to take her to a place with green moss,
giant skunk cabbages, and blue irises all around. She would think
she was in the jungle.

The ride was choppy, and Bill had to steer the boat into the waves
to keep the spray from the whitecaps away. Margaret wanted to sit
next to him on the captain's seat, so he gave her a hand up. They
held on to each other as the boat was lifted high by one big wave
and then dropped back into the sea. Bill promised it would be
smoother sailing once they turned the point.

Margaret felt secure in Bill's closeness on their perch above the
ocean. He turned the boat into the channel of islands. It occurred
to Margaret that those patches of land and trees looked discon-
nected on the surface, but far below, they were the same land. The
trees, rocks, and ocean valleys were all one, standing together
against the endless waves. People were like these islands, she

thought. They live separate lives, but underneath they are all connected. They seek comfort and support through others. No one really stands alone. Margaret nestled in closer to Bill, thrilled to be in his arms in the fresh air and on the exciting seas of her beloved Maine.

By fall, Margaret had won her bet with John McCullough. Gertrude Stein was already at work on *The World Is Round,* a children's manuscript. She promptly finished it for Scott to review. On the evening it arrived, Margaret invited John and Bill Scott to come to her apartment to read through their prize. As was her style, Stein added little punctuation. This didn't surprise Margaret, but John was flummoxed. It was unreadable. Margaret still had hopes of meeting her literary hero, so she wasn't going to cave easily, nor would she second-guess Stein's methods.

For over an hour, they debated whether what Stein had sent was publishable. Margaret defended Stein's view that children naturally knew where pauses in stories fell. John was certain that children would get lost in Stein's train-of-thought style. Scott listened thoughtfully to both of his staff members: he knew that publishing this text would be a financial risk, but he wanted the laurels of having such a famous author on his small company's list. Like Margaret, he believed in challenging the status quo in favor of moving children's literature forward.

Suddenly, the lights went out. This wasn't the first time Margaret had forgotten to pay her bill, but it was an unfortunate time for it to happen. She knew what to do. She found her stash of candles and placed them strategically around the living room. Before long, everyone grew hungry, but the only thing edible in Margaret's apartment was a boat-shaped cake she had ordered for a bon voyage party she was hosting the next day. It was important to keep Scott there until she could convince him to accept Stein's manuscript, so she placed the cake on the coffee table. Between bites, the conversation continued.

Both sides grew more entrenched in their positions, and the discussion turned heated. At its crescendo, Basil stepped inside the apartment to return Margaret's vacuum cleaner. He had heard loud voices on the other side of the door and had come in, unsure of what he might be walking into. When he saw the partially eaten cake, candles burning on every available ledge, and the startled faces gazing up at him, it was more than the shy professor could bear. He dropped the vacuum and scurried down the hall, away from the drama unfolding in Margaret's apartment.

Margaret's laughter broke the tension, and the three editors soon reached a resolution. Margaret felt victorious. They would publish the book. She would edit the manuscript and present her suggested changes to John and Scott. It would be John's responsibility to convince Stein to accept them.

Margaret had arranged to meet Bill Gaston for lunch at the Bear & Bull, part of the Waldorf Astoria hotel. Coming in from the bright day, she had to pause at the entrance for a moment to let her eyes adjust to the cloaked darkness of the room. She didn't see him. This room was rarely empty, but Margaret had never been there for lunch; evenings were always brisk and crowded.

Margaret took a few steps toward the bar and caught the bartender's eyes. He lifted his head toward the back of the room, and she saw Bill sitting at a table in the corner. He wasn't alone. Margaret nodded a quick thanks to the bartender and saw a sympathetic look in his eyes. She took a deep breath and made sure there was a smile on her face before she headed to Bill's table.

The woman sitting with him had on a black silk dress that was totally inappropriate for the early afternoon hour. Her body language indicated that if she hadn't already slept with Bill, it wasn't out of the question. Margaret's name for women like this one was Slitch. These women were always slinking around cocktail parties in low-cut dresses with an air of superiority founded only on their sexuality. Margaret knew that once those Slitches had to carry on a conversation, she could always trump them. Wit was her domain.

Bill said the woman knew how to read palms, and the Slitch offered to read Margaret's. She declined, saying that she would let her foot be read, but never her palm—that she kept a secret. Even the Slitch laughed, but it sounded as forced as the smile on Margaret's face.

Soon the woman said her good-byes, and Margaret was left alone with Bill. He told her that the woman was quite clever at outwitting the government. Her clothes, jewelry, and apartment were all gifts from men she knew, and none of it was documented, so she never filed income taxes. Margaret knew better than to criticize another woman to a man because it always compelled him to defend her. Yes, she agreed, that was very wise of the girl.

Smart, indeed, Margaret thought. That Slitch cut emotions out of the equation. To her, relationships were probably nothing more than business transactions. Maybe that's what Margaret needed to do—build emotional calluses when it came to Bill. But it was too late; she was in love, and the worst part was that she knew for certain there would always be another woman with him at the bar.

Nine

1939

Fog
Like memory
Drifts softly
Softly over the sea
Grey in its mystery
And all we see
Or do not see
Is different
Softened in fog
And memory.

UNPUBLISHED

Margaret sat at the antique dining table that served as her desk at Scott's new offices. Through the glass-paned door behind her, peacocks strutted around the small courtyard. At her feet rested her Kerry blue terrier, Smoke. He appeared to be nothing more than a black mass of curls until he moved or groaned. Across from her sat Leonard Weisgard, an illustrator she hoped to hire. He was gangly with a crest of thick, dark hair that reminded her of a cockatoo. His agent had sent him to meet with Margaret a few days earlier, hoping she would hire him to illustrate Gertrude Stein's book.

Leonard was exceedingly talented. Margaret loved his beautifully blended colors and intricate style. If she couldn't hire him for Stein's book, she had others in mind. Bill Scott, though, found Leonard's art too dark and sophisticated for American children. He wanted Clement Hurd to illustrate Stein's book and didn't want to hire Leonard for any other projects, either. Leonard's style might be more suited to expensive printing techniques than the color-block designs used at Scott, but Margaret was certain Bill's opinion of Leonard's art was based on his wallet, not his eye.

Printing costs and quality were a critical part of publishing. It was the printer's ability to translate the art into press plates for mass production that made or ruined a book. After the illustrator delivered the artwork, printers made pressboards that alternately masked and exposed the corresponding areas to be splashed with either cyan, magenta, yellow, or black ink. If the art was intricate or used blended colors, as Leonard's did, printers created screens that allowed limited amounts of ink to pass from the press to the page. Extra screens drove the cost of printing up. The cheapest books were printed in big blocks of two colors, which was Bill Scott's preferred method. Even more money could be saved by printing half the book in only black ink and placing the colored illustration on the other side of the page spread.

Some of the major publishing houses had recently launched children's book divisions, so more and more juvenile books were making their way to the bookstore shelves. Too many of them looked the same. Margaret longed for more complex illustrations, but, if she had to stick to Bill's preferred two-color books, at least they could be unique. Leonard was talented enough to pull that off, and she had the perfect book in mind for him, but convincing Bill would be difficult.

Margaret wanted Leonard to illustrate a book about sound. The idea for a book that used illustrations representing sounds had first come to her while she was playing a parlor game. Each player declared a street sound to be their own—a car horn, policeman's whistle, or a person shouting "Eyoo-hoo!" Cards were dealt, and if a player's card matched someone else's, they had to be the first to make the other person's sound. It was uproariously fun. Margaret was convinced the game could become a picture book if the right artist could visually marry sound, art, and story. She was certain it would be a hit with children. They loved interacting with a story, and unexpected sounds kept their attention.

Over lunch a few days before, she explained her idea, and Leonard had told her that he, too, believed shapes and colors suggested sounds. As a child, he would walk around London with his father, recording the sounds of the street for a phonograph record, and even then he had imagined how sounds might be drawn. He was willing to take on the challenge without a contract. If it worked, Margaret would try to sell Bill on the idea. After their lunch, Margaret had dashed off a manuscript and handed it to him.

Leonard worked as rapidly as Margaret and returned only three days later with sketches and sample paintings. Her story was of a little dog, Muffin, who gets cinders in his eyes and has to walk around a city blindfolded, guessing what noises are making the sounds around him. This interactive tale presented the perfect way to feature Leonard's brilliant illustrations and bring noises to life.

Margaret was ecstatic. Not only had Leonard fused sound and image in his art, but he had brought the city to life on the page through angular buildings that seemed to overwhelm the little dog. His cars, too, appeared to be in motion. This was exactly what she had hoped for, but she wanted the experts to weigh in.

With art in hand and Smoke in tow, she and Leonard walked over to Bank Street. In minutes, they stood before a kindergarten class with Margaret reading the story and Leonard holding up his art as the young critics reviewed their work. Leonard's wheels looked too much like eggs, the children said, so he made them rounder. The car horn Margaret had described as "Honk Honk" was deemed too dated and promptly replaced by an "Awruuuuugaaa." The story kept everybody's attention, including the dog's.

It wasn't hard to convince Bill Scott to offer Leonard a contract with their standard flat fee for the art. Margaret knew that his work was as vital to the book's success as any word she had written, so she lobbied Bill to pay Leonard royalties. In her role as editor at Scott and at Bank Street, she often negotiated payments to the artists, and she found herself arguing for higher and higher amounts to keep illustrators she knew were talented. There was no room for negotiation on this book—the margins were too thin. Margaret knew there was only one way to assure that the illustrators of her books could make a living wage with their craft: she had to split her royalties with them. She offered this alternative to Bill, with one caveat—he had to publish the book in four-color.

As spring took hold on the streets of Greenwich Village and the flower cart vendors returned, Margaret was pulled to return to

Maine and Sunshine Cottage. She invited her friends and colleagues to visit, and many did. Some came to work in the midst of Maine's beauty and others just to frolic. During the day, everyone did whatever they wished—writing, drawing, sailing, fishing, or island hopping. They napped in hammocks, walked through the forest, and went berry picking. Evenings almost always included a divine meal, interesting conversation, parlor games, or sing-alongs. Margaret paid a local lobsterman to keep her lobster traps full, and a seaplane stopped at her dock weekly to drop off fresh supplies of food and wine.

Over the past year, Margaret and Bill had seen one another frequently. He called almost daily, and they talked about their work, their lives, and their plans for the summer. She accepted that he was unfaithful to her. She once promised Bill that she would never cling to him like other women. She knew that her independence was part of what made her attractive to him. Other women might breeze in and out, but he loved her. She was the one he called late at night and early in the morning.

Bill had gone to Boston at the end of June, and on his return, he told Margaret that he was now married. His new wife, Lucy, was expecting their baby at the end of the year. He said it casually because he fully expected that Margaret would want to continue their relationship. He assured her that he still loved her and wasn't taking this marriage very seriously. Margaret was justifiably angry and hurt. She knew he was a lothario but had every reason to expect that she would become the next Mrs. Gaston. When Bill shared the news of his marriage, Margaret refused to see him again.

All summer, she had done her best to be cheerful for her guests. But they knew she was brokenhearted. It made her feel better to be with her friends, especially Leonard. He was her closest confidant, and he offered her a calm, reliable presence.

Now summer was at an end, and only Leonard and Margaret remained. Leonard painted, using Margaret as his model. The day before, Leonard had painted Margaret sitting in her white rocking chair, looking down while holding a green apple. Today, the fog enveloped the world around them, and he felt inspired to paint her as a heavenly saint. She scoffed but agreed to pose. He placed her on the couch with a drape over her bare legs. She teased him that this painting would ensure her immortality. She wanted to be one of those women who posed for famous artists. He assured her that he had a long way to go before getting famous, so she might want to achieve immortality some other way.

Almost as soon as Margaret got situated and Leonard took out his brushes, they heard a boat pull up to the dock. All they could see out the window was the fog's heavy white mist. Leonard put down his brushes and told Margaret to keep her position; he would go see who was there. She waited for a moment before getting up to look at the painting. He had turned her blond curls a dark brown, but it was her. Those were her own eyes staring back at her.

Margaret was still looking at the painting when she heard Leonard chatting with Bill Gaston. She hurriedly returned to the couch and repositioned herself, pulling the drape on her leg a little higher. Leonard entered the room, but Bill stayed in the entryway. He knew how angry Margaret was with him, and he kept a respectful distance. He asked her to come for dinner to meet his wife, Lucy.

Margaret already knew a great deal about Lucy. Margaret had paid an investigator to dig into Lucy's life and was eager to meet this Texas Slitch, but she feigned disinterest. She sighed in agreement to come over later that day. Bill looked at the painting from where he stood, then skulked out.

The only sound for a long while in the house was that of brushstrokes. Then Margaret realized Leonard was humming. She wondered if he always did that while he painted. She wondered what he was humming. It sounded familiar, like a symphony, but it took time for her to place. It was the song "Bill" from the musical *Show Boat*. The woman sings it through tears, remembering her own husband who abandoned her. Like Margaret, she knows he was no good for her, but can't stop loving him.

At the dinner, Margaret quickly sized up his new wife as a liar. She knew from the investigator's report that Lucy Gaston's background was not the one she had told Bill. Back in the city, Margaret's resolve to keep Bill at bay melted. It wasn't long before Roberta caught him sneaking out of Margaret's apartment early one morning and berated her sister for carrying on with a married man. Margaret also was disappointed in herself. She entered psychoanalysis in the hopes that it would help her to understand why she was drawn to someone like Bill, who was so clearly wrong for her. On her doctor's instruction, she documented her dreams, and each week they discussed their subconscious meanings. Psychoanalysis was emotionally draining for Margaret, but she believed it would heal her.

Many of her dreams centered on her problems with her mother. Her father and sister also figured prominently in those sessions. It didn't take therapy for Margaret to see that she missed the close bonds of the family she'd once had. Her mother and father were separated. Bruce lived on his boat or at his club. Maude lived in Manhattan and worked at B. Altman's department store—a friend of Margaret's who was the manager had hired Maude as a favor to Margaret.

Even though Maude lived close by, Margaret seldom visited her. The times she did were bleak. Maude's health was poor and her attitude downtrodden. Margaret tried to be upbeat, bringing her mother books and flowers, but in a short time, she always became anxious and couldn't wait to leave. Margaret always left her visits with Maude feeling guilty.

Things were not much better with her father. Christmas holidays and summer vacations that had once stretched out for weeks had been reduced to dinners punctuated with casual conversation. Margaret underplayed how much she earned to him, hoping to keep the allowance he handed her each month. Still, she craved his approval and wanted him to be proud of her many career accomplishments, so she always gave him copies of the books she wrote. He seemed not to notice.

Margaret had spent the Christmas of 1939 in Aiken, South Carolina, with Dot, the young girl she had tutored years before in Connecticut. They had remained close over the previous four years, and their relationship had grown from tutor-student to an actual friendship. Dot attended a boarding school in South Carolina and was alone for the holidays. Margaret knew all too well that feeling of loneliness around the holidays and of being trapped at a boarding school. She took the train south, with the hope that the warm weather would help her get rid of a lingering cough.

She soon felt well enough to ride horses with Dot and to chase rabbits with a beagling group based there. Dot was as adventurous as Margaret and, like her, unafraid to take a shortcut through briars when they ran with the dogs. Dot had matured into a beautiful young woman. She and Margaret looked so similar that people often asked if they were sisters.

When Dot returned to New York on spring break, she and Margaret reminisced about their Christmas holiday together. It had been a wonderful time—one of Margaret's happiest holidays in ages. She told Dot that she yearned for Christmases long past when she would sing carols around the piano with her family and then curl up in bed with a cup of eggnog. Dot had an idea: Why not celebrate Christmas whenever you wished? Why not celebrate it now, in the middle of spring? It was a splendid idea. Margaret called friends to join her for a Christmas party that evening. The only stipulation was that each of them had to bring a wacky gift to exchange.

Leonard arrived carrying a large stuffed pheasant, which had brought him lots of stares from his fellow passengers on the city bus. Weather vanes and lobster pots were bargained for, and the whole party was so much fun that the group decided to form a club dedicated to these types of impromptu celebrations. Any member, at any time, could declare it to be Christmas, and they would assemble. They called it the Birdbrain Club, a nod to H. L. Mencken's *Smart Set*, and considered it their own silly Algonquin Round Table. Membership was based on who Margaret, Dot, or Leonard wanted to be included. Proposed inductees, they decided, were required to exhibit a high degree of forgetfulness, an intense curiosity, or, at the very least, a short attention span. This flock of friends became Margaret's closest allies. They were the people she relied on to cheer her up, and they knew all her secrets. They became her new family.

. . .

Margaret's cadre of friends and colleagues came and went that summer at her rented cabin in Maine. Posey Thacher, her friend and fellow writer at Bank Street and W. R. Scott, had married the illustrator Clement Hurd the previous year. The trio carved out time to write, encourage, argue, and create together. Margaret threw out ideas constantly, and her enthusiasm was contagious. Working with Margaret could be exhausting and infuriating but extremely satisfying and never dull. Clem often found himself serving as mediator between his wife and Margaret. Nevertheless, their time together was always productive.

Esphyr "Phyra" Slobodkina, an illustrator Margaret had first hired when she started working for Scott, also visited Maine that summer. Three years earlier, Phyra had walked into Margaret's office at the insistence of her boyfriend, who needed money. He had heard that the pretty blonde at Scott was paying artists advances on books, which meant fast money. Phyra didn't want to disappoint her boyfriend, so she brought Margaret a manuscript illustrated in her collage-style art.

Phyra's style was abstract, somewhat reminiscent of Pablo Picasso's style. Margaret had seen his enormous mural *Guernica,* which depicted the Nazis' Luftwaffe attack on a Basque village, when she visited the Paris Exposition with Roberta and Basil.

As a young girl, Margaret had toured the art museums of Florence, Italy, and she asked the guide why the faces on some of the paintings looked so odd and others so realistic. She was told that artists' perceptions—and mankind's—were always evolving. When she saw Picasso's mural, she finally understood what that Italian museum guide had meant. Picasso's style changed people's perception of art. Margaret hoped that Phyra's art could do the same for children's books.

Margaret didn't buy the manuscript Phyra had so carefully crafted, but she did hire the artist to illustrate one of the first books on the Scott list, *The Little Fireman*. By the time Phyra visited Margaret in Maine, her career was well established. Critics raved about her unique style. But she was struggling to complete one of Margaret's texts for Doubleday; she came to Maine to get help from her favorite editor.

That summer, the nation was deeply divided on whether to join in the European war. Anti-Semitic broadcasts and articles claimed the Jews were forcing America into the war for their own selfish interests.

When Margaret learned that Phyra was Jewish, she confessed that she had to fight her prejudice after listening to those broadcasts. Her confession upset Phyra, who thought of Margaret as one of her closest friends. Margaret's fumbling defense, that she simply didn't know any Jews because there hadn't been any at her schools or in her social circles, only cut Phyra more deeply. The next day, the artist took an early leave from Maine.

Margaret was distraught. She sincerely believed she was democratic and fair-minded, but her conscience bothered her. The sad dismay on Phyra's face even haunted Margaret at night. She dreamed she was on trial for her prejudicial rant, trying to defend her words. In the dream, a wounded Phyra sat in the courtroom, accusing Margaret of never really having been her friend after all. Margaret knew that she would have to make amends, and she hoped Phyra would listen to her sincere apology.

. . .

At the end of the summer, Margaret and Leonard walked to the small café at the center of Vinalhaven. On most summer nights, a small crowd gathered at the town's single restaurant, but the busy season was over and the café was empty. Margaret didn't even see the owner, who usually stood behind the long counter, bellowing greetings when customers walked in the door. Instead, Margaret and Leonard were greeted only with complete silence, and for a moment Margaret wondered if the café was already closed for the season. The sound of a door slamming at the back of the kitchen let her know someone was still there.

The owner's wife came out of the kitchen, wiping her hands on her apron, and told them to sit anywhere they wanted. She looked much younger than her husband, Margaret thought, as they chose a table. The woman explained that she rarely worked there, but her husband had gone fishing with some friends. End of summer, he always left and she closed up, she explained. She asked where they had come from, and Margaret told her they had walked over from Long Cove. The woman nodded and said there wasn't much left in the kitchen, but if they liked steak and tomatoes, she could make them a fine dinner.

Margaret and Leonard gratefully accepted. It had taken them over an hour to get to town, and they were ravenous. Margaret had hiked across the island before, but it had been in daylight, and she had stopped along the way to pick berries. She was surprised by how much farther the walk seemed on a moonless night.

A young couple strode in the door, and the woman came out from the kitchen. The smell and sound of steaks cooking were unmistakable, but the woman told the couple she was closed. They looked quizzically at her, the kitchen, and Margaret, but thanked the woman and left.

The woman brought out Margaret's and Leonard's steaks and pulled up a chair to sit down with them. Knowing they had come from Long Cove, she asked if they knew Bill Gaston. Margaret kept her composure and told her she did, indeed, know him. The woman said she had been good friends with Bill's former wife, Rosamond Pinchot. They used to swim together, back and forth up the slough for hours, talking about children and Maine and most anything. She was the kindest person, the woman said. What a tragedy, and now those poor Gaston boys were losing another mother.

She saw Margaret's surprised face and reported that Bill's new wife had filed for divorce. Margaret and Leonard exchanged knowing looks but asked where she had heard this tidbit. She read it in one of the tabloids, she said, but she couldn't remember which one. She had cut the article out to add to a scrapbook she kept about Rosamond. She could go find it, if they wanted. Margaret said not to bother but that it would be nice to see the scrapbook; she had heard such nice things about Rosamond. The woman assured Margaret that Rosamond had been a wonderful woman, that she treated everyone the same—always a kind word for everyone. And such a good swimmer, she could swim for miles.

While the woman went upstairs, Leonard shared his surprise that Bill and Lucy Gaston's split had already made the news. In July, Lucy had caught Bill and Margaret in bed together at Sunshine Cottage. Lucy had promptly packed her bags. Bill refused to let her take their six-month-old son with her, so she left the island alone.

Now it made sense to Margaret why one of Bill's old lovers,

Blanche Oelrichs, had come to visit. Blanche first found fame when she married John Barrymore and her book of erotic poems inspired by the affair became a bestseller. Blanche's wealthy family had been embarrassed by her affair and poetry, so Blanche had permanently adopted her nom de plume, Michael Strange.

Margaret had rowed over to Bill's house a couple of weeks ago, and she had been surprised to find Michael sunning with Bill and chatting like casual old friends. Margaret detected the sexual undertones Michael laced into their conversation but wasn't as jealous of Michael as she was intrigued. Michael was about twenty years older than Margaret but didn't look it. Her voice was as melodious as a perfectly tuned violin, and her dark looks were exotically haunting. She had once been named the most beautiful woman in Paris. That was decades ago, but she was still beguiling.

Michael was now making news for her political views. She was listed on the exclusive Social Register but also was a registered communist. She was a vocal member of the America First Committee and part of their weekly radio show out of New York. As pressure for America to enter the war raging in Europe grew, the AFC fought for isolationism. They believed that American democracy could only be preserved by staying out of the war and that even sending aid would weaken America's ability to defend itself from attack. They contended that the British, the Roosevelt administration, and "Jewish-owned media" were brainwashing American citizens through propaganda. Bill also supported the AFC's stance and joined the organization, as did hundreds of senators, business tycoons, and celebrities. The pilot Charles Lindbergh often spoke on behalf of the AFC at political rallies and on the group's weekly radio show.

Michael was everything Margaret wished she could be. She was outspoken, sophisticated, and sure of herself. Michael ran in the highest literary and social circles. She was welcomed at the Algon-quin Round Table and was a courtesy niece of the Astors and Vanderbilts. She disdained everything about Hollywood, but actors and movie directors flooded to her doorstep. Even her perfume was seductive. It smelled of lemon verbena and reminded Margaret of tiger lilies. Margaret kept it to herself that the next day she smelled that perfume on one of Bill's pillows.

The owner of the café reappeared with the scrapbook. Page after page of articles had been meticulously preserved. Rosamond's early career, film promotions, marital discord, and suicide were all there. How touching and sad it was that this woman still clung tightly to an occasional friendship that had ended so long ago.

When Margaret and Leonard left the café, she admitted to him she had been the anonymous source for the article about Bill and Lucy's divorce. Making the split public reduced the chance of Lucy Gaston returning to the island. It was a calculated move, but she hadn't counted on it luring other women like Michael Strange to Bill's side.

Tomorrow, she and Leonard would return to the city, where radio and newspapers made the horrors of the world more real. Margaret told Leonard that it was going to be a long, cold walk home—he should button his coat.

Ten
1940

The sound of the wind
Is a wild sound
It bristles the hairs on my back
The sound of the wind
Is the deep sound
Of all that I long for and lack

U<small>NPUBLISHED</small>

Lucy Mitchell sat on the green couch in the Writers Laboratory surrounded by her editors and teachers. Most held black-and-white composition books containing their notes from the week. Some, including Margaret, held manuscripts.

Smoke usually accompanied Margaret to these meetings. He was a fixture at the school and was well behaved around the children, but he was known to nip at other dogs and to piddle on people standing at bus stops. Here, he was relaxed and rested at Margaret's feet, going mostly unnoticed until a writer's story dragged on—then he would issue a soft groan, one that had perhaps been prompted by a nudge of Margaret's foot.

Margaret brought some of the material she was working on for a textbook that D. C. Heath Books contracted with the school to produce. They wanted six social studies books based on the school's teachings and progressive philosophies. Instead of chapter after chapter of fact-filled information, Lucy envisioned the series as fictional stories in which characters learned about the world around them.

Margaret was writing and editing the textbooks for the three younger grades. More than once she had to ask the lead editor what, exactly, social studies were. Each time she was reminded, she would dive right back into her research to align her stories and poems with the theme of the textbooks.

While writing for Bank Street, she kept her manuscripts in the Here-and-Now style, but her own writing was often tinged with fantasy. In Writers Laboratory review sessions, Lucy gently chastised her protégé for straying away from the real world, but her words had little impact. Margaret remembered spending her childhood days in the world of imagination. It was, she believed, an important and natural part of growing up. Lucy had been ill as a child and was not as active as Margaret. Perhaps that shaped her disdain for weaving fantasy into stories. Lucy believed it made more sense to have anthropomorphized animals performing tasks true to their own nature than it did to place them into a human world. Why, she wondered, did Margaret think the real world would be less interesting to a child?

Margaret's work with Disney and editing fables had taught her that children, regardless of their race or gender, connected with stories with animals as main characters. The public seemed to agree with her, judging from the success of the Disney books. She took on more book projects for the studio, including a manners book. She joked that Donald Duck was going to say, "Hell, that ain't polite!" but in reality she believed in the importance of social graces and was proud of all her work. She was also too polite to directly challenge her former mentor. She no longer shared those types of stories in the Writers Laboratory. Instead, she borrowed her friends' children and read her stories to them.

Margaret's career was zooming along. She was part of Bank Street's seminars on how to write for children and was quite proud that the Museum of Modern Art in New York displayed her book *The Little Fireman* in an exhibition of contemporary American art. She was writing for Bank Street, Scott, Harper, and a magazine geared toward children called *Story Parade*. She earned more than most authors, but she usually spent every penny before the next royalty payment arrived. She was an impulsive spender and a poor record keeper, so it wasn't unusual to receive notice her bank account was overdrawn. She took that in stride, rarely worrying about her cash flow. Her father would always loan her what she needed to get by, or she could turn a manuscript into quick cash by selling it to a magazine. As a last resort, she could always sell a book for a flat fee in lieu of royalties. She rarely took that course, but one time she saw a gray fox coat in a store window. She didn't have the money to buy it, but it was gorgeous—worth selling off all the rights to a manuscript. She knew Bennett Cerf at Random House was looking for children's books. Even though at a party long ago she had dumped a drink in his lap for making fun of her "baby" books, they were friends. She called him up and that day walked out of his office with a check.

What Margaret was completely incapable of writing was anything of interest for adults. She submitted short stories, feature articles, and books to editors and publishers she knew, but only one of her articles was picked up. The finished piece was published as a photo essay, so she wasn't even credited.

The short stories she wrote still mirrored her life. In one, she lashed out against her staid brother-in-law, Basil, for criticizing her flitting, uncertain career and romantic life. In another, she recounted meeting the now-married Morrie for a drink in the hope of understanding why he had left her years before. These stories were useful for purging her frustrations and rewriting unsatisfactory endings of relationships and arguments to her own liking, but they were little more than diary entries.

She still yearned to write something of literary merit for adults but couldn't seem to leave the children's book business behind. She assigned days of the week to focus only on serious writing, but found she couldn't schedule what flowed out of her. When she put her pencil to paper to write something for adults, another children's story, poem, or song poured out. She couldn't stop them even when she tried. It felt like automatic writing, as if she was only the medium through which the stories came.

She decided that the only way to jump from juvenile to grown-up writing was to leave children's publishing altogether. Maybe that would turn the spigot of juvenile notions into something she could sell to an adult audience. She had resigned from Scott at the beginning of the year but continued to write books for the small publishing house. She made the rounds of her regular publishers and told them that she would accept no more writing assignments. She turned over most of her Bank Street editorial duties to another editor and, perhaps to convince herself, listed herself as a writer of juvenile books and of a play and stories not intended for children in the annual publication of *Who's Who in America*.

She soon knew that a complete break wasn't possible. There were projects in the works she was contracted to finish. She also wanted to continue some series, like the *Noisy* books, for the sake of her illustrators. Her books were selling, and children's publishing divisions were springing up in almost every publishing house. Many of them called, hoping she would write something for them. She told them she was too busy. Earlier that year, Al Leventhal, the publisher who first hired her to write for Disney, suggested she join a guild of writers and artists that was producing books for a variety of publishers. He was a good friend, and she liked working with him, so it had been tempting. She had initially declined, but after she pared down her schedule to commit herself to writing more for an adult audience, she realized she couldn't support herself if she wasn't writing for children.

Margaret was surprised when Michael Strange called to invite her to lunch. She wondered what spurred this invitation but was excited to see Michael again. At Margaret's suggestion, they planned to meet at the Lafayette, Margaret's favorite restaurant. She chose a seat that gave her a view of the entrance. She wanted to see how the staff reacted to a celebrity coming to their restaurant. People like Michael seldom ventured into the Village.

She ordered a vermouth cassis and tried to shake off the hurriedness that enveloped her. She lived close by but had barely arrived on time. She didn't want to be late—even though Bill had said it was unlikely Michael would show; he had reported to Margaret that Michael rarely did anything she promised.

Michael arrived only a little late. She swirled into the doorway in a huge fur coat topped by a fur hat. She looked like a member of the Russian royal family. The maître d' greeted her with a flourish and showed her to Margaret's table. The waiter, who had been entirely indifferent to Margaret's drink order, praised Michael's choice of sherry effusively. Margaret smiled, happy to see the typically subdued staff in a fluster.

Michael also needed a moment to settle. She had gotten on the wrong subway, and when she emerged at street level, she'd been lost in the angular maze of streets and buildings of the Village. Over drinks, they chatted, and Margaret contemplated why exactly Michael had asked her to lunch. There was a current flowing under this meeting, Margaret could feel it. Michael's eyes danced with anticipation, which told Margaret there was more going on in Michael's mind than her polite conversation let on.

After their first drink, Michael asked Margaret how her love life was faring. Margaret tried to laugh it off, but Michael pressed her. Was she living with a wild musician? Maybe two of them? If so, was the sex good?

Margaret was momentarily stunned by Michael's bold questions but didn't want to dampen the mood of the lunch. She drew in a breath and confessed that her love life was not at all good. She said she was waiting on an old buzzard and then giggled anxiously and lapsed into nervous chatter. It dawned on her as she rambled on that her love life was entirely uncertain. Bill was legally separated but far from getting a divorce. Margaret waited on his calls, waited for him to show up at her door, waited for him to propose.

She brightened, though, as she told Michael that her work life was going very well. Almost everything she wrote for children was snapped up. Her social life, too, was shaping up. She was still active with the Buckram Beagle Club and had made some new, interesting friends through Rosie Bliven's son, Bruce. Bruce was an erudite writer who was freelance writing for half a dozen major magazines. Basil and Roberta had moved to teach at Vassar, so she was now hosting her own dinner parties. She told Michael that she was no longer seeing people she didn't want to see. Michael sniffed. She never saw people she didn't want to see.

She asked Margaret how Bill Gaston was. Margaret considered her response before speaking. Michael had just come from visiting Bill in Maine, so Margaret knew that Michael had a very clear sense of how Bill was doing. Why was she asking? Margaret replied that she and Bill had mostly a telephone relationship these days. Michael chirped that Bill called her, too. In fact, she supposed he sat in his house overlooking the sea, calling women all morning long. She loved him dearly, Michael confessed, but he was such a rascal. She wished she could be a fly on the ceiling of his bedroom, watching him squirm to get away from women after he slept with them. They cling to him, then he never calls them again, she reported to Margaret.

For a moment, Margaret wondered if she had been wrong about Michael and Bill having had an affair; the way Michael was talking made her relationship to Bill seem more like that of an older sister or an old friend. Margaret defended Bill weakly; he made business calls, too, she supposed.

Michael leaned across the table and spoke in hushed tones that drew Margaret in. Michael's voice was musical, and her laugh was rich and deep. Her black eyes moved swiftly around the room every so often, then fell back on Margaret with such intensity that the rest of the room fell away. Margaret couldn't help but feel she and Michael were alone in the restaurant. Waiters brought food, people came and went, but Margaret barely noticed.

"Bill drinks too much," Michael reported. "He gets sad and drinks until all he feels is the warmth of alcohol. Then he surrounds himself with women who are terrible for him, like last weekend. The most horrid woman was there, an actress with a terribly shrill voice that he couldn't possibly be interested in. He was as virtuous as a vestryman with a jackal's morals," Michael said.

Margaret kept her emotions in check. She knew better than to discuss what happened between her and Bill or Bill and other women. Michael was friends with gossip columnists, and Margaret already dreaded being named as a party to Bill's divorce proceedings.

Margaret changed the subject by asking Michael about her work. She told Margaret she was preparing a series of radio shows in which she would read great works of literature set to classical music. She also was working on another book of poetry. Margaret should give up writing all those silly furry stories and write something worth-while.

Years ago, when Michael had been married to John Barrymore, he was too drunk to go onstage one night, so Michael, an occasional actor, stepped into his role. She had relished the limelight. Reluctant to step back into her husband's shadow, she began wearing suits that matched his. He, too, basked in the attention their attire drew. After their divorce, Michael continued to wear clothes that were considered masculine, but tailored to accentuate her feminine body. Many of her society friends were polite to her, but whispers trailed her through a room. The mavens of the Social Register never stripped Michael of her standing in their social club because she was vaguely Austrian royalty. She had always been a curiosity to her friends. Her dark eyes and thick brown hair made her exotic in that crowd. Her rapid wit, pranks, and preening intellect were not, though, considered appropriate female behavior. When she was young, her parents had sent her off to a European boarding school. At seventeen, she returned somewhat tamed and then married into a prominent Philadelphia banking family. But from the moment she met John Barrymore, propriety was forgotten. Michael's book of poetry was a bestselling book. Every society boudoir had a copy, and the nom de plume of Michael Strange on the cover fooled no one. Her divorce from the banker, her marriage to John, and the birth of their daughter, Diana, made headlines around the world. So did their drunken brawls over the next few years, and their divorce.

She was now married to Harrison Tweed, a respected lawyer in Manhattan. They lived in one of the most prestigious addresses in the city, 10 Gracie Square, and flitted from social events in the United States to royal parties in London. It had been years since she was famous for anything but being married to a screen legend. She wanted to write poetry again, but her literary muse had abandoned her long ago. She sat at her desk for hours yet at the end of the day had no worthy words on paper.

They should travel across the country together in a caravan, Michael proposed to Margaret, who was immediately reminded of the rickety wagons pulled by old, bony horses in Ireland. The memory of those poor people who made a living by taking dead or dying horses to slaughter brought a look of horror to Margaret's face. Michael sat back, and Margaret regretted diminishing the frivolous mood, but soon realized that Michael was referring to a motor home. Michael laid out a grand plan in which they would travel west like the Joad family in *The Grapes of Wrath* and pretend to be migrant workers for a couple of hours. They could see if people were really treated that cruelly, then confess they were really society women.

Margaret laughed along with Michael, not quite sure what to make of this incongruous woman. She was drawn to Michael's bravado and enticing androgynous looks. She understood why men like Bill were so attracted to her.

Eleven
1941

If you pursue me
I shall become a fish in the water
And I shall escape you.

And if you become a fish
I shall become an eel
And I shall eat you.

If you become an eel
I shall become a fox
And I shall escape you.

If you become a fox
I shall become a hunter
And I shall hunt you.

If you hunt me
I shall be buried deep, deep in the ground
And you will never have my love.

If you are dead, dead and buried
I will be the dust on your grave
And I will marry you, dead or alive.

"*Les Métamorphoses*"
Provençal French ballad translated by Margaret Wise Brown

By 1941, Margaret's creative focus was far from children's books, although stories and poems for that younger audience continued to pour out onto paper when she sat down to write. She was working on an essay about the life and death of Virginia Woolf and on a play about two lovers torn apart by the war, entitled *I Dare Not Die*. Now that she was no longer on staff at Scott, she didn't have to worry about offending Bill Scott, so she wrote to Gertrude Stein. She explained that when she had heard Stein's speech in Brooklyn years before, she realized Stein's writing was perfect for a children's book. Margaret said that she had many stories about how well children responded to the book, which she would share with Stein when she came back to America in the spring. Corresponding with her literary idol as a colleague was a personal triumph, and Gertrude's kind but short response was carefully added to Margaret's scrapbook. Their correspondence ended there.

Margaret had become good friends with Bruce Bliven and his roommate, E.J. (Ely) Kahn Jr., who wrote for *The New Yorker*. Margaret convinced them to join her and Dot on a beagling excursion, and the jaunt was detailed by Kahn in the magazine. Both Margaret and Dot came away with scratched knees, but Dot declared the wounds added only a healthy glow to her appearance. On that day, the hares were uncooperative, and more than once the hounds bounded off in the opposite direction of their prey. Margaret assured the men this was not the way the hunt usually transpired, but the day's events and Ely's humor made for delightful company. The fourteen-mile run over hills and through trees and brambles wore the two men out. On the ride home, Margaret told Bruce he had never looked better; Bruce said he had never felt worse.

While Margaret admitted to still being in love with Bill Gaston, their relationship was not exclusive. She dated another writer at *The New Yorker* for a brief time and rarely had trouble finding male companionship in the city for dinners or plays. One dinner date turned into a long weekend when her date insisted that Margaret and Monty Hare see the ski slope he recently designed. They drove late into the night to reach Greylock Mountain in Massachusetts.

The next day, Margaret trudged up the slope behind the two men. She wasn't out of shape, but Monty was long-legged, and her date was an Olympic skier. She simply couldn't keep up. They were headed to the top of Thunderbolt Run, considered one of the best wooded ski slopes ever designed. Skiing was just becoming popular in America, and unlike the slopes in Canada and Switzerland, conditions in the United States were primitive. There was no welcoming lodge with a roaring fire at the bottom of this slope, just a little shack that sold admission tickets. A tiny woodstove offered the only bit of warmth.

Margaret hoped to impress Monty with her skiing. He was a member of the Birdbrain Club, known for his impeccable grammar and biting sarcasm. He was one of the funniest people she knew; he was exceedingly charming and reliably cheerful. The same couldn't be said about her date that evening. By the time they arrived at the ski slope, she had already grown tired of him. He was quite handsome but had little to talk about except all the work he had done on this mountain and the races he had won or was going to win.

Marching up this mountain was too much work. They were

going to need a chairlift there if this resort was going to attract anyone but daring young men. Most skiers, like Margaret, preferred a comfortable ride up the hill, bundled in furs and blankets of possum, raccoon, and fox layered on by lift attendants. When she vacationed at other resorts, she loved watching the piles of discarded furs riding past her down the hill on the lift as she rode up. Another set of attendants would remove the pelts and hang them along the fence to be retrieved after the run so skiers were never exposed to the extreme cold for very long.

Halfway up, Margaret had had enough, and besides, she wanted to write down a story that had come to her before she forgot it. She decided to turn back and told the men she would wait for them in the little lodge down the hill.

Margaret had heard a haunting French ballad with a word pattern that she knew would make a good children's story. In the song, a woman attempts to leave her lover by changing into different animals. With each metamorphosis she dreams up, he threatens to transform into something that will keep her close to him. The lyrics were adult and dark, but that "if you, then I" dynamic was something she was certain she could use. She knew that children loved a catchy word pattern simply because they loved language. She once read a story in French to a group of three-year-olds who didn't understand the story but enjoyed it nonetheless simply because of the rhythm of the words.

This idea had been forming in the back of her mind for a while. Four months earlier, she had offered the word pattern to Lucy Mitchell to use in the textbook series but warned her that if it wasn't put to good use, she was going to turn it into one of her own picture books. Lucy was busy with textbooks for older children, so

Margaret decided to make a go of it. She knew from her psychology classes at Hollins that at around the age of two, children began seeing themselves as separate human beings, rather than as part of their parents. That push and pull of wanting to be independent but the fear of leaving the nest is a fraught but necessary stage of development for children. Margaret was convinced it could become the perfect substitute for the obsessive love song in the ballad.

Six of Margaret's books had been published in the last two years, and all the while, she had been rewriting fables into storybooks for the Walt Disney studio and rewriting Brer Rabbit stories for W. R. Scott. It dawned on her that the common threads in those ancient stories was human nature—its failings and triumphs. Such stories had been told for centuries because every culture at every time understood the themes. The characters and way in which the stories were told changed, but the essence of the stories remained the same. Those stories were recounted around campfires, then by troubadours and, eventually, shared in amphitheaters and much later on televisions. Now, she was transforming them into picture books for Disney to animate and show on thirty-foot movie screens. Donald Duck, Mickey Mouse, and their friends replaced those ancient characters, but at the heart, the stories were the same—they were simply being told for a new audience in a new way. Margaret realized that if she could write about the common threads of childhood in her own books, then maybe they, like fables, would last.

As she sped down the slope, the book crystalized in her mind. She settled into the warm, tiny shack and dashed off a story about a child who tells his mother that he is going to run away. He threatens to turn into a variety of things to escape, but she counters each of his metamorphoses by changing into something that will bring him safely back to her. At the end of the story, he decides he might as well stay home. By the time Margaret's date and Monty returned, she had completed the story on the only available piece of paper she had: her ski receipt.

At the beginning of December, Margaret was in Saks Fifth Avenue and stopped at the perfume counter. She asked to sample the perfume she knew Michael wore. It was completely unique and far out of Margaret's price range, but it smelled divine. How smart of Michael to choose an expensive and memorable scent instead of flitting from one perfume to another like most women, Margaret thought. The aroma lingered in Margaret's memory long after she left the store. It triggered a desire to be with the alluring woman, so Margaret invited her for cocktails.

They met in the Village and took a walk after drinks. It was a warm night for that time of the year. A foggy mist blew in from the river and laced the air as they wandered aimlessly down the empty streets. Dark forms scuttled into doorways as they drew close, vanishing by the time the women walked by. Michael threw her arm over Margaret's shoulder and spoke of days in Paris and of walking with school friends through sinister, mysterious streets that felt like this.

At one corner, they saw taxi drivers across the intersection. The drivers stood outside their cabs, smoking cigarettes. Michael shouted out to them, asking if they could tell her where the Grand Theatre was. One shouted back that it had been gone for years but he could take them by the place where it used to be.

Michael waved her thanks. She wanted to walk. She took

Margaret's arm and led her down the street. The driver yelled after them that it wasn't safe for them to walk alone—there were wolves on the way. Michael leaned into Margaret and asked what he had meant by wolves. Bad men, Margaret explained, men lurking in doorways.

Michael howled the word *wolves* over and over, in her low, sensuous voice. As they walked on in the low-hanging fog, danger shrouded the air. It made Margaret feel alive.

That week, Margaret received her first disparaging book review in *The New York Times* for *Polite Little Penguin*. The reviewer found it well-meaning but confusing—the story didn't really make sense. Most likely little attention was paid to the book reviews in that day's paper. It was December 7, 1941—the day the Japanese bombed Pearl Harbor.

Three days later, Michael recorded her last broadcast for the America First Committee and then held a cocktail party. Bill and Margaret went, even though there were rumors there was to be a blackout across Manhattan that night amid fears that the city might be attacked. Margaret and Michael were amused that they both wore black dresses with bright red belts.

Michael offered to let Margaret use one of the spare rooms in her apartment as a writing studio. That way they could read each other's work at the end of the day. Bill warned Margaret to be careful or she would wind up being Michael's Boswell—a reference to the eighteenth-century biographer James Boswell, who kept meticulously detailed notes on the life of his friend and subject Dr. Samuel Johnson. Margaret protested but knew he wasn't too far off the mark—Michael confessed she collected biographers and journalists as friends in the hope they would write about her.

Margaret envisioned herself writing in Michael's lavish apartment. One of Tweed's relatives had been the architect and another the owner of the development, so he and Michael had one of the best apartments in the building. It had a dramatic view of the East River, and whenever Margaret entered it, she felt like she had stepped into a home on the coast of France. Floor-length Venetian mirrors hung on the walls. At each turn, large vases of flowers the size of bushes were strategically placed. Over the huge Renaissance fireplace, a mantel was lined with tiny glass animals, and above it hung a sketch of Michael by a famous French artist. In those pencil lines, Margaret saw Michael's exceptional beauty in her youth.

When Margaret first walked into Michael's bedroom, she wondered if she had stepped into her daughter Diana's bedroom by mistake. Stuffed animals were stacked high on the bed. It turned out they were all Michael's; she confessed that she'd collected them her whole life. The room itself was sophisticated, decorated in blue velvet baroque fabrics. Heavy blue drapes framed the window. From there, the river looked like a silver ribbon winding its way around the city. At night, the lights along the shore lined the river as it faded from sight.

Although Michael and Tweed appeared to be a happy couple while they entertained in their magnificent home, Margaret knew it was a façade. Michael was miserable in her marriage. She confessed that she was incapable of being faithful to her husband, or any man, and had learned the art of discreet affairs when she visited Spain during her boarding school days. She had asked someone why Spanish women were so close to their maids, why they always rushed off to the movies together in the afternoon. She was told that the women weren't really going to the movies. The minute they turned the corner, the women walked off to meet their lovers while the maids went on to the movies. American women, Michael said, want to talk about their affairs. If they had the good sense to keep quiet, there would be far less trouble.

Twelve

1942

For having felt well loved by you
For having felt no shyness that you should watch my face
For the joyous meeting of eyes in laughter
The fling of your head
And the dark bright look of you
The warm flowing laughter
From a hundred hidden springs in other years
And for the constant uncertainty
Of when you would laugh

"In Greater Amicus"
White Freesias

Margaret walked along the Central Park Zoo's gray concrete path to the seal pen, straining to see Michael through the crowds of people and pink balloons. It was chilly. Men and women were dressed in dark overcoats. What would Michael be wearing? she wondered. Her hair would be wild and free to catch the wind, as always, not hidden beneath a dull, dark hat. She remembered that Michael was tall and statuesque because she had to lift her eyes up to meet Michael's. Margaret looked over the top of the crowd but didn't see her anywhere.

She waited for a long time and wondered if she was mistaken about where they were supposed to meet. She remembered that, as a child, Michael had run away from her nanny to the zoo. They had found her at her favorite place in the zoo, the polar bear pen. Margaret walked to the bear's cage but didn't see Michael. The polar bear, too, was nowhere to be seen, submerged somewhere in the water. She returned to the seal's pool and looked through the crowd again; no Michael.

She must have changed her mind about coming, Margaret thought and turned to leave. Then she heard a familiar "Yoo-hoo!" behind her. She looked around, and there was Michael dressed in a dark coat, and on her head was a springy blue straw hat accented by a white grosgrain ribbon. A little white veil covered her face, and in her white gloved hands she held a bouquet of white flowers. Michael laughed, delighted she had fooled Margaret. Tweed had said Margaret would never recognize her in those clothes, and he was right. Michael had been following Margaret around the whole time.

It still felt like winter, so they walked briskly around the zoo arm in arm, gossiping about the writers they knew. Michael complained about the intellectual crowd. They were humorless; they wore the clothes of artists, but were, at heart, without creativity. Michael told Margaret that she and Margaret weren't like those boring intellectuals; they were poets at heart.

As the two women continued their tour through the zoo, Margaret thought about her deepening relationship with the entrancing Michael. Michael frequently invited Margaret to the Colony Club, the most exclusive women's club in the city, for lunches and dinners. The luxurious club had every comfort of the grand resorts, including bedrooms, servants' quarters, a gymnasium, and a rooftop garden, but it was only a cab ride away on Park Avenue. For Michael, it was a second home and frequent getaway after arguments with her husband.

Margaret delighted in watching Michael move through the club's elegant dining room. Michael designed her own suits in an androgynous style that mixed tight pants cropped above the ankle, fitted vests, and V-neck blouses topped with a long-tailed blazer. She sometimes added gold epaulets to the shoulders of the jacket or pinned on the stunning diamond brooch John Barrymore had designed for her. Her flamboyant attire stood out against the backdrop of society ladies dressed in lace and long gloves. Margaret heard the hushed comments some of the women made as Michael walked by. Michael assured her she'd grown used to the comments and jealousy. She was living the dream they secretly desired. She was beautiful and wealthy. She had been married to a Hollywood star; she was an actress and an author. She had made the fairy tale come true, and they could never forgive her.

Margaret and Michael called each other at any hour of the night, chortling together about their days. They talked about the parties they'd gone to and the men who had flirted with them while they were there. Each admitted she'd had an affair with Thomas Wolfe. Margaret's had been brief, but not Michael's.

Now, although winter still gripped the air, holding Michael's arm in her own, Margaret began to feel that her friendship with Michael made all her other friendships seem half-asleep. Margaret still loved Bill, and the time she spent with him was comfortable, but when she was with Michael, she felt clever, young, and beautiful. Times with her were an adventure. They walked to the amphitheater, where a chamber orchestra was performing, and took seats. Margaret wondered how the musicians could play in this cold weather. She and Michael snuggled close for warmth and listened to the music.

Over the last few months, Margaret had also formed a bond with Michael's daughter, Diana. They learned that intervening on each other's behalf when Michael became unduly stubborn could aid all concerned. When a movie studio had offered Diana a contract and wanted her in Hollywood right away, her mother refused to let her go. Michael knew enough about the business to know the studio only wanted the Barrymore name on a marquee; she worried that Diana's acting fell short of the public's expectations of a Barrymore and that the press would take pleasure in tearing the girl apart. Michael wanted Diana to use her real last name, Blythe, until she gained more experience, but the deal was contingent on using the Barrymore name.

Diana was only nineteen, and Michael still held guardianship over her career. The studio couldn't hire Diana without her mother's signature, so the girl pleaded to Margaret for help. She and Diana waited for Michael to join them for dinner at the Algonquin Hotel. The hotel had aged along with its clientele, but it held firmly to its literary cachet and reputation. Diana was early, as usual, and her mother was late, as usual. Michael had finally arrived with Tweed in tow, looking mischievous. More telling were the smudges of Michael's lipstick on the side of Tweed's face. They seemed terribly pleased with themselves as he ordered a scotch and soda. When

Michael ordered nothing, Margaret and Diana exchanged quizzical glances. For an uncomfortable period, the four sat in silence.

To Margaret, the scene had been surreal: waiters with trays of old-fashioneds moved around the crowded tables; eccentric old ladies shuffled off to their rooms; people arriving for dinner in formal evening clothes filled the restaurant. All the while, Margaret watched Diana succumb to nervousness. Michael was right; Diana would be destroyed. She didn't have her mother's calm, Margaret thought. If she went to Hollywood, she would never overcome her insecurities.

Once the drinks arrived and the waiter had stepped away, Michael launched a verbal attack on her daughter. She knew Diana had just given an interview to a Hollywood reporter about her movie deal. Michael said that if the article mentioned her in any way without her approval, she would sue the magazine without hesitation. The year before, Diana gave an interview to *Life* magazine which depicted Michael as a controlling stage mother, and she was clearly still angry about it.

Diana, though, believed that Michael had blinders on when it came to film. Diana would never be able to earn the same kind of money on Broadway. Her brothers had inherited millions from their father, but Diana's only inheritance was the Barrymore name, and she intended to use it.

The next day, Margaret intervened and helped Michael negotiate a shrewd deal for Diana with the producer at Universal Pictures. Diana was only required to make three pictures per year, and if she was contracted for a part in a play, she could spend up to six months in New York. She would earn up to $2,500 a week, making her one of the top-earning film actresses—even before her first film. Michael insisted Diana have a female chaperone and that she live away from her father because things went on at his house that his daughter shouldn't see.

After Michael's farewell cocktail party for Diana at the Gracie Square apartment, Margaret stayed on after the other guests left. She sat with Michael on her bed. They were tired and inebriated. Over the past months, the two women had engaged in a slow dance of mutual seduction. Michael was sometimes wearing her negligee when Margaret arrived and asked her to come sit by her bed for a morning chat. She read poetry to Margaret in her lovely low voice. It was beautiful, lulling.

Michael crooned her complaints about Tweed to Margaret. He treated her like a child instead of like the artist she was. He embarrassed her in front of the household staff. She suspected he was having an affair, but the final blow was when she asked him what he thought of her poetry. He admitted he had no opinion on her poetry because he never read it.

Michael said that she was beginning to feel very close to Margaret. She would never be that close or love anyone like she did Margaret. She promised to love her until the day she died. Then she called her a son of a bitch. She said they should write something together full of tenderness and poetry. They needed to do it for humanity. Michael insisted, though, that Margaret had to stop writing the fairy stories and get to work.

Margaret couldn't be sure how much of what Michael had said was true and how much of it had been infused by alcohol. She knew Michael's passions were fleeting; her sentiments might easily blow away. But until they did, Margaret decided, she would be by

Michael's side. Michael had promised her that she meant it when she said she'd love her until the day she died. She would call forth the best in Margaret—she knew she would.

Margaret was trying to leave the fairy stories behind, but writing anything for adults was still a struggle. She tried to capture the story of Michael surprising her at the zoo in an adult love story. What came out was a children's story about a dog who wants to go to the zoo, but the guard won't let him in. He dresses in a straw hat, sunglasses, a floral dress, and white gloves to slip past the unsuspecting guard.

Fortunately for Margaret, her editor at Harper & Brothers, Ursula Nordstrom, was pragmatic. Margaret might one day succeed at writing serious literature, but until then, Harper would publish and heavily promote her children's books. Ursula had a knack for spotting talented writers and illustrators. She paired Margaret's zoo story with the illustrator H. A. Rey. The book, *Don't Frighten the Lion!*, came with a paper cutout of the story's main character that could be dressed in the same disguise the dog used to fool the guard.

Ursula believed in Margaret's ability, and that year, her faith paid off. In its review of *Don't Frighten the Lion!*, the *Boston Herald* crowned Margaret the premier juvenile author in the country and praised her for consistently turning out good stories. At the same time, Harper was promoting Margaret's book *The Runaway Bunny* very heavily. They mailed prepublication press packets to newspapers and librarians, containing oversized, unbound pages of the colorful book to be read to large groups of children in libraries or schools.

Reviewers raved about Clem Hurd's illustrations. The story

Margaret had first thought up while on the ski slope—about a child who tries to run away from his mother and a mother who changes herself into a dozen different animals and things in order to stay with her child—had transformed into a playful back and forth about the same shape-shifting between a mother and a baby bunny. *Library Journal*'s reviewer predicted this would become an enduring work and hailed the rhythm and beauty of the dialogue as authentic poetry.

Instead of merely promoting this book in trade publications, Harper took its marketing campaign directly to parents and grand-parents. It placed ads in consumer magazines, promoting it as the perfect Easter gift. It sent toy stores and bookstores stacks of post-cards to mail to customers or slip in bags at the cash register. The campaign worked exceedingly well. Stores stocked and sold the book in huge numbers.

Three of Margaret's books were published that spring, and another three were to be published that fall. It was customary for reviewers to forward a copy of their final reviews to the publisher. Then an editorial assistant would type a letter containing the most impor-tant part of each review to send to the author. But Margaret wanted her own copy of every review for her scrapbook. She hired a clip-ping service to read through hundreds of newspapers and maga-zines and cut out each mention of her name. The service tagged and dated the clippings, forwarding them along to Margaret, who duti-fully glued each into her ever-expanding scrapbook.

Margaret was eager to introduce her friends to Michael, so the women planned a dinner at Michael's apartment. The small group included Bruce Bliven, who was now a regular contributor to *The New Yorker;* Monty Hare, who was producing a play off Broadway; and Clem and Posey Hurd. Michael promised to help Margaret prepare the meal, but when guests arrived, she was nowhere to be found. Bill Gaston took over cohosting duties. He mixed martinis as the group waited for Michael to show up. She flew in the door almost an hour late in full evening attire and carrying a huge basket of gourmet delicacies to serve for dinner. Margaret wasn't perturbed; she had grown used to Michael's dramatic entrances. Whenever Michael finally did appear, Margaret felt the room come alive. She assumed everyone else felt that way, too.

After introductions, Margaret proudly showed off hers and Clem's new book. Michael flipped through it and guffawed at its last line, "Have a carrot!" It was so like Margaret, she said, to treat someone who loved her with such disregard. Margaret was bruised by the comment but laughed it off to keep the dinner party light. She placed Michael between Bruce and Clem at the table. As they ate, she kept an eye on their conversation. Bruce and Michael chatted effortlessly while Clem sat almost silent.

Monty and Clem knew more about Michael than Margaret was aware. They had been college friends with Michael's second son, Leonard, and had heard his stories of how terribly his mother treated him and his siblings. As they ate, Michael constantly picked at Margaret. She corrected her grammar and dismissed her children's books as silly endeavors. It made the guests uncomfortable.

At the end of the night, Margaret declared the dinner a success with the exception of Clem's silence. Margaret assumed Clem hadn't talked because he couldn't find anything in common with Michael. Margaret was oblivious that her friends resented Michael's cruel remarks. They wondered what redeeming qualities Margaret saw in this vainglorious semi-celebrity with her swallowtail eyebrows.

In June, Margaret joined Michael at a rented house on Long Island Sound. They were alone for a week and spent the time writing and reading together. They took long swims and longer walks in the rain. They talked about what they wanted in a relationship and how the men in their lives had failed them. That week, they became lovers, and for the first time in her life, Margaret understood why men went to war for women they loved. To Margaret, Michael was a goddess.

That Friday evening, Tweed and his guests arrived for the weekend. Tweed must have noticed the change in the women's relationship. He most likely knew of Michael's prior infidelities and saw Margaret as another passing fancy. At dinner that night, the tension among Margaret, Michael, and Tweed was palpable.

Michael's frustration with her husband was laid out as plainly as the ham on the table. She talked of the life she was planning without him. She raised her voice so that even with his slight hearing impairment he could hear what she said. She described the house where she was going to live and write. She planned to live there alone, she announced loudly.

Tweed had grown used to Michael's ways. He calmly stood and offered second helpings of the ham to their guests. Putting more ham on Margaret's plate than she could ever possibly eat, he taunted her for drinking wine instead of scotch. She responded with biting sarcasm. She knew she could hold her own with Tweed. At the end of dinner, everyone rose to retire to the porch, but Tweed bade them good night and went straight to bed.

Until the early hours of the morning, Michael kept the conversation on the porch lively. All the guests watched her, entranced—especially Margaret. Entertaining was where Michael truly shined. She found other people's lives enthralling and could elicit secrets they never planned on sharing. She studied politics and formed resolute opinions and relished debate. At her table, bishops, actors, and royalty might find themselves engaged in a discussion on the war, predestination, or the history of the theater.

That night, Michael and her guests argued about psychoanalysis. Margaret strongly believed in the benefits of her therapy. She felt that the one hour a week she spent dredging up emotional wounds helped her achieve clarity and settle her internal turmoil. Michael stridently disagreed. In Michael's opinion, analysis was, at the very least, useless and indulgent. More than that, it brought up a cascade of memories that became a focus of a patient's life. Margaret stood her ground. Focusing on her problems with her psychiatrist freed her mind the rest of the week. Neither backed down. Alone in her room, Margaret stayed up until the early hours of the morning, writing a long letter to Michael explaining her belief in psychoanalysis.

The next day, Michael and Tweed appeared to be a loving couple once again. It was Margaret's turn to feel bereft. Maybe Michael was punishing her for defending psychoanalysis, or maybe she didn't really love her. Margaret knew that Michael also longed for someone who loved you completely, someone who would be by your side when you were sick and who wouldn't want to be anywhere else. Someone who believed in you as an artist and did everything they could to support you.

Margaret went to her room to pack her things. The week had been magical when it was just the two of them, but with the intrusion of the outside world, it had become a disaster. She collapsed on the bed in tears. She tore up the letter. There was nothing she could do to stop how she felt about Michael. She wanted to be more than friends. She was desperately in love.

Margaret resigned herself to life without Michael and returned to Sunshine Cottage in Vinalhaven alone. She had had minor surgery to remove a small tumor on her breast and wanted to recuperate in the midst of Maine's woods and swim in its waters. She believed in the healing properties of that shore and felt parched from having been away from its waters too long. She was not allowed to use her left arm until she was well, so rowing a boat was impossible. Lifting anything heavy was also out, so Bill and his oldest son helped her with chores. The lobsterman's wife prepared her meals.

As the days passed, she grew grateful for her returning health and was happy in her solitude. She loved it when the fog settled in and blanketed her little house. With the exception of her work on the Heath social studies textbook series for Bank Street, she spent her time reading. She wanted to take life more slowly. Her stay in the hospital had helped her to realize how busy she had been. She needed quiet, time to absorb the sounds around her and the words in front of her.

The Heath series had become an unending nightmare for Lucy Mitchell. As Lucy planned, the series took fictional characters into different worlds where they learned about a subject, and it was Margaret's idea to open each chapter with a song. But Heath thought the books strayed too far from the standard textbook model. Dozens of pages of written material were tossed aside when Heath decided the series was too liberal and the style too narrative.

Margaret, Lucy, and scores of other writers at Bank Street had devoted countless hours to creating the readers, but after four years of struggle trying to please Heath's editors, Lucy's good humor ebbed. Her hope of bringing the Bank Street philosophy to a wider audience now looked unlikely. Margaret was especially disappointed when the songs she had written were rejected as too novel an addition. A compromise on that was reached when it was decided poems would replace songs—a more traditional approach to chapter openings.

Before she had come to Maine, Margaret had promised Lucy she would forge ahead as quickly as possible. Once they got these books behind them, they decided they would get together in New York to celebrate.

As she recuperated in Maine, Margaret wrote a poem with a memorable word pattern to introduce a story in the textbook. In the story, a little girl moves from a country home to a skyscraper in the city and is relieved to see that all her cherished items from her old room are there with her, in her new bedroom. It brought back Margaret's memory of moving to their new house on Long Island after her boarding school years. She was so comforted to see her childhood furniture and possessions settled into her new room and easily placed herself in this little girl's world where she found security from her familiar furniture and things. She paired those emotions with her own childhood ritual of saying good night to the things in her room and drafted a poem called "Good Night, Room." In it, the little girl said good night to all the things in her room she found dear.

Until Margaret was better, she couldn't use a typewriter, so she sent handwritten versions of her poems to Bank Street by way of the lobster boat that picked up outgoing mail. She told Lucy that if Heath didn't like any of the works she submitted to just throw them away. She would start over again.

That summer, Margaret's dog, Smoke, swam from Sunshine Cottage to Bill's house and mated with Bill's standard poodle. By the end of the summer, Bill, Margaret, and Leonard sat on Bill's lawn, watching their four black puppies tumble and play. Leonard was scheduled to illustrate a book based on Margaret's observations of the puppies copying the "big dog" actions of their father. She saw the way the little dogs mimicked their parents and how their little world was a mirror of the bigger dog's world—big and little beds and bowls and bones. What was different was how the little dogs reacted to the world around them. They yapped at everything that startled them while their father stood observing silently. Smoke was unafraid of what frightened his puppies because those experiences weren't new to him. Once the puppies saw how their brave father reacted, they followed suit.

Margaret noticed the same pattern with Bill and his sons. They, like the puppies, often copied their father's actions. It was human nature as much as it was a dog's nature to want to be like its parents. Margaret loved Bill's boys. They were kind and always willing to help her around the house, head out on an adventure to pick blueberries, and gather kelp, fish, or lobsters for their dinner.

She continued to hold out hope that Bill would marry her after his divorce was final. She loved Michael, but wanted a family and longed for the security marriage would give her. Margaret had to settle for Bill's companionship to plays, restaurants, and soirées in New York. Here in Maine, though, they were a couple, and when Bill's boys were around, they were a family. Marriage to Bill was a waiting game she was sure she would win. He would never be monogamous, but she loved him madly and knew he felt the same.

As she sat beside Bill and Leonard, looking over the glistening sea, she was content. That night, she stayed at Bill's and sent two of the puppies back with Leonard to be used as models. It was always best when Leonard had the studio to himself. His level of messiness while he painted was more than Margaret could tolerate. He worked furiously, tossing sketches and rejected paintings to the floor.

Like Margaret, Leonard studied the dogs to understand their behaviors. He always turned over a story in his mind for a long time before picking up a brush. Once he started painting, his visions were swiftly converted into watercolors. It wasn't unusual for him to paint an entire book in a single day because the images were so well formed in his mind by the time he began.

The book about the big and little dogs was to be published by Doubleday under one of Margaret's noms de plume, Golden MacDonald, a name she co-opted from Bill's handyman. She liked that the name paid homage to her Irish heritage and her golden hair. Both Doubleday and Golden Books published her work under that name.

It didn't really matter to her because children rarely noticed the name of the person who wrote a book they liked.

When Margaret returned to New York, Michael called her late one night. She begged Margaret to find a taxi and to come get her. She had locked herself in her room and was packing a bag. Somehow Tweed had found proof of her affair with Margaret. Homosexuality was considered a mental illness to be treated in asylums or with drugs. Tweed's doctor was on his way over. It was certain he would place Michael on medication and, most likely, into an institution. She had to leave their Gracie Square apartment right away.

Margaret dashed downstairs to find a cab while Michael's maid helped her flee through the back staircase. It was a narrow escape, and they had the driver cruise around the city as they considered Michael's options. For the first time Margaret could remember, Michael didn't tell the cab driver that she had a bad back so he needed to drive slow.

Michael knew she would be safe at the Colony Club, so Margaret delivered her to that sanctuary. From there, Michael telephoned her lawyer to demand an apology from Tweed and to work out a formal separation. Within days, she had both and was allowed to move back into Gracie Square. With Tweed gone, Margaret stayed with Michael on some nights. They dined by candlelight as they looked out on the river, making plans for their future together. Margaret was going to give up her apartment and move in with Michael. They would document their lives together, a sort of biography that would write itself as their lives went along. They would be like Gauguin and Van Gogh—artists who understood each other and lived together, supporting each other in their craft.

Close friends teased Margaret about how much time she and Michael spent together. Bill Gaston told Margaret that he thought Michael had had her fill of men and had turned to a girl and that from there she would likely go on to goats. Margaret let them believe what they wished—that Michael was a substitute mother, a friend, or a lover. Many of her closest friends knew she loved Michael, but she confessed to only a few that she and Michael were more than friends.

In August, they went to Michael's new country home in Milford, Connecticut. The house was near Michael's son Robin's home. By all accounts, Michael was a distant mother, far more concerned with herself and her own happiness than her children's, but she was obsessed with Robin. She told her other children that he was her favorite while also openly and constantly criticizing him for his lack of ambition and failed career as an actor.

She had always been jealous of Robin's lovers, often seeing them as a threat to her relationship with him. Michael was always looking for ways to get them out of Robin's life. When he inherited a portion of his father's vast estate, he bought a quaint farm in Connecticut, just far enough away from his mother for comfort. His parties seemed to never end. He lived the life of an English squire and entertained friends on long drink-filled weekends, serving champagne and caviar for breakfast and gourmet meals for dinner. He was quite creative and took up a variety of hobbies. He grew an abundance of flowers and an assortment of vegetables in his quaint gardens. He liked his life the way it was and was not pleased his mother had bought a house nearby.

Before leaving New York, Michael met with her accountant, who told her she had to find a way to make an income. Her divorce settlement and savings would not support her for long. She was terrified she couldn't support herself. Her recent autobiography hadn't sold well, and none of her poetry had been published in years. Her agent was trying to sell a collection of letters between her and John Barrymore, but there was little interest. Barrymore had died in May, and the stardust that once surrounded the couple was fading. Worse, the legacy he built was being dismantled by Diana's bad behavior. The only headlines the young starlet made were for throwing punches at Hollywood parties or producers. Always mercurial, Michael was now even more sensitive and irritable.

When Margaret made a seemingly innocuous comment that she liked lightning and thunder as she watched a storm turn the sky black, Michael raged at her. How could she be so insensitive? Margaret knew she had a terrible fear of storms, and her remark was inconsiderate. Michael retreated to her bedroom, and Margaret slept on the couch that night. She was angry with herself that she'd ruined Michael's first day in her new house. She reflected on the shifting sands that were Michael's moods and on her own desire to please. What did Michael really want—a friend with her own thoughts and opinions, or a statue standing silent? She was tyrannical with Margaret, then wanted her to stand as an independent person. The situation was impossible!

As she lay there, she wondered if the relationship she hoped for could ever be. She slept fitfully and was awakened by Michael making coffee downstairs. Margaret waited quietly as she wondered what this day would hold. Michael asked Margaret to join her for breakfast, and everything seemed to be back to normal. They chattered to their dogs and talked about where to place a vegetable garden. When Michael rose to go write in her studio, Margaret flippantly told Michael to work hard, and Michael responded with a torrent of complaints. Michael criticized Margaret for mispronouncing her words; she said her remarks weren't clear in their connotations or meanings; she wanted everything brought to her lower level of understanding; she intentionally found ways to aggravate others—just to get a reaction from them. She said Margaret's inability to write anything except children's nonsense was because she had no deep emotions. Her writing could only become more serious if she, too, became more serious. Margaret needed to grow up, Michael raged.

Michael's words stung, but Margaret knew some of her accusations were valid. There was, indeed, something within her that wrecked relationships. She obsessed over trying to please lovers and then found ways to undermine and irritate them. She recognized that quality in her own mother and was afraid it was an inherited curse. Her habit of using the wrong word and losing her train of thought when she spoke was embarrassing. She struggled with self-confidence and knew Michael did, as well, but the face Michael was able to show the world was one of confidence, courage, and intelligence. Margaret wanted that for herself. She wished she could cut the damaged part of her psyche out of her brain and heart, but she would take this bitter medicine from Michael in the hope of sweet things to come. She told herself that Michael was not lecturing her out of cruelty but out of a loving desire to fix her. She, too, wanted their relationship to be one between equals.

Michael had no desire to be with a childlike version of herself, skipping along. If she was to keep Michael's love, she had to come forth as herself, pure and relaxed, uncompromising and ruthless. She apologized to Michael.

That evening, Michael received a phone call from a reporter at a major New York newspaper, the *New York Journal-American,* asking about her divorce. He told her that Tweed had flown to Reno and filed for divorce. Margaret listened to Michael's laugh and her flippant responses. How easy it was for her to shape editorial policy. How wise of her to be charming and cheerful instead of defensive. Michael called her lawyer and had him countersue Tweed for divorce on the grounds of mental cruelty.

The two women spent the next few days reading and gardening. Margaret planted tomato vines along the fence, and Michael planted chrysanthemums in beds near the house. They dug a winter garden and talked about the soups they would make from their carrots and beets. When they wore their dirty clothes and muddy boots into town, Margaret teased Michael that she would need to hide if she saw any of her social club friends. They surely wouldn't allow someone who tromped around in filthy clothes like hers as a member.

When they returned to New York, the article on Michael's divorce was published. Michael's charm on the phone with the reporter had counted for nothing. Tweed had tipped off the reporter to Michael's affair with Margaret. Tweed had obviously worked closely with the reporter to craft the vicious exposé, which dismissed Michael's stage career and poetry as insignificant. To make certain she knew he was the source, Tweed provided the sketch that hung above their fireplace for the article. The article branded Michael as the "Sappho of Long Island."

Margaret at five.

(Courtesy of Westerly Public Library)

Margaret (right) and her sister, Roberta. Part of the family menagerie in-cluded a squirrel, rabbits, guinea pig, and dog that shared their father's name, Bruce. *(Courtesy of Westerly Public Library)*

A glamour shot of Margaret from her Hollins yearbook, something her father paid additional fees for each year. *(Courtesy of Hollins University)*

Margaret (fourth from the left) riding with other members of the equestrian club at Hollins. *(Courtesy of Hollins University)*

Margaret with John Eyre (left) and Brooke Stoddard (middle), fellow members of the Buckram Beagle Club at Locust Valley, New York, on April 16, 1939. *(Courtesy of Bert Morgan)*

Lucy Sprague Mitchell.
(Courtesy of Bank Street College Archives, Bank Street College of Education)

Margaret with quill pen, her preferred writing instrument. *(Photo by Consuelo Karaga. Courtesy of the Brooklyn Museum)*

Edith "Posey" Thacher (left) and Clem Hurt with Margaret at the publication party for Gertrude Stein's *The World Is Round*. *(Courtesy of Thacher Hurd)*

Margaret (left) with Mary Phelps, another member of the Writers Lab, outside of Bank Street School. *(Photo by Elisabeth Garvais. Courtesy of Bank Street College)*

Michael Strange. At the time this photo was
taken she was married to John Barrymore.
*(Bain News Service, Publisher. Retrieved from the Library
of Congress)*

Ursula Nordstrom,
Margaret's editor at
Harper & Brothers.
*(Used by permission of
Magnum Photos)*

Margaret was photo-
graphed with her dog,
Crispin's Crispian, as
part of a publisher's
promotional cam-
paign. *(Photo by Consuelo
Kanaga. Courtesy of the
Brooklyn Museum)*

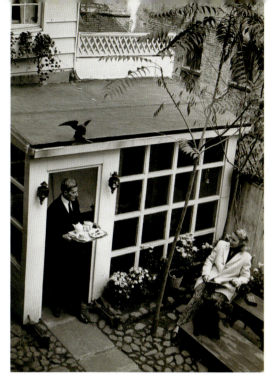

At Cobble Court,
being served tea by
Pietro Ricci, her
valet. *(Used by permission
from Philippe Halsman
Archives and Magnum
Photos)*

Margaret in front
of the fireplace that
was the model for
the one in *Good-
night Moon.* *(Used by
permission of Philippe
Halsman Archives and
Magnum Photos)*

Margaret standing in "Witch's Wink" or the "door to nowhere" at the Only House. *(Photo by Jim S. Rockefeller, Jr.)*

With Crispin's Crispian at her writing studio on Vinalhaven. *(Photo by Jim S. Rockefeller, Jr.)*

Page from a dummy book Margaret created to show Golden Books. She noted that each page number should be placed on the bunny's eye to give differing facial expressions. *(Courtesy of the Westerly Public Library)*

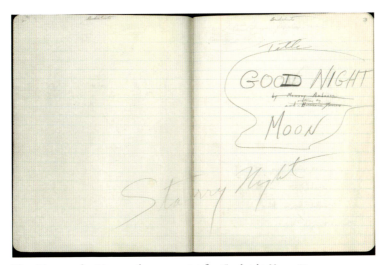

The title page for Margaret's manuscript for *Goodnight Moon*. *(Courtesy of HarperCollins and the University of Minnesota, Children's Literature Research Collection)*

Margaret at her desk in the Only House with the view of the island Leonard Weisgard illustrated in their Caldecott Medal winner, *The Little Island*. *(Photo by Jim S. Rockefeller, Jr.)*

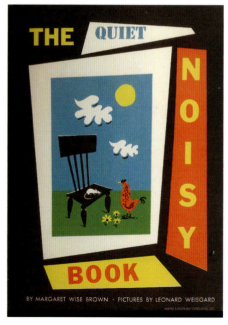

Margaret was sued by her former publisher and friend Bill Scott for publishing *The Quiet Noisy Book* with Harper. *(Used by permission of HarperCollins Publishers)*

Margaret painted this sample of how she wanted Clem Hurd to illustrate *The Little Brass Band*. *(Courtesy of the Westerly Public Library)*

Margaret at Stafford House on Cumberland Island, holding her first copy of *Fox Eyes*, illustrated by Jean Charlot. This story was inspired by her time on Cumberland as a teenager. *(Photo by Jim S. Rockefeller, Jr.)*

Margaret and Crispian with Big Bill Gaston (right) and Leonard Weisgard (left) in her Town & Country convertible at Rockland, Maine. *(Courtesy of Laurel Ripley Galloway)*

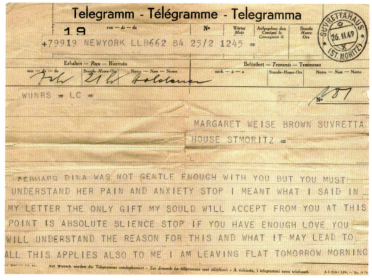

Telegram Michael Strange sent to Margaret demanding all communication between them cease. *(Courtesy of the Westerly Public Library)*

With Dot Wagstaff Ripley (right) at Dot's wedding. *(Courtesy of Laurel Ripley Galloway)*

On Cumberland Island Margaret continued to write about and sketch things that inspired her, even while sitting on a piece of driftwood at the beach. *(Photo by Jim S. Rockefeller, Jr.)*

Margaret with Jim Rock-
efeller (Pebble) on the stairs
of Plum Orchard, the house
where they met. *(Courtesy of
Jim S. Rockefeller, Jr.)*

Christening Pebble's
boat, the *Mandalay*.
*(Courtesy of Jim S.
Rockefeller, Jr.)*

In Eze with Walter Varney. Margaret's note on the front is a nod to T. S. Eliot's *The Waste Land*. She refers to Crispian and his canine companion [Mistinquett], who was named after a French femme fatale. *(Courtesy of Jim S. Rockefeller, Jr.)*

In 1967, Cobble Court was moved from the Upper East Side of Manhattan to Greenwich Village, where it resides today. *(Courtesy of Jack Manning/The New York Times/Redux)*

Memorial stone in grassy clearing near the Only House.
(Courtesy of the author)

The Only House today. *(Courtesy of the author)*

Michael was shattered. Being an avant-garde, somewhat androgynous poet was considered eccentric and was tolerated in her circle of society friends like the Vanderbilts and Astors, but being called a lesbian in the paper of record almost certainly meant social banishment.

Michael hid away at the Colony Club worried that she might lose friends, family, and her inheritance after the scathing article. She told Margaret to stay away. It was better for both of them if they weren't seen together until Michael's lawyers settled the financial details of her divorce.

Michael refused Margaret's calls, but a month after the article ran, she invited her to lunch at the Plaza Hotel. Margaret arrived first and took a table at the back of the room so she could watch for Michael. She didn't recognize her until a strange woman sat down at her table in the seat opposite her. Michael had hidden her bushy brown hair by a veil tied close to her head and under her chin. She told Margaret she was incognito—she'd grown tired of hearing the whispers of "There goes Michael Strange" as she walked by.

Her voice was strident, not at all like her usual calm, musical tone. She had been very busy trying to settle the whole mess with Tweed. Their plans to live together at Gracie Square were out. Tweed would be keeping the apartment. Michael had to find a new place to live. She wouldn't be able to see or call Margaret for a long time. Margaret needed to stop asking where Michael had been and what she had been doing with her days. She already had enough to worry about.

Michael worked hard to maintain her androgynous, mysterious allure; she would not put that at risk for a relationship with Margaret. Neither would she give up her social standing for anyone. After her pronouncement, Michael was happy and light again. Margaret's mind raced with responses she kept to herself. She mourned for the lost closeness with Michael but knew there was nothing else they could do.

Michael had never been alone in her life, and Margaret doubted it was really what she wanted, either. They both longed for something beyond love and friendship—a relationship so deep they could call on that other person any time of the day or night. People learned to live without that, but Margaret didn't want to.

After lunch, they stepped outside to watch the Navy Day Parade. The military men marching past the Plaza wore uniforms, but to Margaret, they didn't look like soldiers yet. Most still wore the demeanor of their civilian trades. Only the sportsmen and officers wore their uniforms with any martial bearing.

Michael said it reminded her of the time she carried the American flag in a suffragette march. The flag was too long, and at Forty-second Street, a policeman had stopped and helped her fix it. As Margaret and Michael watched the men march off to their uncertain fate, Michael pulled off her veil and vowed not to wear it again.

Thirteen
1943

Put a he on a he
Or a she on a she
And it never adds up to 1 2 3.
Put a he on a she
Or a she on a he
And before you can even say Jack Robinson
You've made 3.
He times she divided by he
Then take away she
And now what have you left?
A he or a she.
And what's this strange geometry
Within the heart of you and me?
This place apart
This secret heart
When all is what it seems to be.

"HE AND SHE"
White Freesias

Michael rented two apartments on East End Avenue. The flats were at the end of a hall across from each other, and she planned to live in one. The other she intended to use as a writing studio. She planned a New Year's party at her new apartments and fretfully waited for guests to arrive. If all went well—if people came—then her reputation had survived the vicious article. She wasn't sure if Tweed's influence could sway the Social Register to remove her from the list, but this party would give her an indication.

The next day, she called Margaret, ecstatic that the newspaper piece actually served to make her more attractive to the men in her circle. Among the women, it elevated her mystique. She was, without a doubt, still part of the social set that mattered so much to her. Finances, though, would be a problem. She asked Margaret if she wanted to give up her place in the Village and move into the apartment Michael was going to use as a writing studio.

The new apartments were only two blocks from Michael's Gracie Square apartment but were a world away from Margaret's bohemian enclave in Greenwich Village. She would only have to pay Michael for half of the rent, the same amount she was already paying for her old apartment. Unlike her ancient building in the Village, this one had hot and cold running water. An arched marble fireplace graced the room. But a wall of windows looking out on the East River as it curved around the building was the most dramatic feature in the space. Having apartments at the end of the hall gave the women similarly spectacular views that glistened in the day and sparkled at night as the boats moved up and down the water.

Michael's proximity meant frequent interruptions. Michael simply couldn't force herself to sit down and work. One day she claimed to have gotten a great deal done, but Margaret was surprised to see that the work she had done was party planning, not poetry.

Michael's inability to concentrate had become a problem for Margaret. Lunches at the Plaza, Diana's latest drama, and a busy social calendar were easy distractions. If Margaret didn't get her writing done between eight in the morning, when she woke, and ten, when Michael stirred, then it was unlikely she would write at all that day. She needed a place away from Michael's hubbub. Deadlines were upon her.

She remembered a book of New York architecture Tweed had that included a photo of a tiny antebellum farmhouse nestled among tall buildings somewhere on the Upper East Side. If the house still existed, it would make a fine writing studio. Its size and cobblestone courtyard reminded Margaret of the house she had rented from Stringfellow Barr while at UVA, but she couldn't remember exactly where it was. Margaret spent a morning walking around the Upper East Side looking for the little cottage. She peered around buildings and down alleys for hours. Finally, on York Avenue, she saw a building that looked familiar. She walked through the entryway of a tenement and found it. The little clapboard house was tucked away underneath a peach tree. It was just as she remembered in the photograph. It was painted white with angles of roof betraying addition after addition. Somehow all the changes only made the home more charming. She located the landlord of the tenement building and found that she owned this little home, too. She told Margaret it had once been a goat hut, which only added to its appeal for the whimsical writer. Margaret rented it on the spot.

The house was nestled behind the tenement, a series of brown-stones, and a Greek Orthodox monastery. It had only four rooms—two upstairs and two down. The floors were connected by a stairway outside. An attached room housed the bathroom, and a tall stucco wall at the north end of the courtyard was accented by a medieval-looking wooden door that led to the monastery's garden. There was no electricity, and two drafty fireplaces were the home's only sources of heat. The cold seemed to radiate from the old brick floor, so Margaret filled the house with plenty of furs. In front of one small window, she hooked a hammock into a small nook. Michael decorated the little house with antique furniture, and together they planted flowers in the courtyard. A friend donated two geranium trees that had once stood at the entrance of a horse track. Their colorful flowers bloomed high on either side of the front door. Margaret christened her little hidden home Cobble Court.

A few days after settling into Cobble Court, Margaret returned home to the apartments to find Michael in a meeting with a promoter. She seemed quite nervous, so Margaret quickly retreated to her own apartment.

Later, Michael told Margaret the promoter had called her, hoping to hire her to perform a series of concerts around the country that, like her short-lived radio show, married great works of literature with classical music. Given Michael's uncharacteristic jumpiness, Margaret was certain it had been the other way around. Regardless, the promoter and Michael had reached an agreement. The tour would start in small concert halls and churches and run for six months before finishing at Carnegie Hall in New York. Michael was elated. She was going to have an income that came with a spotlight.

This was Michael's tacit admission she was not going to succeed as a writer. The recital readings and their accompanying music would take weeks to plan, but she was at last motivated to work. Margaret was relieved. She still wrote short stories and had written a play for an adult audience, but it was clear she couldn't soon support herself as a writer of anything besides children's books. Those stories about furry little animals that Michael made fun of might not be serious literature, but they paid the bills.

When summer came, Margaret's desire to see the wild woods and smell the sea air of Maine grew too strong to ignore. She longed to shake off the city's dreary winter days, to leave the business side of writing behind, and to refill her well of creativity. She routinely issued invitations to her editors and friends in publishing to join her when they could, and the members of the Birdbrain Club knew they were welcome anytime. Margaret often said she went there alone to think and write, but that usually lasted about two weeks, then visitors to Sunshine Cottage arrived steadily. Her annual routine was to meet with her editors, make a list of things to do, and gather research materials. On the day of departure, she filled her car with groceries and alcohol, then headed north.

Michael preferred to spend her summers in tony Bar Harbor. For decades, it was where her family and friends had gathered. When she was still known as Blanche and was a wealthy banker's wife, she had lived at Le Selva, a castle-like home along the shore. She was active in the suffragette movement and was a leading hostess along that haute coastline. The superb Maine summer stock theater also was a draw for Michael. Famous actors, including Ethel Barrymore, Michael's former sister-in-law, frequently made their way to those stages.

Michael rarely brought Margaret into her Social Register world. Early on, Margaret realized that the women of that set whispered among themselves that she was merely another of Michael's eccentric adornments—a quiet wallflower with no noticeable personality. It was true that Margaret was fearful of speaking around that crowd for fear of embarrassing Michael because of her poor grammar and diction. However, the idea that she was merely a satellite hovering around Michael was insulting. So while Margaret was in Maine, she spent most of her time with Bill Gaston. She loved both him and Michael deeply but knew neither would ever fully commit to her. Bill teased Margaret about Michael and their attraction to one another but didn't question her about it. She was happy to be with each of them whenever she could.

On this trip, Margaret stopped to pick up Dot, who was at home with her mother in Litchfield, Connecticut. The two remained close, and Dot, more than ever, looked like Margaret's little sister. Dot continued to write and draw, contributing many works to her school's literary journal before she graduated. She had completed her debutante season the year before and was working part-time at Abercrombie & Fitch. It was common for Margaret to spend a night with Dot and her mother on her way to and from Maine. They rode horses and let their dogs romp together.

Smoke, Margaret's Kerry blue, was aging rapidly by now, but he was still a terror almost anywhere he went. Monty Hare, grateful to Margaret for buying up all the unsold seats on the opening night of his off-Broadway play, gave her a calmer Kerry blue. She named him Crispin's Crispian, in homage to Shakespeare's King Henry V's rousing speech. Unlike Smoke, Crispian didn't piddle on people at bus stops or attack other dogs on sight. He was fond of chasing cats and cattle, however, and on occasion nipped at people he thought threatened his mistress.

Once in Maine, Margaret and Dot parked in Rockland to wait for the ferry. They made a last-minute stop at the grocery store for long loaves of French bread, cubes of beef for the dogs' stew, steaks, chops, and butter. The boat was delayed, so they stepped into the county clerk's office to see what land or homes might be for sale. They were shown a list of properties, and a little house with a peaked roof looked just right. It was adjacent to the property Bill had shown her years earlier, where skunk cabbages and lush forests gave one the impression of being in the midst of a jungle.

That same afternoon, Margaret and Dot decided to tour the property with Bill. The little house was nestled into the hillside and backed by trees. There was no road, so it could be approached only by sea. The house had once been the home of the quarry master, and the land was dotted with pieces of granite—huge, rough slabs as well as smooth-cut columns—that never made it to their intended architectural structures. Where stones were extracted, large quarry holes were filled by underground springs. Like Cobble Court, the home's basement had served as a winter shelter for goats and sheep and also had no electricity or running water. That didn't dissuade Margaret. She was charmed by the apple orchard in the back and a door upstairs that opened out onto thin air. Its staircase had long ago become the victim of too many brutal Maine winters. Margaret quickly returned to the clerk's office and bought it. The price was so low she was able to write a check on the spot for the full amount.

Margaret placed her rocking chair in front of the door that opened to nothing. In the mornings she watched the sun illuminate the flower-filled meadow, the sea, and the islands beyond. She watched the seals play in the ocean and the fog roll in over the hills. She placed her desk by the adjacent window and hung mirrors around the room to reflect the sea and light from every direction.

In the front of the house, there were stone steps to the first-floor entrance. Two small bedrooms lay off the main room, and a set of steep steps led to an upstairs kitchen with a small table and woodstove. If she needed to accommodate a large crowd of friends, rental houses nearby were usually available.

Margaret turned the well into a makeshift refrigerator. Perishables like butter and milk were suspended by appropriately labeled ropes. She stored wine in streams to be plucked out while on hikes or picnics. One of the granite quarry pools on the property was designated as a cold-water bathing spot. For those who didn't want to plunge into the quarry's freezing water, Margaret created an outside vanity next to a tree. She turned an old washtub upside down and placed a washbasin and pitcher on top. Above, she tacked a gold leaf mirror to the tree.

Margaret boldly named her new home the Only House. It was the only house that could be seen from the water, and it was the only home she truly owned. She was a writer who could support herself, and this little house on a flowery hill was all hers.

Fourteen
1944

So all the bunnies put their heads together—
as close as their whiskers would let them get.
And they wiggled their noses.
And hoisted their ears up and down.
And thumped their heels on the ground.
And they thought the way bunnies think.

"BOMB PROOF BUNNIES"
Unpublished

In the spring of 1944, Margaret and Michael were living peacefully together. Margaret's time away in Maine and her cozy writing refuge in the city allowed her ample opportunity to reflect and write. Michael, too, was happily working on her performances. They told themselves they were allowed one drink per day, although sometimes they gave in to an extra martini or two, especially if they asked Bill to join them for dinner or drinks.

Michael didn't want to be the sole focus of Margaret's romantic desires—she thought the younger woman too needy. Margaret doubted Michael's love for her on an almost daily basis. What she didn't question was her love for Michael.

In the moment she saw Michael lying back in her bed like a God in repose—noble, beautiful, and free—Margaret understood why people would die for another and why she fought so hard for this relationship. She prayed that if Michael's words once again speared her heart, she would remember that moment—remember Michael's swept-back hair, her lean face, the way she lifted her head, and the tone of her voice.

In April, Michael's son Robin died in his sleep. His boyfriend, Billy Rambo, had committed suicide the prior year by jumping off the Empire State Building. Billy had been questioned in a murder case that was making tabloid headlines. After that tragedy, Robin began drinking more heavily and almost never left his house. Michael brought a priest by to talk to her son and tried to cheer him up, but nothing she did lifted his spirits. He sank deeper into a depression and rarely got out of bed. He complained to Michael that he felt abandoned not only by his lover but also by her. He confessed that he was jealous of Margaret.

On the night he died, he wrote farewell notes to friends, his mother and sister, and one to Margaret. Then he took an overdose of sleeping pills. He said that he wanted to be with Billy, and he requested that his body be buried next to his lover's in Indiana. In the letter to Margaret, he apologized for treating her with such bitterness.

Grief-stricken, Michael moved into Robin's house and stayed for months. Margaret and Diana implored her to come back to New

York, but Michael wanted to be alone with Robin's things. She wrote letters on Robin's stationery and had everything in Robin's bedroom moved to the study in the Connecticut home. She kept everything exactly as it was in his house, down to the papers on his desk. The only change she made was to swap her bed for his.

Margaret tried to assuage Michael's grief the only way she knew how—by memorializing Robin in a story. She asked Leonard over to lunch, but when he arrived she told him he would not get to eat unless he agreed to illustrate a manuscript she had written called *Robin's House*. It was the story of an inventive boy who turned the rooms of his house into a creative paradise. He never needed to leave his home because it had everything he needed. Leonard knew right away why she had written the book and refused to agree without thoroughly considering the story. Margaret caved and served him lunch anyway.

Many of Margaret's male friends were serving in the military, but Leonard didn't pass the physical exam for service. Bruce Bliven and Margaret spent Bruce's last night before deployment traipsing around the city. Clem Hurd was to be stationed in the South Pacific, so Posey also left for the West Coast to stay with her parents. That way she could be closer to her husband.

Most everyone was involved in the war effort one way or another. Michael was a volunteer with the Red Cross, and Dot was an official spotter along the Connecticut coast. Margaret wrote a series of stories for children who might be frightened while huddling in bomb shelters, but "The Bombproof Bunnies" never made it past the rough-draft stage. Neither did "The War in the Woods," a comical story in which a bear declares that all the animals in the forest must behave like him, even the bees. All the other animals try to be gruff and eat bark like a bear and follow the bear's ridiculous ultimatums, such as one that states wildflowers may no longer be wild. Eventually, the bear realizes that it is best for the animals to be themselves, and peace is again restored to the woods.

Like most businesses during the war, publishing had to adapt to the reduction in materials, as well as in sales. To reduce the cost of printing, some publishers decreased the number of pages in their children's books. Margaret railed against the reductions—it was almost impossible for her to reduce the conventional forty-eight-page storybook to twenty-four pages. In addition, fewer books were being published in general.

The economic slowdown of publishing during the war, coupled with Margaret's earlier failure to agree to contracts, took a toll on her finances. Frustrated with a now-unreliable income, she worked out an agreement with Golden that guaranteed her a monthly payment. She struck a deal that paid her $300 per month on future royalty earnings. In exchange, she granted Golden the rights to three books per year.

When Michael returned to the apartments in the fall, she teased Margaret about her prolific nature. If Bank Street wanted Margaret to write four hundred pages on a mouse's squeak—she could do it. This time, Margaret was good-natured about the jab. It was unlikely Margaret would ever leave children's books for a career as a serious author of adult literature. Like Michael, it seemed everything came easier to Margaret than writing something of merit for adults. When Michael suggested they work together on a musical for children based loosely on the Bible, Margaret leaped at the idea.

Michael could forgive her anything except faults that were her own, and this would be a good distraction.

Lucy Mitchell sent Margaret copies of the textbooks they had written and edited for D. C. Heath, along with the teacher's editions she'd been paid extra to write. In those, Margaret created ways for teachers to use her material in the classrooms—projects, discussions, and questions were a few of the ways she guided the teachers to make the textbooks more interesting. In the package, Lucy added a note relaying how disappointed she was by the final product and a comical eulogy she wrote about the demise of a textbook. Her dream was dashed, but her sense of humor had returned.

In the textbooks was the beguiling word-patterned poem "Good Night, Room" Margaret wrote as a substitute for one of the nixed songs. Being reminded of the nighttime ritual she shared with her sister so long ago spurred an incredibly detailed dream that night. In the dream, the room was hers, but the color scheme was that of her downstairs neighbor's—bright green walls in the living room accented by red furniture with yellow trim. It felt like stepping into a colorful Spanish painting.

Instead of saying good night to the things in her childhood room, in the dream it was her black telephone, lamp, and brush she bade good night. She wrote the story down as soon as she woke. Too impatient to wait for a typist, she called Ursula Nordstrom and read it to her. Ursula agreed it was almost perfect and decided to publish it.

Afraid of losing the visions in the dream, she included more notes than usual in the manuscript. She wanted the light in the room to subtly illuminate each object as it was mentioned. The entire room was to slowly dim as the story came to a close. The window was to be like her own, large enough to feel like the moon hung in the sky just for her. She chose a new title, more fitting with the way the moon loomed in her dream—*Goodnight Moon*. For both Margaret and Ursula, Clem was the logical choice as illustrator, but it would have to wait until he returned from the war.

Inspired by her neighbor, Margaret eventually painted her own apartment walls green and yellow. She also bought a red velvet cover for her antique poster bed, confessing to Michael her fear that the room would look like Christmas décor. But in the end, Margaret loved the bright colors of her revamped room.

Fifteen
1945–1946

In every book
At every film, I look
At the chorus or the star
I'm reminded of you
And of only you only and
That's the way things are.

If I were now to die
I would be most happy
For I've never gone so far
As to love someone more
Than sun and the moon and star and
That's the way things are.

"THAT'S THE WAY THINGS ARE"
White Freesias

As usual, Margaret spent her summer in Vinalhaven. She also went to Vermont for a week while Leonard stayed at the Only House, working on a story she wrote while looking out at the little island in front of her new home. When she came back, she found he had spent the entire time lying around and had not painted a single picture. At first, she was furious that he had wasted so many days. Then, as he painted, she realized he had been carefully studying the island. Like her, he had watched how the weather and waves created an ever-changing view of the tiny island to create stunning illustrations for *The Little Island*.

Other friends, too, came to visit the Only House. This time, they came ready to improve the little cabin. Dorothy Bennett, her Golden editor, added on a chimney and fireplace. Margaret watched her work, fascinated by the intensity with which her editor slung mortar and laid the bricks. For three days, Dorothy, her tongue held in the corner of her mouth, worked from morning until the last rays of the sun vanished from the sky to finish. Other friends helped Margaret construct a porch and build an outhouse. By the end of September, her house on the flowery hill was shaping up.

The world, too, seemed brighter. The war had ended, and by December, Margaret was in Cobble Court waiting for Clem and Posey to arrive from the airport on a snowy evening. Margaret's valet, Pietro Ricci, had lit a good fire before he left and had stacked more wood neatly beside the fireplace. There was enough there to keep Clem and Posey warm through the night, and Pietro would return the next day with food and more fuel for the couple.

Clem's tour of military duty in the South Pacific was over. He and Posey were returning from the West Coast and needed to find a new place to live. Margaret offered them Cobble Court as a temporary residence while they searched.

As Margaret waited for them to arrive from the airport, she admired her and Pietro's handiwork. Pietro had worked for Michael's son Robin for many years. After Robin's death, Michael hired him to work for Margaret and herself. Pietro was born in Italy and, like Margaret, was fluent in French, so she nicknamed him "Pierre." He walked the dogs, kept the apartments and Cobble Court clean, and could substitute as a cook if other household staff weren't available.

Pietro had polished the interior brick floor of Cobble Court and Margaret the brass. She had spent two Christmas seasons working at Altman's in their silver department and had come to love polishing silver and brass; it always gave her a sense of accomplishment. Her little living room glowed in the firelight.

Margaret would have Christmas dinner with her father later that month, but her mother was in poor health and living with Margaret's brother, Gratz, in Ann Arbor, Michigan. Margaret would not be visiting there anytime soon. Whenever she thought about her mother, pangs of guilt struck. She regretted not visiting more often when her mother had lived in New York.

Margaret was very excited about the Hurds' return. She'd kept in contact with Posey, and they had collaborated on a couple of Golden books, but nothing was better than working together in person. When the three of them were in one another's company, they inspired each other.

Ursula made only a few changes from the penciled *Goodnight Moon* manuscript Margaret submitted. She didn't keep the bit of humor Margaret added at the end in tiny script. She wanted a little drawing of the child saying good night to a cucumber and a fly.

Her draft listed the author as Memory Ambrose, a pen name she adopted from Bill Gaston's housekeeper. She gave Clem the nom de plume "Hurricane Jones" after one of the islands near her house in Maine. Ursula deleted those noms de plume but kept Margaret's title of *Goodnight Moon*.

The baby boom that followed the end of World War II brought with it the golden age of picture books. More sales meant publishers could afford new printing and manufacturing techniques. This inspired Margaret to think more broadly about what might be possible in book design. Pop-ups, die-cuts, shaped books, and novelty add-ons were a few of the ideas Margaret handcrafted in the dummy books she created to pitch to her publishers. She found a luminous paint that would glow in the dark and tried to get a printer to make an ink that would do the same on the pages of a book. That experiment didn't work, but she painted stars on the ceiling of her apartment that glowed down on her as she slept.

Not only were books including novelties, but the marketing of books also stretched in new directions. Margaret and Leonard's next book, *Little Lost Lamb,* came with a full-color poster that was suitable for framing. It was such a new concept that the publisher had to reassure buyers that the removal of the poster would not damage the book.

One of Margaret's cleverest ideas was immediately picked up by Ursula for Harper. Margaret made a petite, hand-sewn book she called *Little Fur Family* and wrapped it in real rabbit fur. Garth Williams illustrated the fur-covered book that was placed into a slip-cover box with a round hole to showcase the fur. Harper advertised it to the publishing trade as the year's best book, and *Publisher's Weekly* agreed, declaring that not since *Pat the Bunny* had there been a novelty book so novel. The retail price was $1.75, and a mink version was available on a limited basis for $15. Harper printed seventy-five thousand copies, and fortunately, parents and children found the book irresistible. Unfortunately, so did the moths in Harper's warehouse. A vast portion of the inventory was ruined. The next edition was covered in faux fur.

That summer, Margaret was the maid of honor at Dot Wagstaff's wedding. Margaret heartily approved of Dot's new husband, Louis Ripley, whose wealthy family owned a cattle farm in Litchfield. The wedding, though, caused Margaret to feel the sting of her age and her single life. She was ready to make a change.

Bill's divorce proceedings had not yet concluded. Weeks before, Margaret sat with Bill and a few of their friends outside a courtroom door as his lawyers negotiated an arrangement. Margaret was convinced that Lucy was dragging this out to keep Bill from marrying her, but as she watched the attorneys enter and exit, she came to see that Bill could have bought his freedom long ago—he simply didn't like the price tag Lucy had placed on the settlement. After that, it wasn't unusual for Margaret to place a wall of pillows between her and Bill if he wanted to spend the night in her bed.

As Margaret distanced herself from Bill, she was needier of Michael's attention and affection. In letters, Michael professed her love and devotion to Margaret. Once home though, Michael quickly grew tired of Margaret's neediness and sought to escape their claustrophobic apartments. Diana's career was in a tailspin, so Michael often traipsed after her daughter from set to set between her own performances. Margaret sometimes followed, if Michael asked her to come along and she could spare the time. Margaret's world seemed to revolve around the telephone these days. She was working on books for six different publishers, and everyone needed answers or approvals.

On a cold day in October, Philippe Halsman, a photographer from *Life* magazine, posed Margaret in the hammock that hung in a window of Cobble Court. Her longtime friend Bruce Bliven sat beside her in a chair with a pad on his lap, suggesting that the photographer was capturing the interview Bruce had completed for an article in the magazine. In actuality, the interview had occurred two months earlier when Bruce came to the Only House. Bruce was still regular contributor to *The New Yorker,* but also was a prolific freelance writer. Over chuckles and wine, he penned a whimsical piece about Margaret that would appear in the December issue of *Life.* The short feature highlighted her colorful career and declared her to be not only the most prolific children's book writer but the prettiest. It declared that anyone who met her would find her exceedingly sophisticated and claimed that she fooled her city friends into thinking she had a green thumb by tying cherries or oranges to the green bay tree she kept in her apartment. Margaret was elated by the article and being photographed for one of the world's most famous magazines thrilled her beyond even her own vivid imagination.

Halsman wanted to capture the little house where she wrote, so he stood on a ladder outside of Cobble Court. To include the house and courtyard, he needed a higher vantage point and found it through a window in the tenement building owned by Margaret's landlord. He photographed Margaret being served tea by an elegantly attired Pietro and opening the door for Crispian to enter.

Inside the tiny house, he positioned Margaret at her desk with a blue heron quill pen and then on the floor with copies of her books surrounding her. In another photograph, she was in repose on her zebra-skin couch as she tried to look pensive in an awkward pose.

She felt completely comfortable, though, when Halsman photographed her sitting in her rocking chair and lighting a fire.

Michael continued to perform her Great Words with Great Music recitals around the country, and the pace was grinding, so she was frequently tired and irritable. While Michael traveled, Margaret cared for the apartment and the house in Connecticut. She watched over their dogs and Diana's, too. The pets had become Margaret's own little fur family, and each of her letters to Michael included updates on their dogs. The letters Margaret received from Michael as she traveled were mostly tender, but with both Margaret and Diana, Michael was alternately supportive and dismissive of their accomplishments. The two women knew Michael was jealous of their successes. Diana's career had eclipsed Michael's, and newspapers usually referred to Michael only as Diana's mother; Michael's own poetry and performances were secondary tidbits of information. As Michael's audience declined, her producer had to move most of her shows to churches. Those were easier to fill.

Diana had asked Michael to come see her in the road-show production of *Joan of Lorraine* and was thrilled when she came to see her in Atlanta. Diana's performance that night as Joan was so moving that members of the cast watching from the wings were in tears. She received numerous curtain calls and was ebullient as she waited backstage for her mother to congratulate her. But Michael left the theater without a word. Michael had always hoped to play the role of her heroine, Joan of Arc. Well practiced at wounding her daughter, Michael knew that ignoring her after such a marvelous turn was the cruelest thing she could do.

Likewise, Michael had continued criticizing Margaret and her books. Many of Margaret's longtime friends and collaborators inched away. They couldn't bear to watch how cruelly Michael treated Margaret, who tried so desperately to please her.

The *Life* article became a high point in Margaret's career. The issue's cover featured Ingrid Bergman in the Broadway production *Joan of Lorraine,* which must have felt like a double blow to Michael. Margaret said little about the article in her letters but carefully pasted the cover and article into her scrapbook. It was an affirmation of her talent; she might never be a serious writer of adult literature, but she was one of the best writers of children's books. That, for now, was enough.

Sixteen
1947

Who does your heart return to?
Who do you really love?
In that blue hour of evening
Who are you thinking of?

Who does your wild young heart turn to
In those dark dreams of night?
Whose is the face before you
When you turn out the light?

"WHO DOES YOUR HEART RETURN TO?"
White Freesias

Margaret's mother passed away in January of 1947. Margaret and Roberta traveled to Ann Arbor for the funeral. Margaret took a circuitous route home, going to her mother's interment in Kirkwood, Missouri, and then to Connecticut to see Dot's newborn daughter, Laurel. Margaret was Laurel's godmother, and the christening took place at the same picturesque church where Dot and Louis had been married. Margaret heaped attention and gifts on the little girl, on whom she bestowed the nickname Pookie.

Dot and Margaret still hunted with the Buckram Beagles. They were at work on a collection of horse stories and poems but had not yet found a publisher. Two years earlier, they wrote and illustrated a book about the circus under the pseudonyms Timothy Hay (Margaret) and Wag (Dot). On a trip to the circus at Madison Square Garden in Manhattan, they had watched as the dazzling white Liberty horses began their intricate stepping routine. They turned to each other with the same idea—*this* could be a book! *Horses,* about a little horse who goes to his first circus, was on the shelves the following year. The art featured pops of red throughout, and the eye-catching cover showcased a red-and-white striped tent. A small circle on each spread displayed a fact about horses. Two years later, Margaret was revising and writing a voluminous horse story collection that she wanted Dot to illustrate. It would include facts, folktales, stories, and songs—almost two hundred works in total.

Margaret wanted to sell this collection to Golden because her collections with them earned her twice the royalty rate of a storybook. The publisher also was producing some of her books in an oversized format that Margaret adored. A larger size allowed more action to transpire across a double-page spread. Margaret had written a story of a bunny who rolled an egg from one page to the next, and she felt her text had really been brought to life on the book's large pages by Leonard's blended art. There was so much room on each spread that they decided to fill the expansive backgrounds with lush wildflowers. Margaret had picked as many different flowers as she could find for Leonard to use as models. They hadn't known he was allergic. The next morning, he woke with eyes so swollen he couldn't open them.

Margaret had been sending more and more manuscripts to Golden Books. Their line of Little Golden Books was exceedingly popular and was being sold in department stores around the country. Those huge print runs made their books affordable for families who once considered children's books a luxury. The low cost, rugged cardboard binding, and eye-catching designs encouraged parents to buy more than one book at a time, too. The sales of the pretty little books with the signature bright gold spine were skyrocketing—and so did Margaret's royalties. She was stunned by the first Golden royalty check she received and celebrated by hopping on a plane to Florida to buy a car. She returned in a yellow Town & Country convertible that matched her golden hair.

Margaret also encouraged many of her friends to submit books to Golden. She and Posey Hurd had cowritten a book called *The Man in the Manhole and the Fix-it Men,* which featured characters in the workaday world. Margaret had written the book for Scott, and she had more ideas for those sorts of stories, but her allegiance to the publisher was waning. Advance payments were often calculated on potential earnings, so based on her book sales, Margaret had been negotiating higher advances with Golden and Harper. Scott refused to grant Margaret an increase on her advances or royalty percentages. They also continued to use outdated printing techniques, even though Margaret had successfully negotiated affordable printing on new presses in Sweden.

Margaret and Leonard had been working with Scott for over a year on another book with an appealing word pattern. This one engaged children by describing something in their world—a daisy, a shoe, rain—and then deciding what was the most important thing about that subject. She called it *The Important Book* and wanted it printed in four colors as Golden and Harper were doing. Bill Scott refused, so Margaret decided to sell the book to Harper. Royalty negotiations and Margaret's demand for higher-quality printing had stalled the final contract, so she was within her legal rights to give the book to Harper. Margaret knew pulling the book would be a financial blow to Scott, but she was certain that any manuscripts she gave to the small publisher had little chance of success against the more attractive books on store shelves.

Bill Scott's books looked dated. Margaret's last book with him had been a huge disappointment. The colors weren't at all close to Phyra's original illustrations, and the printer haphazardly altered the featureless faces she gave her characters. The results gave the book a comical look. Margaret sent him a telegram at 2:43 in the morning registering a "full protest" and demanding that Bill print the book as Phyra had illustrated it.

Margaret wrote Bill a letter officially terminating their publishing relationship. She would no longer send Scott new manuscripts. Scott editor John McCullough dug in his heels, too. He canceled Margaret's other books that were scheduled to be published. Without explanation, he told Phyra to return a manuscript she was illustrating, *The Little Farmer,* to Margaret. Phyra was bewildered but nonetheless did as she was instructed.

In July, Leonard won the Caldecott Medal for his illustration of *The Little Island.* He had captured the island in front of the Only House so beautifully. Margaret was happy that the critics had recognized his talent with the highest award in the industry, so in commemoration of the award, she gave Leonard a wafer-thin Gubelin watch. In return, he gave her a box of gold Caldecott Award stickers. He couldn't have given her a more delightful gift. She stuck them to the dummy books and manuscripts she submitted to publishers—and even some copies of her finished books on her shelves.

Margaret was asked to write a piece about Leonard for *Publishers Weekly*. In it, she ticked off his many artistic accomplishments, behind-the-scenes stories of their collaborations, and his one publishing failure. This, she noted, was no fault of his as the illustrator, nor was it hers as the author; she laid the blame squarely at the feet of the publisher who had refused to print with the additional colors she and Leonard had been promised.

Bill Scott knew this was a jab at his dated printing techniques. Ethel Scott, too, must have taken offense at Margaret's claim in the article to be the one who wrote *Cottontails*, even though Ethel was listed as the author. Whether or not Margaret intentionally used this piece to distance herself from her old employer didn't matter. Bill Scott saw it as a declaration of war.

For a long time, Margaret had longed to return to Ireland to see the place where her ancestors lived. To her, everything about Ireland was more charming than America, and when she finally made her way there, she stayed much longer than originally planned. A month there did nothing to diminish her appetite for her family's homeland.

She stayed first in Liston, then traveled on to Dingle, where her ancestors had boarded boats bound for America centuries before.

She bicycled to scenic spots and ancient churches, stopping to talk to almost anyone she met along the way. The beauty of the dramatic cliff-lined beaches, with shawled women walking enormous gray wolfhounds on long leather leashes, struck a chord of primeval longing Margaret felt in her blood.

Everywhere was the smell of peat moss burning. That aroma was so specific to this land and evoked visions of cozy rooms with warm fireplaces. She understood why that scent brought tears to the eyes of her transplanted Irish friends in New York—to them, it smelled of home. She mailed swaths of it back to her apartment. She would share most of it, but she wanted to keep some for herself to burn when she wanted to remember this beautiful land.

She found that the humblest things, like bread and butter, were far more delicious in Ireland than at home. The people took great pleasure in their unpretentious lives; the land, rock walls, and roads had character. She loved hearing the hooves of donkeys on the stone streets and the tinkling bells on the carts they pulled. Margaret adored how these villagers accepted people as they were—you could sit down and have a conversation with anyone.

She spent her last week at a little house that belonged to a welcoming couple. She stayed at their inn for several nights, and they were so charmed with Margaret they insisted she stay at their private retreat on a tiny island. It was only a short row away, and the house overlooked a sandy beach with an ocean of crystal-clear water in front. Behind were the cliffs and shores of Dingle. It was clean as a whistle and positively enchanting. At low tide, she gathered shells to add to her collection inside the little cottage that sat alone on a tiny island.

Margaret wanted to bring Michael to this little house when she came to Europe at the end of the month. On the trip from New York to Ireland, Margaret had reflected on her relationships with Bill and Michael. She was tired of Bill's philandering and drinking, although she still loved him. His divorce was still dragging on, but she had adjusted to her life as it was. She no longer wanted to marry him, and her physical attraction to him was slowly dying. Before she left for Ireland, he had confessed with a laugh that he could never change his adolescent approach to romance. Maybe that's why he was attracted to her. She, too, was unable to grow up. Each summer they would return to Maine and become a temporary family. Together they created the eternal prom he wished life could be—a place where they could dance the night away on his ballroom under the stars and relive the summers of their youths in Maine.

On her way to Ireland, Margaret realized that even if she was intellectually ready to leave adolescence behind, she had no idea how to do it. If she calmed her racing mind, then perhaps she could analyze her life. Maybe maturity was the ability to calm your mind and emotions—an ability to discard the love you have for someone like Bill simply because you knew it was going to lead nowhere. Was that what growing up was? Choosing what you didn't want to do instead of where your heart leads you?

Margaret decided she would not invest any more of her emotional energy into a romantic relationship with Bill. She loved Michael more than anyone else. Margaret hoped she could grow up enough for Michael to feel the same. Michael would never be faithful, but Margaret knew she could count on Michael to be there if she needed her. She knew the person behind the extravagant ego and had witnessed the failings of her fragile self-confidence. It was Michael who wrote letters full of love and encouragement to her and whose phone calls she hoped for at the end of the day. Michael was the one who draped warm furs over Margaret when it was cold. When Michael came home from the road, Margaret welcomed her with a cup of peppermint tea. It was her life with Michael that was secreted into her books time and again. They had cobbled their lives together the best they could, and it was enough to make Margaret happy.

Michael would be attending the royal wedding of Princess Elizabeth and Prince Philip Mountbatten and was then scheduled to perform at Wigmore Hall in London. Margaret thought that a relaxing stay in Ireland would be beneficial to Michael, who continued to tire easily. This small cottage near Dingle would be the perfect place for Michael to come rest.

In her letters, Margaret described the place and her days of traveling through Ireland to Michael. She wrote using the coded language Michael insisted upon. At times, they attached emotions they had for each other to their dogs or had imaginary characters speak for them in their letters. Michael's was Rabbit and Margaret, Bunny. Michael's dog, Cricket, might speak for her, telling Margaret how much she was missed and loved. If their letters were ever discovered, they would read like nonsense, yet the two women knew the veiled meaning of every word. When Margaret wrote, she would touch the gold wishbone necklace Michael had given her. She sometimes doubted how much Michael loved her. At those times, she needed Michael to reassure her, which she often did. However, at other times, Margaret's neediness irritated Michael. She wanted Margaret to stand on her own two feet instead of clinging to her. Those arguments could last for days. The wishbone necklace had been Michael's way of silently reassuring Margaret. All she had to do was touch it to remember that someone did love her very much.

Over the last year, Michael had been frequently absent from their apartments, still busy touring with her show. Diana had begun using her mother's apartment as a home base when she took on the lead role in the traveling production of *The Philadelphia Story*. Again, Margaret cared for their dogs while they were away, sending a stream of letters that included updates from their dogs Mocha and Cricket. Smoke had died two years earlier, but the letters invariably reported on Crispian's bad behavior toward the smaller dogs.

Michael was to perform in London at Wigmore Hall and then travel on to Paris, returning to the United States in time for Thanksgiving. Margaret asked her to visit a bookseller who was holding French editions of *The Runaway Bunny* and *Little Fur Family* for her. Margaret had also arranged for the bookseller to bind a copy of Michael's performance script in leather as a keepsake of the long years' labors. Margaret was certain Michael would be completely charmed by the gift.

From Ireland, Margaret traveled to Lausanne, Switzerland, to ski. The now married Infante Juan Carlos was there, as well. She was thrilled to see him again, and they dined together. Although their reunion was anything but serious, Michael and Charles Shaw, an abstract artist Margaret convinced to illustrate books, surreptitiously planted a story with a gossip columnist. It declared that Margaret had "thrown over" Juan Carlos in favor of Charles. They thought the prank quite humorous, and Margaret complimented them on an "extraordinarily extraordinary stunt."

On her return to New York, the printer's proof pages of Clem Hurd's illustrations for *Goodnight Moon* were awaiting her. Clem's illustrations perfectly captured Margaret's dream and had used her own living-room-turned-bedroom as the story's setting. Her own green walls, accents of yellow, and her big bed with its bright red spread were perfectly captured in Clem's illustrations. So were her rocking chair, table, and black telephone. The great green room with the red balloon was her own bedroom and, like her, the little bunny in the story looked out at the moon and stars through the room's huge window. She also recognized the arched marble fireplace Clem used in his paintings. It was one he knew well from his stay at Cobble Court.

The reviews of *Goodnight Moon* were positive, and the reviewers appreciated Margaret's intention to create a book that was lulling and comforting—a style that evoked Gertrude Stein's repetitions but was also layered with Margaret's own thorough understanding of a child's world. *The New York Times* praised the book's rhythms and claimed that the pictures were a perfect complement to the drowsy phrases. However, the head librarian at the New York Public Library was still resistant to the Here and Now style of writing and saw little need for a go-to-sleep book; she refused to purchase the book for her library.

At the end of November, Michael collapsed at her hotel. She was rushed to a London hospital and then was ordered to rest and recuperate for a few days at the Savoy hotel. The traveling and performing had exhausted her. Margaret boxed up a traditional Thanksgiving meal and sent it to Michael at the Savoy with a promise to be waiting at the port in New York when she returned in December. She would bring along a chauffeur to carry her bags and make her peppermint tea back at home to help her relax.

Diana also would be home for Christmas and would have her new beau, Bob Wilcox, with her. She first met the fellow actor during her summer stock tour and demanded he be hired as her costar for this road show. He was an alcoholic, and soon Diana adopted his habit of drinking before the curtain rose. Her state was not lost on the critics. When Michael read a review that declared Diana to be wobbly-legged onstage and forgetful of her lines, she was furious.

Margaret tried to soothe Michael's anger toward Diana and Bob by praising his kindness and support for Diana's talent. Diana and Bob lived together openly at Michael's apartment, even though she was still married to a tennis pro she had met in California. That was not considered appropriate among the highbrow set, but Diana was unperturbed by what her old friends might think. She hosted large parties and invited friends she knew from the theater instead of debutante balls.

Margaret often stepped across the hall to join in the merriment and was there one night when the legendary stripper Gypsy Rose Lee came for dinner. Gypsy wore a gorgeous flowing black fur coat with a red silk lining. Both Margaret and Diana tried to buy it from her. When their offers were turned down, they pretended to steal it, saying the only person who should own a coat like that was Michael. Margaret entertained some of the guests by walking around the apartment, pointing out places where Michael would have stood, if she had been there, and drolly imitating what she would have said. In her letter to Michael describing the evening, Margaret said she did this because everyone there missed her so, but Michael felt betrayed by Margaret's allegiance to Diana. After two bad relationships and a wrecked movie career, Diana was now drinking herself out of any possible stage roles. Michael ordered Diana to find her own apartment right away.

When Michael returned to New York, she invited Diana, Bob, and his brother, a renowned New York surgeon, over to tea. Diana knew from the moment she walked in the apartment just what her mother had in mind. Dressed dramatically in a long white stage gown, Michael implored Bob's brother to get Bob help for his drinking. She then berated Diana for living with an alcoholic actor—it was ruining her career and her reputation, she said. Bob jumped in, telling Michael she had no right to attack Diana or to disparage her love life. He reminded Michael that she was married when she began an affair with John Barrymore. Bob's brother, who had been expecting a pleasant visit, sat in stunned silence as Bob and Diana stormed out of Michael's apartment.

This was the first time Diana had firmly chosen someone else over her mother. Diana broke off all contact, and there was little Margaret or anyone else could do to cheer Michael up. Most likely, Bob had also mocked Michael for her lesbian lifestyle.

On New Year's Eve, Margaret brought home some friends late at night to continue their celebrations. They were loud and happy, singing songs as they entered Margaret's apartment, but the fun was cut short. Their party woke Michael, who threw a tantrum. She was feeling ill, she said, and wanted peace and quiet. She berated Margaret for her selfishness and told her friends to leave.

Michael became less tolerant of Margaret and more critical of their relationship. Margaret felt the distance between them growing. Giving up her relationship with Bill Gaston had had repercussions for Margaret. She relied more on Michael, who did not want to be the sole focus of Margaret's neediness or her love. Michael's resentment bred more insecurity. Occasionally, Michael promised Margaret that she loved her, once even giving her a ring as a token of her affection. Behind Margaret's back, though, she complained that Margaret was too much of a burden. She hoped Margaret would soon find some man to marry.

Seventeen
1948

When spring comes around
And the cherries are red
I dream of your eyes
And all that they said.

In those shadows of spring
When the cherries were red
The songs were all sung
And the sweet words all said.

I remember the time
Of that wild blooming tree
I was with you
And you were with me.

We lay on the grass
And sweet nothings were said
We gazed up at the tree
Where the cherries were red.

"TIME OF THE CHERRIES"
Unpublished

In April of 1948, Margaret sat at her desk with a copy of a *Publishers Weekly* article in front of her. It had a lengthy feature on her old employer, William R. Scott Inc., celebrating the publishing company's tenth anniversary. Bill was commended for the many advances Scott had made in children's books, but it was clear he had made certain Margaret's name appeared only as an author in the article. There was no mention of her instrumental role in the company and how many of her innovative story ideas and developments in book design had led to the success of the struggling little company. Instead, Bill took full credit for all her ideas.

She seethed at the slight and marked up the pages of the magazine, bearing down her pencil in anger. She underlined the parts where Bill had revised history, dotting it with question marks and exclamation points. Where he claimed that he was the one who got his staff to write books of their own, she scrawled, "Nuts!!" It was ridiculous for him to grab the credit for starting her off as a writer.

Perhaps Bill Scott was upset by her refusal to submit new manuscripts to him, but until this article, she had thought they were still friends. Bill had criticized Margaret for working with Golden. Other publishers also complained that Golden books were cheap and threatened not to work with authors or illustrators who published with Golden. Margaret huffily defended her decision to write for them. The art and writing was as good, if not better, than the sugary, overwritten books some publishers were racing to throw onto the bookshelves. The story and illustrations were what lifted a book's standards; sentimentality was cheap, not binding and paper.

Margaret's reputation for shouting down her editors was, by now, well known in the children's publishing world. She usually caved the next day and sent an apologetic letter or telegram but often regretted backing down. Michael convinced her to hire Harriet Pilpel, a respected intellectual property attorney, to review her contracts. In addition, Margaret hired an agent to act as a go-between with her editors and to place her manuscripts. Her time was better spent writing than arguing with publishers and walking around town selling her manuscripts. It had the added benefit of letting her lawyer and agent fight on her behalf for better printing and quirky words she liked to insert in her stories. She knew she needed more time to write.

Before turning over a manuscript to any of her publishers, Margaret would calculate how much it would earn in their hands. Time and again, she earned the most money by publishing with Golden or Harper. Those two publishers encouraged Margaret to let her imagination run wild and wanted her to write books they could publish in wonderful new ways. After Harper's success with *Little Fur Family,* Golden paid Margaret extra for first refusal on her novelty book ideas. Some of those ideas were so ahead of anything that had been produced, she needed to make sample books to explain her ideas to their editors.

Margaret made a handmade bunny book shaped like a rabbit, books with foils that shined or glowed in the dark with luminous inks. She cut holes in one book for a stuffed mouse on a ribbon to wind his way into the story. On another she cut an oval hole for an egg to tumble out. She wrote a story that helped a child learn how to tell time that was to come with a pocket watch. Almost anything was possible including books with vinyl records. Both book publishers and record companies were racing to produce recorded stories and songs for radio and television. Neither was producing anything of quality. She knew she could do better and decided to learn everything she could about the music business.

From the moment they drove into the gate at the Connecticut house, Crispian began barking with joy. He recognized where they were and leaped from the car when Margaret let him out. He ran circles around the house and over the hill, yipping excitedly to be back at this farm. In the distance, Margaret heard the sound of cattle mooing on their way home to the barn, then the honking of geese warning Crispian not to get too close.

Margaret walked on the still-green grass in the warmth of an Indian summer evening. The leaves on the lilacs and trees had disappeared, but a few tomatoes clung to the vine along the fence. The once lush forest had dropped its leaves, and the pasture beyond the house was now visible. Margaret stared at the property she once shared with Michael. It was closed now, in preparation for the winter. The house appeared to be asleep, and it crossed Margaret's mind that a story about a dreaming house had potential. If she had had time, she would have written it down, perhaps even continued on to a rough draft, but the sun was setting. She had come here to sear the moments she shared with Michael in her mind in case she didn't return. In case Michael, too, never came back.

In September, Michael had once again collapsed after one of her performances, and the source of her exhaustion over the last two years was finally diagnosed as leukemia. Her doctor believed it was an aggressive form of the disease and estimated she had less than a year to live. He recommended she quit her tour and simply rest.

Instead of following his orders, Michael obstinately refused to cancel any of her performances. She also decided that, if her time was limited, she wanted to experience new places and make new friends. She no longer wanted to live with Margaret and told her to find another place to live.

Margaret was desperate to remain in Michael's life. At first, Margaret thought she couldn't live without her. She flirted with the idea of suicide, but Leonard convinced her that it was quite likely Michael would change her mind. So she had continued to write love letters to Michael, reminding her of what they meant to each other. Margaret wrote Michael that they had come to this world separately, but somehow they had found one another. They had once loved each other deeply, and her love was still there for Michael. She once promised to take care of Michael through any sickness. All Michael had to do was give her a chance.

She walked over to the small graveyard where they had buried their dogs. Bright yellow whirls of marigolds dotted the grass. She picked one to press into a letter for Michael. The chrysanthemums they had planted the first year they moved here were in bloom, and the mint they had transplanted from Maine looked healthy. No leaves or fruit were left on the apple tree, but she walked over to it anyway. She found a yellow apple on the ground and picked it up. The fallen apple and gray branches of the tree reminded her of a song she heard as a schoolgirl in Switzerland long ago. She couldn't recall the title, but she remembered the haunting, emotional voice of the singer. Something about cherry trees and not appreciating the people who really love you. Maybe if she played that song for Michael, it would convince her to come home, that this was the time for them to be together. Margaret put the apple in her pocket and called Crispian back to the car. They drove out of the gate and past the barren trees toward Dot's home.

Michael grew steadily more exhausted but hadn't stopped touring or missed a single curtain call. She and Margaret wrote to each other, but Michael kept her distance from Margaret. She was convinced that the stress of her relationship with Margaret had caused her leukemia. She grew more and more religious as her health diminished and decided her attraction to Margaret was a sin. She concluded that if she was to regain her health, then their physical relationship had to end. If they were really Christians, as both professed, then they should be able to fight their desire to be together physically. They should be able to love one another only as friends.

At first, Margaret was only wounded by Michael's words, but then she grew angry. She wrote letter after letter to Michael defending the nature of their love. Those letters only grew the divide, but Margaret couldn't stay silent. She knew Michael's time was limited and pressed her to remember their old life together. Margaret vowed to change and become someone else. Someone less needy and, if an asexual relationship was what would help Michael heal, then she could become the friend she needed. Margaret simply wanted to be with her before it was too late. Michael's response was a terse telegram stating that the only communication she could accept from Margaret was complete silence.

Eighteen
1949

Margaret's Root Soup Recipe

Boil small amount of water and salt. Dice onions and potatoes as you go into boiled water and also chopped parsley
and leeks. Take off the minute potatoes are cooked and add
more chopped parsley and butter, and cream if you like.
The trick is to cook quickly and unevenly, and not for long.

In the midst of all this personal turmoil, Margaret's professional life
was thriving. Golden had offered to renew Margaret's contract and
to increase the number of books of hers that they would produce to
four per year. She was in negotiations with Harper for another six
books, and three more were coming out from other publishers. Television and radio shows for children were on a rapid rise and had
caught Margaret's fancy. She saw how the blending of sound, images,
and emotion she and Leonard aimed to create in the *Noisy* book series
was manifest in television. Even with radio and records, it was possible to mix music, stories, and poems in exciting new ways.

Fortunately, she still held music and performance rights to most of her poems. She could rewrite those and sell them as she wished. She also could rewrite her stories into audio scripts. She went to record companies with samples in hand and walked away with deals from Young People's Records and Columbia.

Golden, too, was intent on turning their extensive line of books into recorded stories with songs. At first, Margaret fought with Golden's publisher, Georges Duplaix, to keep her rights. Georges offered to discuss a deal with her, but she had to keep in mind that Golden also intended to develop television and audio recordings on all their forthcoming books. They could no longer allow Margaret to hold back rights or cut her own deals with other companies. Georges warned her that no matter how much they liked a work, they would decline to publish it if they could not have all rights.

After looking at the numbers, Margaret saw that, over time, she stood to earn much more money with Golden than with Columbia and Young People's Records. They were producing many more records than either of the other companies and printing more copies of each record they made. Even though the other companies paid Margaret a higher royalty, a record with Golden stood to be the most financially fruitful for her. Harriet Pilpel had negotiated a fair split on those rights, and Margaret quickly rewrote her Golden stories so that they could be performed as songs or sound-rich stories on the radio.

At this time, Margaret joined ASCAP, an association for songwriters and composers, so she could meet composers who could help put her words to music. Burl Ives, the exceedingly popular folksinger, agreed to lend his voice to one of her songs. She met with Oscar Hammerstein II, Alec Wilder, Rube Goldberg, and a host of other composers. She knew that, as she had with Gertrude Stein and so many of her illustrator friends, she could train songwriters and popular singers to tweak their talents toward what would appeal to a child.

She imagined different ways to combine music and books. For Young People's Records, she added sound effects to her stories and songs. She wanted Golden to publish an illustrated book of music that could be placed flat on a piano. They could place a sleeve in the front of the book to hold a record album. If they made it oversized, it would stand out on the shelves of a bookstore and couldn't possibly be ignored.

When preparing to leave for Maine that summer, she packed copies of her books so she could mine new songs from those pages. She also shipped fur pillows and a lion-skin rug that included a fang-bearing head up to the Only House. The previous year, she had hired a local contractor to build a small house on a rock outcropping at the edge of her property, and it was almost complete. Margaret wanted to give the little home to Michael but had little hope Michael would ever see it. Her old lover remained steadfast in her refusal to see Margaret.

When Michael was on breaks from her tour, Margaret left the apartment to stay at Cobble Court or the Only House. Alternatively, Michael took up residence at the Colony Club. That summer, friends came and went, but Margaret wasn't her usual self. She was brusque with Clem and Posey when they came to visit and often spent her days writing alone or working on the new house she planned to give to Michael.

She was still friends with Bill Gaston, but their love affair was over. He and his boys visited regularly, but her nights were spent alone. The sound of her pencil scratching on paper, the wind outside, and the crackling fire were often the only things she heard except the chatter in her head. She was too sentimental, she decided. And still overweight. It was time to cut out sugar, fat, and starch from her diet. She limited herself to only half a bottle of wine each evening.

She kept busy converting the new house into a writing studio. She had a window added to the back of the house, framed like a picture. It showcased the forest like a live painting. She painted the exterior of the house but miscalculated how much paint the job would entail. There was only a smidgeon of paint remaining and a whole wall left to cover, so she used the last of it to paint the same fish her sister had drawn years before for the cover of Margaret's *The Fish with the Deep Sea Smile* right onto the bare wall.

The cottage was charming and airy, even though it was small. Margaret had a great deal of work to finish that summer. In addition to writing books, she recorded the melodies of her latest songs and sample radio shows on a wire recorder she kept in the house. She was working on two articles about writing for children, and both were due soon. The first was for Hollins's alumnae magazine and the other for Grolier's *Book of Knowledge*. The Grolier's series was the very one that had lined her shelves as a child. Margaret's parents had revered the books, and she knew her father would be proud of his daughter for contributing that piece. He could no longer doubt that Margaret had lived up to the standards of his illustrious family. She hadn't fought in wars or argued on the floor of Congress, but she was leaving her mark as her ancestors had before her. She was no longer just a writer of silly stories and songs. She was an expert on how to write children's literature. *The Book of Knowledge* would say it was so.

When Margaret was hired to write a monthly children's page for *Good Housekeeping* magazine, her name became more widely known to the public. The magazine introduced Margaret to its readers as a modern, pretty woman who happened to craft her works in a fairy-tale hideaway. The editor painted a perfect picture of Cobble Court as a little house aglow by firelight and ruby-red kerosene lamps— exactly the type of place from which children's stories should come.

She also was asked to submit a menu to be included in *The American Woman's Cook Book,* along with other notable women, such as Mrs. Calvin Coolidge and Lillian Hellman. Margaret's menu for a "Lunch under the Apple Trees" featured a recipe for root soup to be served with a salad of umbrella mushrooms and sliced avocados.

The tumultuous relationship with Michael had strained Margaret terribly. On top of that, Margaret would have to find somewhere to live away from Michael, who was on tour until the end of the year. Cobble Court was uninsulated and too cold for New York's winters. Likewise, it would have been impossible to survive the brutally frigid Maine temperatures at the Only House in winter, so she would have to find an apartment when Michael returned.

She distracted herself by staying busy with her writing. She had eight other books in the works for five different publishers. She recently had an article published on how to select the proper book for a child. In it, she encouraged parents to find stories told in simple words about familiar things. The color of the sky, the feel of rain, even tables and telephones might be commonplace to parents, but to children, everything in the world is new and wildly exciting. She believed frightening fairy tales should be avoided for younger children who had yet to learn what is real and what is not. To them, a witch or goblin is as real as a horse or chicken. Older children, depending on their environment, understood the difference between fantasy and reality; they could enjoy those stories without harmful results. It was important for children to find the fun and adventure in folktales and legends since they were based in nature and were often a window into human nature. Word patterns, rhymes, and rhythms were also something she suggested parents look for in a book because they mimicked children's playful language. Sudden changes and sharp contrasts in sound kept their attention, and it delighted them to hear a cat meow or a train go *pocketa-pocketa-pocketa*. Stories should be short—no more than ten or fifteen minutes—unless the readers involved the children in the stories through questions, which gave them a chance to be part of the narratives. Margaret explained that the purpose of books for young children was not so much to educate them as to echo their laughter and sadness, to capture the reality of the world they loved. Children were sensitive to subtle overtones and rhythms and eager to hear them reflected in stories, songs, and poems. She believed that unless parents encouraged those senses, they became blunted by the age of five. Literature gave them back their own world and kept the keenness of their senses alive.

Margaret's circle of publishing friends had dwindled. Leonard was busy with his new wife and the Hurds with their young son, Thacher. Margaret was spending more time with composers than illustrators, editors, or book publishers these days. She no longer went to Bank Street to test her material. Margaret used her neighbor's boys and her goddaughter, Laurel, as her guinea pigs.

When she was asked to write a version of the Christmas story for one of her publishers, she went to visit Dot. Margaret had no idea what animals did at night in a barn, so in Bank Street fashion, she wanted to observe their nocturnal activities firsthand.

Dot's barn was sturdy enough to keep Margaret from freezing, although it was a cold November night in Connecticut. Dot bundled Margaret up in a huge raccoon fur coat and made a comfy nest of blankets and sweet-smelling clover hay in one of the stalls. The Ripleys' herd of fawn-colored Swiss cattle curiously sniffed their new barn mate as night settled in. Two cats slept next to Margaret's head, but their purrs didn't drown out the constant digestive noises of the cows or the loud urination of the horses that made her dream of Niagara Falls.

Around five in the morning, the barn manager came in to feed and water the animals. He proceeded to stick a pitchfork in the stack of hay. A surprised and fur-draped Margaret leaped up. The man was startled, terrified that he had roused the biggest raccoon ever. It took a round of coffee and shots of whiskey to calm both of them down.

The night in the barn gave Margaret half a dozen other ideas. The sounds of barnyard animals might make a good piece for *Good Housekeeping*. She wrote a song for Young People's Records and a barn story for Golden. There were so many possibilities; everything was a discovery to a toddler, and almost every discovery could be turned into a book, poem, or song. Dot telegrammed, wrote, or called to share what Laurel and her new baby, Louis, said or did, and Margaret documented their lives as if they were the subject for one of Lucy's textbooks.

Through Dot's life, Margaret witnessed motherhood firsthand. Margaret watched Dot open her children to the world around them in the day and comfort them at bedtime. She loved how every day was different but reassuringly the same. Wake, tend to the cattle, ride horses, play with the dogs, bathe, and go to bed. Days were simple and slow. Margaret pondered how this might have been her own life if she had married George Armistead so many years ago. She wondered if she would have been happier with a husband and children. Her books were her legacy. They felt like her children. She had an enviable life, but the fear of what was next was never far from the front of her mind, especially after Michael had ordered her to find a new place to live.

As Christmas approached, a musical version of Margaret's book *The Little Brass Band* was being performed by the New York Philharmonic at Carnegie Hall. To a sellout crowd of children and parents, Santa Claus used a huge thermometer to register how well they all sang along to "Silent Night." Margaret sat in the audience in a new wool suit she bought especially for this occasion. She longed to share this moment with Michael, but it had been almost three months since they had last seen or spoken to each other. They did, though, continue to exchange letters.

It was clear from Michael's last letter that she was pessimistic about her chances for recovery. She had received a blood transfusion that she hoped would send her illness into remission, but instead, it had made her feel even weaker. Another letter arrived asking Margaret to help settle her estate if she were to die. Michael still wanted to keep her distance from Margaret, but knew she would do as Michael asked, so she sent a letter of instructions for Margaret to follow if "a refrigerator suddenly fell on her head." She didn't trust Diana or anyone else to follow her requests. She specified how to claim her insurance policy's proceeds and how her furniture and jewelry should be distributed. Anything not specifically covered was to be split between Margaret and Diana. She also warned that the cleaning out of her apartment shouldn't be left to her daughter-in-law because she hated to throw things away.

Michael concluded that burying Robin in Indiana had been a hastily made decision. Mother and son should be buried next to each other as they originally planned, she said. Being away from him in death frightened her, so she asked that his body be exhumed and transferred to the family plot in the Bronx. She asked Margaret to make certain that request was followed.

Michael's last stop on her Great Words with Great Music tour for the year was at Times Hall in New York. This venue was the smallest of Broadway's theaters and held only around five hundred people. Even so, the ticket sales to the show were slow, so the house would be almost empty that night. Margaret bought a block of empty seats and distributed them to her friends, hoping to fill the house.

Backstage, she left a vase of camellias and a note in Michael's dressing room. She also left her keys to the Connecticut house. In the note, she apologized for not yet having found a new place to live, and she promised to move from their apartments as soon as the weather warmed. Michael sent a response by messenger, thanking Margaret for the flowers and promising to call the next day. She reiterated that their relationship was stealing the little amount of energy she had and asked Margaret to refrain from contacting her. If she could do that, then perhaps they could have a relationship in the future.

Margaret succeeded in getting a larger audience into Times Hall, although the venue was far from full. When an emaciated Michael walked out in her white Grecian gown, a gasp from Diana could be heard in the audience. She had not seen her mother for almost four months and was shocked by her appearance. Two hands could easily fit around her waist. Her face was desperately thin, and her skin was sickly white. It was clear to everyone in that little theater that the woman onstage didn't have long to live.

Margaret was not part of the audience that evening. Michael's doctor had called Margaret on Michael's behalf and explained that his patient was under a great deal of stress already and that being around Margaret compounded her anxiety. It was best for Michael for Margaret to stay away from the theater that night.

Nineteen
1950

I will light one cigarette
And when it is ended I will go
I will not smoke it fast
Or slow
Just in the way of everyday
I look at you and your
Familiar changing face
I see the moment ended
In this familiar room
From which I will go
With the grey curls of cigarette smoke
Rising slowly
To linger a little longer
On the air

"THE END"
White Freesias

Michael disappeared after her show, and Margaret had no idea where she was. When her mail piled up at the apartment, Margaret hounded Diana, trying to find out where Michael was. At first, Diana refused to tell Margaret. She didn't want to cross her mother, who was in Switzerland receiving an experimental form of treatment for her leukemia. Doctors at the Hirslanden Clinic in Lausanne disagreed with Michael's initial diagnosis of acute leukemia. Instead, they confirmed she had chronic leukemia, and if it went into remission, then her life could be extended by a few more years. They told her, however, that she had arrived not at the eleventh hour or the twelfth, but at half past twelve. She might have arrived too late for the treatments to work.

Blood transfusions, daily injections of vitamins, and x-rays made Michael feel better. A former acquaintance of Robin's, who was a professional male escort, tagged along to help Michael with whatever she needed. When Diana found out he had helped Michael spend her limited dollars on flowers, limousine rides, and private chefs, she was outraged. At Michael's request, he also had bought matching suits for them to wear on walks around the clinic grounds. Michael was almost out of money, and to waste it on useless treatments, flowers, and car rides was more than Diana could bear. She convinced her mother to call Margaret.

On Valentine's Day, Margaret sat in her bed with her big red comforter, looking over the river as snow fell on the city. She was relieved to have heard Michael's voice on the phone and thrilled to be exchanging loving letters once more instead of nasty telegrams. She wanted to be by Michael's side while there was still time and made plans to visit her at the clinic. Both were hopeful Michael's renewed vigor meant the illness was in remission. Margaret conferred with Michael's doctor in New York about follow-up treatments. Remission meant a second chance, and Margaret wasn't going to let her pride lead her into any more arguments with

Michael. She was eager to have Michael back at home where she could take care of her.

A few days later, Margaret checked into her hotel in Lausanne, and a letter from Michael was waiting. It said that Michael's doctor was ordering Margaret to stay away because their relationship was a source of strain for Michael. If they were to achieve remission, all stress must be eliminated.

Margaret was crushed, but she responded with calm and kindness. She said she would do anything to help Michael get well, including staying away. Her only desire was for Michael to get well.

Margaret stayed on in Switzerland for a few days in the hope Michael would change her mind. When she didn't, Margaret got on a train to visit Garth Williams in Italy. Garth had moved back to Rome, where he had studied art years before. He and Margaret were working on *Fox Eyes,* a manuscript of Margaret's that had not yet found a publisher. She loved his illustrations for the book and was sure she would eventually find someone to produce the book.

While on board the train to Rome, a man sitting in the same compartment as Margaret placed chloroform over her face. When she woke, she had been robbed, although the thief fortunately left her journal and manuscripts behind.

Her luck didn't improve on her return home to the United States. *Publishers Weekly* announced that *The Quiet Noisy Book* was to be published by Harper. The idea she and Leonard Weisgard had years before to blend story, sound, and images in *The Noisy Book* had been a huge success. Four more stories featuring the little dog Muffin had been published, and contractually, it was clear that the rights to the series belonged to W. R. Scott. When Bill Scott read that the next book in the series was being produced without his consent, he promptly sued Margaret and Harper.

It had been Margaret's understanding that her publishing relationship with Scott was over. She had told Bill months earlier that she would no longer send him manuscripts when he failed to print her last book in four colors as he had promised. He completely ruined her last two books on press by using an inferior printer. She had tried to help him, but his reluctance to move to modern presses placed his house at a competitive disadvantage. That directly affected Margaret's royalty earnings, so she really could not afford to let him have any further manuscripts. In her mind, it had been an agreeable parting of the ways.

Bill might not have the opportunity to publish new books by Margaret, but that didn't mean he would let a competitor take over his bestselling series. He was going to hold Margaret to her contract even if it meant a legal battle.

She was infuriated. She was still hurt by the *Publishers Weekly* feature and bitter that Bill had taken credit for her ideas. She dashed off an angry letter to him. She could not believe this was how he was reacting after all she had done for him over the years. She had given up royalties on books that were still earning money for him. She had brought him the best illustrators in the business. She had promoted his company in every interview. Yet he didn't even respond to a letter she recently wrote about an underpayment. She was shocked he was suing her after stealing her ideas and taking credit for her work. Therefore, she counted her friendship with him as bad judgment and his friendship with her as hogwash.

She asked Harriet Pilpel to countersue on the basis that Scott repeatedly violated their contracts. She wanted retroactive payments on verbal agreements Bill had made with her. She also wanted to file a legal complaint with the Writers Guild and get them to review Scott's royalty payments for discrepancies.

Harriet knew Margaret's legal stance was weak. It was in Margaret's best interest to stay on Bill's good side and settle this amicably. She talked Margaret out of sending the poisonous letter. Harriet also was Michael's lawyer and knew she didn't have long to live. There had been no remission, so Michael returned to the apartments at East End. A lawsuit would be costly and emotionally draining at a time when Margaret was overworked and exhausted. It was time for Margaret to make peace with her former boss.

Margaret helped care for the very sick Michael and cheered her on as Michael wrote a series of children's stories about the adventures of two bunnies living together—"The Rabbit M.D." and "The Bunny No Good." Margaret served as Michael's editor for the stories, and Ursula had agreed to publish them. There were many flaws in the stories, but Margaret wanted to give Michael something to look forward to as she wasted away. She replaced her characteristically snarky comments with exclamatory remarks about how funny the stories were. It wasn't long, though, before Michael was back in the hospital, this time in Boston at a clinic that specialized in the latest treatments for leukemia.

By fall, Michael was the size of a child, and her skin had turned a sickly yellow. It was obvious she was close to death, so Margaret rented a hotel suite close to the Boston hospital to be near Michael. She did her best to keep up with her work by mail, phone, and telegram, but for the first time in her career, she was behind schedule and wrote very little. She was at the hospital most of the day and often into the night.

Sleep would give Michael a reprieve from the unending pain, but nothing the doctor ordered allowed her to rest. At the end of October, she writhed in pain day and night for almost a week. Morphine eased the pain, but her heart could only take so much. Her body went through crisis after crisis—internal bleeding, bedsores, and fluid-filled lungs that had to be drained through punctures in her back. It seemed the only things that kept death at bay were transfusions.

After watching Michael suffer day after day, Margaret asked the doctor to try something other than anesthetics to help Michael sleep. Maybe hypnosis would help. The suggestion brought a sneer to his handsome, professional face, but he went into Michael's room and came out with a smile. With a laugh, he announced that Michael's pulse was still strong as an ox. The only thing keeping her awake was hysteria.

Margaret was incensed. How dare he laugh at her friend's suffering and dismiss it so easily. The doctor's face drew pinched. He snapped that he would order a new painkiller and a transfusion for his patient. Margaret walked past him into Michael's room and closed the door.

Michael was hunched over in a chair. Her breathing was labored, and in the corners of her mouth there was blood. Margaret knew it was time for Michael to stop fighting. She took Michael's hands into her own and told her not to be afraid to die. Her mother and son, all the people she loved the most, were already there. Life here was just a promise, just a beginning. Somewhere there was the completeness, the continuation of what started here. Michael grew calmer and quiet. This was what she needed. She lapsed into rest.

Margaret held her hand through the transfusion. Afterward, the doctor ordered that Michael was to receive no more visitors. She was not to contact anyone except through him. Michael was too weak to protest loudly but scrawled a note to Margaret. The doctor snatched it away before Margaret could read it and declared that she was to do as he said—"or else."

Margaret knew what the "or else" was. Two weeks before, a psychiatrist had told Michael that there was a ward for people who cracked. These treatments were torture enough. Margaret didn't want Michael to lose the special care of her private nurse or the kindly head nurse she had befriended.

Margaret returned to the hospital that afternoon with a small bouquet of primroses—Michael's favorite flower. She sat in the hall outside Michael's door until nightfall. Before leaving, she gave the bouquet to a nurse to put by Michael's bed.

At one o'clock in the morning, Michael called Margaret, begging her to come to the hospital. Michael believed these were her last two days on earth and wanted Margaret by her side. Margaret rose and started to dress, then thought about the threat Michael's doctor had made the day before and paused. She didn't want to offend the doctor further for fear of what he might do to Michael, so she called the nurse on duty to ask permission to come. The nurse refused.

By sunrise, though, Michael's private nurse called and told her to come as quickly as she could. The doctor couldn't be reached and had left no standing order for any painkillers. Michael was in agony.

When Margaret arrived, she saw the primroses by Michael's bed. The sick woman summoned her strength and declared that from now on her friends were to take orders from her, not her doctor. The head nurse agreed and promised to take responsibility for letting Michael's friends into her room. The nurse also found another doctor who agreed to give Michael morphine to ease her pain.

She was soon calm. She asked to see her son, Leonard Thomas. Margaret knew Leonard refused to come visit his mother but didn't want Michael to know. She said Leonard had a cold and the doctor was keeping him away. It seemed the kindest thing to do.

The next day, Margaret maintained a vigil outside Michael's hospital room. She heard Michael crying for her, begging Margaret to be with her, but the doctor forbade it. She had promised Michael she would hold her hand as she faced her last moments, and this last act by the doctor was sadistic, not compassionate. Michael should have someone by her side who loved her.

Margaret stood by the door, listening to Michael's calls grow faint. Before long, a nurse stepped outside the room and said Margaret could go in. Michael had died.

Margaret longed to lift Michael out of the bed and hold her in her arms, but nurses still bustled about the room. They brusquely came between her and Michael, like adults keeping children at bay, then suddenly, they were through. They told Margaret she could wait until the doctor returned and swept out of the room. Michael was no longer their patient. She was someone else's responsibility now.

Margaret stepped to the bedside and closed Michael's eyes. She kissed them quietly, tenderly. She took Michael's hand in hers and felt it curve into her own. Michael's hand answered her touch, and

Margaret knew that the nurses had been wrong; death had not yet come.

Margaret took the pearls from Michael's neck to give to Michael's son, as she had requested. She draped the strand around her own neck and then crossed the room to retrieve Michael's large gray robe she always slept under. In some maternal way, she wanted to keep Michael warm. She removed the towel that propped Michael's head up at an odd angle and held Michael's head close to her own. Margaret wondered what thoughts Michael had at these last moments. What part of her consciousness would live on after she died?

These last few days, Margaret and Michael talked about what happened to the soul after death. Margaret still held to some of the tenets of the Theosophical Society and was inspired to write a book for Michael, *The Dark Wood of the Golden Birds*. In it, beautiful birds disappear each night into the forest. People who try to follow them never return, until the day when a boy has to enter the woods to save a friend. He comes back but is forever changed by the beautiful world he saw on the other side of the forest. Michael was going into the forest, on a journey that would leave Margaret behind. Having been witness to the séances and readings by mediums for so many years, Margaret believed that some souls could come back and communicate from the other side. She hoped this book would be a guide for Michael to do the same. It was a vanity project, too obscure to sell very well, but Ursula and Leonard helped their grieving friend with the book. Leonard illustrated the book quickly, and Ursula rushed it to press so Margaret could give a copy to Michael before she died.

In addition to talks about life after death, Margaret and Michael talked about Margaret's life alone to come. For the first time, Margaret confessed to Michael that when they first met she kept a diary about their days together. Even then, she had hoped to write about a life they would share. She promised to finish that book and to read from Michael's collection of poetry each morning. Michael's memory and spirit would be with Margaret always because she loved her most of all. Their bond was unrefined, Margaret thought, and stronger than love. They got lost in each other. Separation from each other was no longer possible. Michael would take a part of Margaret with her, but part of her would live on in Margaret.

Michael's death was noted in papers around the world. Numerous obituaries described her as the former Mrs. John Barrymore and as a poet. They reported that her son Leonard Thomas had been at her side when she passed.

Twenty
1951

When I fly away which way is best
North, East, South or West?

North, East, South, West

In Michael's absence, friends who had once distanced themselves began to reenter Margaret's life. Some may have disapproved of her relationship with Michael; others had just hated to see Michael's condescension of Margaret and her career. Rosie Bliven urged Lucy Mitchell to invite Margaret back to the Writers Laboratory. Rosie had told Lucy that their friend was still up to madcap adventures. As she saw it, Margaret had been entranced by Michael because she needed a mother figure in her life. Margaret filled her time with crazy, amusing activities because she was a lonely soul. She was, though, loveable—still the old imaginative person they knew.

Condolences from Margaret's friends poured forth. Dot encouraged Margaret to remember the good days and happy hours. Though this chapter of her life with Michael was closed, the vibrancy of their life together would linger. There was much to look forward to in life, Dot promised her grieving friend. She had a host of people who loved her, and though that wouldn't take away the sorrow, she should know she was much loved. She encouraged Margaret to come visit whenever she wished. Other friends also invited her to spend time with them——in Virginia, Connecticut, and France. One friend in Key West urged Margaret to throw Crispian in her jalopy and head south.

Posey Hurd's note was one of pure sympathy, even though she and Clem had not liked the way Michael had treated Margaret. They loved Margaret and grieved for her loss. Bruce Bliven urged Margaret to remember that Michael would be the one snorting at her sad solitude. She knew the line between sorrow and self-pity, and, as Michael would have wanted, Margaret should remember the happy moments of their time together.

Lucy Mitchell did invite Margaret to come back to the Writers Laboratory for a visit. Both were aware that their writing styles had landed on opposite ends of realism. Lucy was working on a geography book, and Margaret was writing a tale about fairies in the woods. Lucy knew full well the grief of losing the person closest to you because her husband had died two years earlier. She had just recently completed a biography on their life together. Margaret was honored when her old mentor and friend asked her to edit her biography of her late husband.

The majority of Michael's estate had been left to her children, who were considerate of Margaret's relationship with their mother. They gave Margaret the use of Michael's furniture and deeded the house in Maine Margaret had built for Michael back to her. Michael had appointed Margaret as her literary executor, which made Margaret consider her own publishing legacy. Too many of Margaret's own manuscripts were lying fallow at publishing houses as editors delayed their decisions to accept or reject them. When Margaret reviewed the status of her projects still awaiting approval, she was livid. Golden had over a dozen manuscripts pending for more than a year, as did Harper. She wanted them to commit to the works or let her sell them elsewhere. Margaret accused both Ursula and Georges of trying to control her output by slowing down their decisions to commit to a manuscript.

She had agreed to Golden's paltry monthly advance only because Georges said he would publish four of her books per year, not accept and then hold on to the manuscripts. If he didn't publish her manuscripts, there was no way for her to earn anything past the advance. She would have no more of it. If Golden wasn't going to publish the manuscripts they were holding on to, then she wanted a kill fee and demanded those works be returned. She refused to sign the new deal with Golden and demanded a quick review of her projects with Harper.

Ursula responded quickly. She told Margaret that she had always appreciated the informality of their working relationship, and she assumed Margaret did, too. She didn't want to lose the good things about their closeness but was eager to settle the messier aspects that casualness wrought. She promised to give Margaret concrete decisions on submissions quickly and to schedule the publication of accepted manuscripts promptly. She was certain they could find a happy medium of friendship and professionalism. She told Margaret how much it meant to work with her as an editor but also as someone who appreciated Margaret's talent, then she joked that they should now sing a hymn together.

Margaret did value Ursula as an editor and a friend, so she

quickly backed down. She didn't feel quite the same way about Georges. She gave him a set of dueling pistols and joked that this might be the better way to settle their contract negotiations. She also complained about a small underpayment on a recent royalty statement. Georges sarcastically feigned shock at the company's gross negligence. He promised to have their accountant shot by firing squad at dawn.

In October, Margaret and her valet, Pietro, were in her apartment when her ancient refrigerator's icebox exploded, leaking ammonia gas throughout the rooms. There was no way to escape the long, narrow apartment without going back through the smoke and gas. They were able to grab Crispian and make it to Margaret's bedroom at the far end of the apartment. Gasping for air, they flung open the window and breathed in the clean air. There was no fire escape, ladder, or rope. They screamed for help and kept their heads out the window. Margaret held the wriggling dog so that his nose, too, would not take in the toxic fumes.

Finally, her upstairs neighbor who had lived through the London Blitz came to their rescue. He brought wet towels to shield them from the gas as they fled the apartment. The gas was so noxious that it peeled the paint off her walls, removed the varnish on her furniture, and killed all her plants. Pietro remained sick for months afterward, and Margaret developed a bronchial condition that lasted into the following year. She became exceedingly frustrated in her dealings with her landlord, Captain Vincent Astor, whose often-unresponsive company had finally replaced the damaged refrigerator with one that was similar in age and just as hazardous. She eventually turned the whole matter over to Harriet, commenting that her landlord's lackadaisical ways were irritating—who did he think he was? A writer?

The lawsuit with Scott about *The Noisy Book* series was settled at the beginning of the year, although there were too many personal affronts for Margaret and Bill Scott to ever again be close. However, he did want Margaret back on board as a Scott author. He asked her to write a companion for *A Child's Goodnight Book* they had published years before.

Michael's death and the exploding icebox gave Margaret a new perspective on the preciousness of life. She wrote letters to three of her illustrators, praising the work they did on their recent books with her. When she realized that a manuscript she had sent to Phyra Slobodkina to illustrate was too similar to Harper's *Goodnight Moon,* she asked Golden to nix the project. She didn't want to end up in another legal battle because she had stepped on another publisher's rights. She reestablished a friendship with John McCullough, her old Scott colleague. She let him know that she appreciated his thoughtful comments on her manuscripts and respected his editorial talent.

Ursula, too, was once again a trusted friend. They went together to the Book Week ceremony at the New York Public Library, but when they arrived, Margaret realized she had left her invitation behind. The librarian standing guard at the door knew Margaret and her books well but refused to let her enter until all other guests arrived. There were plenty of empty seats, but the librarian wasn't going to bend the rules for her.

Ursula stood with Margaret in the hall, chatting as their colleagues were ushered in. Margaret felt spurned once again by this group of self-important librarians. She grew more agitated as the time for the ceremony drew closer and the room was still far from full. These librarians enjoyed looking down on her. They would never accept her as a serious writer.

Angry tears formed in Margaret's eyes, and she told Ursula she was leaving. Ursula didn't want to abandon her friend and sometimes-favorite author, especially when it was obvious how upset she was. So the two women parked themselves on the front steps of the library, next to the lions. There, they held their own awards for Book Week and celebrated privately.

Margaret spent much of 1951 traveling to see friends, including a trip to upstate New York to be with Monty Hare for opening night of his tent road show of *The Tempest*. He had been director of the Barter Theatre in Abingdon, Virginia, for the last five years, and whenever possible, Margaret had driven to see his new shows and then on to Hollins for reunions or visits.

Monty had faced great difficulty getting the road show production off the ground. The union for stagehands struck the show, and costly delays set in. When opening night finally arrived, thunderstorms ripped away part of the large performance tent, and Monty was convinced their first show would be their last. Just then, Margaret arrived on the scene with a hot dog cart in the back of her convertible. She sang silly made-up songs about hot dogs and dispensed her wares to the arriving audience with good cheer. Monty was, as ever, grateful to his Birdbrain friend. Before Margaret returned to Manhattan, she had a draft for a song-filled story about a street vendor and his shiny hot dog wagon.

As promised, Margaret read from Michael's poetry collection each morning. She longed to have Michael to explain obscure passages or to relish the beauty of some lines. Margaret was, though, learning to live for herself for the first time. Michael was gone, and Bill was no more than an old friend. This newfound independence spurred a story about a dog who was free to do as he wished, *Mister Dog*. It was the story of her and Crispian living together, but alone, both doing as they wished in their hidden world of Cobble Court. She was comfortable in her solitude. She belonged to herself and only herself.

Twenty-one
1952

The day before I met you
The sky was Cobalt blue
The trees were green
The birds were still
The day before I met you

    The day before I met you
    The earth was flat as flat
    My heart was cold
    My thoughts were old
    The day before I met you

        And then that day I met you
        That glorious golden sky
        As you walked in my hair rose up
        My heart was beating too
        I knew your face, I had dreamed your eyes
        Before the day I met you

"THE DAY BEFORE I MET YOU"
Unpublished

In late March, Margaret sat down in her Cobble Court living room for a lengthy interview with a reporter from the *News Leader* in Richmond, Virginia. Margaret's hair was cut in a short poodle style, and her curls rested on top of her head. She looked elegant in a tailored gray suit with a beige wrap over her shoulders. The room was decorated with touches of Virginia—dogwood blossoms set off by magnolia leaves. Margaret served tea on her antique French Quimper china, and on the table was a plate of freshly prepared hot cross buns. Margaret and the reporter discussed her strong ties with Virginia, her college days, and childhood visits there. Crispian soon grew impatient waiting for one of the buns and upset the butler's table, snatching one of the treats and running away, effectively ending the interview. Regardless, Margaret liked what the reporter ended up writing. She weighed twenty pounds more than she wanted, so she was thrilled when she was described as tall and slender in the article. When her clipping service sent her the piece, she underlined those words and added exclamation marks then placed this revised version of the article in her scrapbook. Perhaps it was that article that spurred her cousin Morrie Johnston to invite her to Cumberland Island for an end-of-March vacation.

Within the week, Margaret was back at Plum Orchard. It was marvelous to see the Johnstons once again. It was still tradition for the Carnegie families to rotate dinners from house to house, and when it was the Johnstons' turn to host, they held a casual dinner party.

Margaret took notice when a strikingly handsome young man arrived with a growler of the home brew they called "Sweet Lucy" as his family's contribution to the meal. He, too, noticed Margaret. She stood at the foot of the house's grand staircase, inside a graceful wooden alcove. To this man, she looked like a work of art. He made a beeline for her and stayed by her side for the rest of the evening. His name was James Stillman Rockefeller Jr., but he was known to family members as Pebble. He was fifteen years younger than Margaret and was one of the little children she'd played with at his grandparents' home decades before.

Their attraction to each other was immediate and grew steadily as they talked throughout dinner and on into the late hours of the night. In the morning, they went for a walk on the beach. Like Margaret, Pebble treasured the sea and the breathtaking beauty of this island paradise. He loved how her golden hair was the same color as the glowing marshlands that surrounded the island. For the rest of her time on the island, Margaret and Pebble seldom left one another's side. When she had to return to the deadlines and telephones of the publishing world, he made her promise to return as soon as she could.

Back in New York, Margaret questioned the new relationship. Only weeks before, she had been certain she would never love someone again, and now she was just as certain she couldn't live without Pebble. She'd spent a decade on an analyst's couch dissecting her dreams and emotions to understand why she chose relationships that were wrong for her. She'd spent her life trying to avoid the same fate as her parents, who had been miserable in their marriage, but she had settled for a miserable love life. Her attraction to Bill Gaston had been detrimental to her self-esteem from the moment she

met him. He was a serial philanderer, and she had allowed him to
hurt her time and time again. Then there was Michael, whose huge
and fragile ego often cloaked their happiness in angst and anger.
Margaret had never had a full, mature, and loving relationship. Now
she was in love with a much younger man, which Freud would most
likely have attributed to a skipped stage in her emotional growth.

Before long, though, Margaret forced herself to stop worrying.
She knew she would damage this relationship by second-guessing
every statement, emotion, and motivation. Had a technical explanation of what she was feeling ever changed what she felt? She decided that the scrutiny she put herself through in the past had
amounted to nothing more than wasted energy. At the center of it
all was fear: fear of being her mother, fear of losing her family, fear
of losing Bill or Michael. This time, she wasn't going to be afraid
of what came next. She loved him and knew he loved her. She wasn't
going to miss this chance for happiness. She had spent years in analysis, but this time, she didn't want to analyze why she was attracted
to Pebble. They loved each other. It was as simple as that. She finally felt healed.

Before returning to Cumberland to be with Pebble, she had to
straighten out her contract with Golden Books. Georges Duplaix was
still in Paris, so she met with her Golden editor, Lucille Ogle, who
described the details of the new contract to Margaret. Golden
would only be required to accept three, not four, manuscripts per
year from Margaret. They weren't, though, required to publish any
of the manuscripts they accepted, but would pay her a small kill
fee for any they did not agree to publish. Nor was Golden required

to let her know which manuscripts they rejected or accepted until the contract expired. Margaret realized that this could tie up many of her works for years. This was not at all what she and Georges discussed. She was furious and dictated a scathing telegram to Lucille, threatening to never work with Golden again if they didn't live up to the arrangement she and Georges had first discussed.

To Georges, Margaret wrote that he should be glad the ocean was between them. She confessed to having lost her temper with Lucille and to having sent a nasty telegram. Then she said that after reflecting on the situation, she would like to send that telegram again. She knew she was his prize author, and the deal was simply unfair. If he didn't live up to what he had promised, then when she came to France in August she would shoot him with her bow and arrow.

Georges's recollection of their agreement differed greatly from Margaret's. In his letter, he tried to lighten the situation by saying he wasn't certain if the ripples he felt all the way in France came from America's testing of the atomic bomb or from the explosion between Cobble Court and his offices at Rockefeller Center.

However frustrated Margaret was, she also knew it was in her best interest to keep her business dealings productive. She was not going to let her relationship with Golden be derailed the way hers had been with Bill Scott. Eager to leave New York, she turned the issue over to Harriet Pilpel to resolve. She also asked Harriet to prepare a will, but to only draft it in a provisional way because she would surely change it many times before it was complete. Short of money once again, she asked Harriet how much it would cost to prepare the will, because most of her money was tied up in Golden's profits. She wanted to get as far away from the whole mess as possible. She packed her bags, put Crispian in the car, and drove to Florida. She couldn't wait to be by Pebble's side again.

Three days later, she was on a dock, listening to a chorus of insects and birds play against the constant swoosh of metal on wood as Pebble drew his plane over his boat, the *Mandalay*. Pebble was busy preparing the vessel for its maiden voyage around the world. Moored to a small wooden boathouse in the waters of the marsh-lined Intracoastal Waterway, the *Mandalay* glistened in the bright Florida morning sunlight. Margaret sat and watched Pebble work—his brown back bent over the hull as he slid a plane across the wood, smoothing out the rough edges of the boat. He whistled softly while she looked on with affection. Pebble climbed up to the halyards of the mast and secured the O in the rigging. He shimmied down with his hunting knife in his belt. *He is completely comfortable with himself,* Margaret thought. *This is a man doing something he loves.* Their month together had brought them much closer. Without Pebble ever uttering a formal proposal, both understood that they would spend the rest of their lives together.

Later that afternoon, Pebble needed to go hunting; it was his turn to find a deer for the family larder. Margaret wanted to go with him. It surprised him that someone who wrote so dearly of little bunnies and furry things also was a hunter. They set off in the family car and parked where the sea and the forest met, where the shoreline was dotted with weathered white branches of ancient oaks. In the wooded dunes, huge tree branches towered high and dipped low to the ground in graceful curves. Margaret remembered these trees from the walks she had taken in these woods with her cousins, how as a child she'd flashed a light into the eyes of toads and a whip-poor-will, then something more frightening. Now, with Pebble by her side, she saw these twisted trees only as a wonderland of plants, animals, sea, and freshwater. He selected a spot beside some bushes, and they perched on a dune to await their prey. A doe passed by, and even though he saw no fawn, Pebble held his fire. Later, when a buck peeked around a tree, he shot, and the deer fell.

He scrambled down the dune with Margaret right behind, and together they hauled the deer to the shoreline. Pebble used his hunting knife to cut into the deer and remove the organs. Margaret held the still-warm heart in her hands and looked at Pebble. She understood that this wild place and this type of experience made him the man he was, and she loved him all the more for it. Margaret, with the blood of the deer on her hands, her shirt askew and missing a button, could not have been more captivating to Pebble. They rode home in silence, holding hands.

Days later, as Margaret and Pebble drove along the shore, they spotted a group of people standing at the water's edge, looking at a shrimper's little green boat that was caught on the rocks. The boat's owner and his son stood by, gravely watching as their livelihood and most prized possession got tossed against the rocks with each wave that rolled in. Pebble parked the car and went to talk to the shrimper, who was black, and the island's caretaker, who was from India and a firm believer in his country's caste system. The caretaker made it clear he had more important things to do than tow the boat off the rocks. From his manner, Pebble could see that the caretaker thought it was beneath him to help the shrimper, even though losing the boat would cause the shrimper's financial ruin. Margaret held an excited Crispian away from the crowd and watched as Pebble took off his shirt and shoes. He dove into the surf and swam to the edge of the breakers. From there, he climbed the rocks and boarded the boat. He struggled to free it from the jagged boulders but quickly saw it was no use. The engine was submerged, and the hull was filling with water. He swam back, and Margaret stood close enough to hear him tell the shrimper that he would have to wait for the tide to go out. Maybe, he said, they could make the boat watertight by patching the hole, but she saw from their faces that no one believed the boat could actually be saved.

The only thing they could do was drive the shrimper and his son to a telephone and arrange a salvage crew for the boat. Later that night, as Pebble and Margaret sat on the front porch, she reflected on the day's events. She told him the opening line of a story that was forming in her mind. It was about a windup toy boat dancing on the sea that didn't know it was the last time it would dance. Pebble said it didn't sound like a children's story. She assured him it would be. She was only comfortable writing about animals and children—she lost her way when she tried to write for grownups.

Pebble and the men working on his boat lived in old servant quarters on the property. He had hired three men to help build the boat, and two of them would stay on as crew. One night as Margaret made dinner for Pebble's family, the crew showed up in their sweaty work clothes, expecting to join the feast. Margaret chastised them, saying she couldn't have all these attractive men wandering around half-naked at her dinner party. One joked that he was wearing his best shirt. Margaret pointed out that it was time to get new clothes when the holes got ahead of the material.

Then, pointing at Pebble, who was attired only in very short shorts, Margaret said he was going to get all the attention from the ladies that night in the hair shirt he had on. He laughed, but no one changed, hoping to make Pebble's family and the other dinner guests feel stuffy in their nice clothes.

The largest mansion on the island was still Mama Carnegie's Dungeness, although it was abandoned and in slight disrepair. After her death, the fortune of the family had been divided, and no one wanted to take on the costly upkeep of the big house. Pebble and Margaret climbed to the top of the house's towering cupola and looked out over the marsh. There, they planned their future, and Pebble gave her an engagement ring to formalize their plans to marry. Before the wedding, Pebble and his crew would first sail to Miami, pick up supplies, and then meet Margaret in Panama. Meanwhile, Margaret had to return to New York, organize her affairs for their long getaway, and then meet with music producers in France. Looking out over the marsh, Margaret was reflective. She said she had been only half alive before she met Pebble. She had at last found happiness and peace, adventure, and boundless love, with him.

When it came time for Pebble to set sail, Margaret christened the boat with a bottle of champagne. Pebble didn't want to leave, but the sooner he left, the sooner they could be married. They parted the next day, eager to see one another again in three months.

When Pebble reached Miami, letters from Margaret were waiting for him. He had no ship-to-shore phone, so the letters were their only way to communicate. A crewmate's girlfriend met the crew there and planned to stay while they restocked the boat and headed on to Panama. However, the whole crew's plans quickly changed when an opportunity to earn some extra cash on a shrimp boat arose. They decided they would dock in Miami for a month. The girlfriend's plans soon changed, too. She wanted to stay on with her boyfriend instead of boarding her flight to New York City. She offered Pebble her ticket, and he seized the opportunity to go visit Margaret. He jumped on the flight with nothing but what he was wearing—a pair of shorts, sneakers, and a T-shirt.

Margaret loved surprises, and this was one of the best. She and Pebble stayed for a short time at her high-rise apartment. Margaret borrowed clothes for him and introduced him to her friends. On Cumberland, Pebble had shown Margaret his world; now it was her turn to show him the facets of Manhattan she loved. They had never discussed their age difference; it was of little importance to either of them, and although her friends noticed, it was inconsequential. Margaret had found her match in spirit and adventure. They were thrilled for her and could see how happy she was.

Crispian, though, wasn't too sure about Pebble invading their dwellings. The dog only begrudgingly accepted Pebble at the end of his leash if a walk in the park was involved. Pebble believed the best way to someone's heart was through his or her dog, so he was determined to make friends with the jealous Kerry blue.

The couple cozied up in Cobble Court for a few days in Margaret's enchanting fur-covered home. Pebble was fascinated by the eccentric touches of Margaret's writing refuge and the way they had to wind their way through the tenement building. It was like entering a secret world. Pietro kept them fed and cared for as they escaped the real world outside of the tiny house in the middle of skyscrapers.

Margaret was lost in love. She loved lying together with Pebble's head on her chest. She loved his curls and the weight of his body on hers. When she first met Pebble, she had worried that he was too much of a boy for someone her age. Now she only saw him as a man.

After a few days, she took him to the Only House. It had always been a creative getaway filled with unique touches of a life well lived. Now it was infused with the bliss of romance. Margaret placed wildflowers in tiny vases around the house. Pebble watched her plunge into blackberry bushes, seemingly oblivious to their scratchy threats. Her skill at subduing the vines, learned while beagling, reminded him of a pet bear he once had. Oblivious to the thorns, Margaret brought out the best berries from the depths of the bushes.

When Dot and her children came to visit, they pulled kelp from the seafloor and made grass skirts. One evening, they went on a walk in the setting sun behind her house through the woods. As they drew near to a huge circular stone at the edge of the forest, Margaret shushed the group, warning them to be quiet so they wouldn't scare the fairy people away. They lay on their bellies in the soft moss, looking under toadstools and leaves for the little people. Laurel swore she saw a little fairy dressed in a purple chiffon dress with blue shoes. As they walked past the rock, Margaret pointed at the pools of water where rainwater collected in the depressions on the rock's surface. Those, she explained, are where the fairies go to cool off after a night of dancing.

Alone at the Only House again, Pebble and Margaret watched dusk settle in over their little kingdom. They sat through the rising of the moon, the stars appearing in the dark, dark sky, and the noises of the night animals stirring. During the day, they rowed or sailed around the islands with a bottle of wine cooling in the waters of the sea on a rope that trailed behind them. When a storm blew up, even an expert sailor like Pebble couldn't right her dilapidated sailboat when it was swamped by the waves. Fortunately, Margaret's handyman happened by and brought a wet Margaret and Pebble aboard. He told Margaret that she looked better wet than she did dry. Margaret laughed and puffed on her pipe, which was still lit.

When they returned to New York, Margaret made preparations for France and life on a boat. She met with her publishers, picked up checks, and dropped off manuscripts. Lucille Ogle at Golden let her see Garth Williams's art for the book that had come from watching Pebble try to save the shrimper's sinking ship, *The Sailor Dog*. It was to be Margaret's wedding present to him.

Margaret loved Garth's illustrations but asked that the name "Kitty" etched on the boat in the story be replaced with the name of Pebble's boat, *Mandalay*. Margaret also turned in a revision of a book that was to accompany a clever song by Rube Goldberg entitled *Willie the Whistling Giraffe*. Rosemary Clooney, a popular singer whose songs were frequently heard on radio and jukeboxes, agreed to sing *Willie*. Margaret had written several songs she was sure would make popular adult records if someone like Clooney were to sign on to perform them. She turned over a batch of songs to a composer she met through ASCAP, including one she was particularly fond of called "I Like People" that Golden planned to package with a book. She knew that one had jukebox potential.

At Harriet's office, Margaret delivered signed contracts and copyright registrations for her latest songs. The will Harriet had prepared for her was ready to sign, although she had to give Margaret the disappointing news that the United States Coast Guard had turned down her request to be buried at sea. The Coast Guard had sent a mocking letter, declaring that this was the first time they received such a request, which couldn't be granted because it was against public policy. They suggested Harriet tell her client to make other arrangements.

While in France, Margaret had plans to meet with the beloved French composer of the Babar musical, Jacques Prévert. She hoped to compare notes on writing music and get his advice on writing for the stage and screen, a new frontier for her. She had corresponded with Jacques the year before when they were part of a publishing experiment. They both wrote books based on the same photographs by Osa Johnson, a famous wildlife photographer, which had been published simultaneously in French and English, but the stories they created to go along with the photographs were completely different.

Margaret and Pebble planned to sail where they wished without a final destination or timetable, which made packing a challenge. She bought some clothes for France at Bloomingdale's and ordered six months of her prescriptions from the apothecary. At last, she was ready to set sail.

Dot and her children accompanied Pebble to the dock to see

Margaret and Crispian off. They boarded the ocean liner with Margaret and walked up and down the ship's long hallways in search of Margaret's cabin. When they finally found it, a steward explained he would take Crispian each morning and evening for a walk around the boat and then feed him on the deck. Margaret told Laurel he was a special dog. After all, he had his own book, and they had to treat him like a celebrity.

As tugs pulled her boat away from the docks she knew so well, Margaret's friends and lover waved good-bye to her from the docks. There were tears in her eyes. Her life would never be the same. She confessed to Dot that she didn't think she would ever return to her old life in New York. After being on Cumberland with Pebble, New York City felt like a phone booth.

Although some of Margaret's friends questioned the wisdom of taking Crispian to France, Margaret knew it was the right place for him. Walter Varney, the manager of the château where she would stay, was the one other person in the world who loved the cantankerous Crispian as much as she did. He would take great care of her dog. He had once had his own Kerry blue, and he knew how obstinate that breed of dog could be. On the boat during the way over, Margaret trained Crispian to understand basic commands in French. She had no idea how long she would be gone on her extended honeymoon, and she wanted him to know the language.

Her hotel, Château Barlow, had once been a castle. It sat atop a hill in the ancient village Èze and had one of the best views of the French Riviera. The owner, Samuel Barlow, was a music producer. He had visited this hillside town and had fallen in love with the crumbling old castle. He turned the ancient building into a rambling hotel that became a mecca for musicians, writers, painters, and actors—one never knew who might be dining or staying at his famous hot spot.

The twists and turns of the hallways and the multitude of windows reminded Margaret of her book *The House of a Hundred Windows,* which featured a cat peering out from the many different windows of a castle onto famous paintings. Margaret picnicked on the hillside, staring down at the Côte d'Azur that sparkled below. She was eager to join Pebble every time she looked at the sea. She understood why he said the sea was uncomplicated. Unlike land, you knew your adversaries, and it was always a clean fight.

One night at a dinner with Walter and his friends, Margaret was invited to go sightseeing in Italy and to stay at a palace in Florence. She was short on funds, but another dinner companion offered to loan her the money needed for the excursion. She traveled to the palace, located along the Arno River. She wrote to her sister that Crispian chased cats all around the palace and that she was very near the pension where they had stayed with their mother before going to Brillantmont.

On the train back to France, Margaret's side began to ache. She thought it might be an ovarian cyst, something she had experienced before. The pain usually passed after a day, but by the time she arrived at the station in Èze, her pain was unbearable. Instead of returning to the Château Barlow, she went directly to a hospital in Nice.

She was examined and told to prepare for a possible surgery. Symptoms of an ovarian cyst and appendicitis are similar, and the doctor wanted to wait a day to see if her pain would pass. If not, he would operate in the morning. Margaret hurriedly put things in order. Her checking account was overdrawn, and she had no money to pay the hospital or the man who had loaned her money to travel to Italy. She asked Walter to send her father a telegram asking him to deposit money in her checking account. Bruce Brown, however, didn't like or trust Walter. He told Margaret he thought the man was a crook. Besides, Bruce also was quite sick—far too ill to go to the bank. Margaret cabled Roberta asking for the money, and her sister sent it right away.

Margaret wrote a codicil to her will naming Pebble her closest of kin and dashed off letters and telegrams to editors and friends. Dr. Daviau performed surgery the next day and found that a cyst was not the issue but that Margaret's appendix was about to burst. Once it was removed, he placed it in a jar that Margaret kept by her hospital bed. He ordered her to lie still while she recovered.

Margaret knew that staying in bed after surgery wasn't recommended. Blood clots could form if a patient didn't get up and move around. She questioned the doctor's orders and called her physician in America to ask him to intervene. He tried, but to no avail. Even after two more calls to her doctor in the States, the order for absolute bed rest remained. Margaret was irritated but tried to be as friendly as possible with the doctor and hospital staff. Dr. Daviau brought her wine from his own cellar. She also charmed the stereotypically strict nurses to let Crispian in for a short visit. Walter was attentive to her every need and brought her meals from local restaurants. He moved her bed to an open window so she could watch a parade passing by.

The hospital's nurses were nuns, and their caps with wings extending from either side reminded Margaret of Babar's adventures. She spent her recuperation time writing letters and working on manuscripts. This health scare had made her all the more eager to begin her new life with Pebble as soon as possible. She dispatched a postcard to Monty Hare, telling him about her appendectomy; other than that, she said, she was having a marvelous time and doing well. In a postscript, she wrote that she was having two boxes of Michael's papers delivered to him.

On the morning of November 13, Walter arrived at the hospital early in the morning to help move Margaret to his hotel. She would complete her recuperation at Château Barlow and then meet Pebble in Panama. He had chosen a location for their wedding on the island of Saint Thomas and set sail to meet her plane.

The nurse came in to prepare Margaret for release and asked how she felt. Margaret pulled back her bedcovers and kicked her leg up can-can style and said, "Grand!" But then, she immediately collapsed. A blood clot that had formed in her leg had broken free and cut off the blood supply to her brain. To the nurse and Walter, it appeared as if Margaret had suffered a stroke. She regained consciousness briefly, but her words were unintelligible.

Walter dashed off telegrams to Pebble and Margaret's father at 8:15 A.M. to let them know Margaret was seriously ill. He told them she had suffered an embolism but promised to send them an update the next day. Two hours later, though, he issued another telegram to tell them Margaret had died.

The business of an American dying overseas was handled by the American Consulate. Their crisply written telegrams and letters were practiced in sympathy, formality, and efficiency. Walter Varney was willing to accompany Margaret's remains back to the United

States, but funds would have to be wired. The codicil to the will Margaret had written almost two weeks before requested that she be cremated and her ashes spread at her beloved Only House.

The thank-you letter Margaret had written to Roberta for sending her money arrived a few days later. Margaret had promised to pay her sister back in December. She had joked that she was grateful for the money because it meant that if the surgery didn't go well, at least she wouldn't die a pauper.

Pebble arrived in port expecting to meet Margaret. Instead, he was handed Walter Varney's telegrams. For almost a month, he stayed on his boat, deep in mourning. He didn't have the heart to go on with his journey, so he returned to New York. He moved into Cobble Court with plans to stay there until the lease expired.

Dot took care of shuttering the Only House. When Margaret's possessions arrived from the American Consulate in France, it was Pebble's mother who sorted Margaret's clothes and forwarded the gifts Margaret had bought for her friends. On Margaret's stationery, Pebble wrote a letter to her father, telling him how honored he felt to have loved her and to have been loved by her. He said that Margaret had been a rare individual, the kind that comes along only once in a long, long time. She would never really die because she lived on in him, and through her books, she would live on in many, many other people. The next year, Pebble left Cobble Court. He returned to his boat and the uncomplicated sea.

Epilogue

After Margaret's death, Bruce Bliven joined a group of Margaret's friends for a dinner to memorialize her. Her Birdbrain Club, editors from different publishing houses, and beagling club members gathered, but when the dinner was over, Bruce knew they would never gather together again. Margaret had been the architect of the web that connected them; without her, there was little to keep them united.

Roberta and Bruce had been named executors of her estate and were suddenly thrown into the middle of Margaret's copious business affairs. Deadlines and decisions were heaped upon them. Some of Margaret's collaborators finished songs and books of hers that were in progress, but most of her projects were stalled by the lengthy probate of Margaret's will. It took almost five years for the courts to sort out the contracts, copyrights, and value of Margaret's publications. At that time, *Goodnight Moon* was earning very little per year, so they estimated the value of the book to be $200, and it would be another twenty years before the New York Public Library would add the book to its stacks. At last tally, the book has sold more than forty-eight million copies.

The clipping service Margaret had hired years before forwarded her obituary from dozens of newspapers to Roberta. They were stamped as "No Charge" along with the date. Because Margaret had been Michael's literary executor, Roberta and Bruce had to settle Michael's publishing affairs, as well. When boxes of Michael's manuscripts were delivered to Roberta, she contacted Diana for help. Diana told her to burn it all—there was nothing worth keeping.

Margaret's prediction that Diana's lack of self-confidence would derail her acting career was correct. Diana's candid autobiography, *Too Much, Too Soon,* detailed her troubled marriages, addiction to alcohol, and life in the shadow of a domineering mother. Diana never received another film role after her mother died, but her autobiography was made into a movie and was said to be the inspiration, in great measure, for *The Bad and the Beautiful,* a blockbuster that won five Oscars. Diana died at the age of thirty-eight from an overdose of alcohol and Seconal. The week before she died, she made news when four policemen removed her from the audience of a Broadway theater for being drunk and unruly.

Margaret's relationship with Bill Scott had never fully mended. Other than the single manuscript she was required to give him in the settlement, she never turned over another story to him. Bill tried to arrange a scholarship in her memory, but that never came to pass.

The illustrators and authors Margaret worked most closely with all had long, successful careers in children's books. Clem and Edith "Posey" Hurd collaborated on more than seventy-five books. The ones they worked on with Margaret remain their bestselling publications. Their son, Thacher, is a bestselling and award-winning illustrator. He had the idea to put his father's art for *Goodnight Moon* onto a poster and sell it. That idea eventually turned into A Peaceable Kingdom, a successful company dedicated to placing independent artists' work onto a variety of paper products.

Garth Williams went on to illustrate *Charlotte's Web* and Laura Ingalls Wilder's Little House on the Prairie series. His name, like Margaret's, was not as well known as his work.

Dot lost her best friend, but it felt like she lost her sister. She kept Margaret's spirit alive in stories she told her children. Her daughter, Laurel, distinctly remembers seeing the fairy under the toadstool, dancing the hula with Margaret while wearing a grass skirt fashioned from kelp, and how her godmother declared a handful of champagne corks to be boats as she tossed them into Laurel's bathwater. For many years, Laurel had no idea that her godmother was famous or that her real name was Margaret—she only knew her as Goldie. Unlike the millions of children who can only imagine themselves to be the bunny in *Goodnight Moon,* Laurel knows the comfort of scrambling up Margaret's leopard-skin step stool onto that big bed with its red comforter. With awe, she recalls the view of the moon from Margaret's wall of windows and how it seemed to hang in the sky only for her.

Dot wanted to write a biography of Margaret and contacted all the members of the Birdbrain Club to collect their memories of Margaret. The members of that group were loyal to Margaret to the end. When journalists and potential biographers began asking questions about Margaret's relationship with Michael, they collectively agreed to lie. It would be many years before Bruce Bliven broke his silence and shared the truth of his friend's love life. Dot never found a publisher for her biography.

When a photograph of Lucy Gaston lounging on a yacht in the Caribbean was published in a 1949 issue of *Life* magazine, Bill Gaston penned a clever letter to the editor exclaiming his gratitude that his soon-to-be former wife was not suffering as much as her divorce lawyers declared. He kept that letter pinned to his wall the rest of his life. After Margaret died, he begged Leonard Weisgard to sell him the portrait he had painted of Margaret. Leonard refused.

Margaret's estate faced additional problems when Walter Varney returned to the United States the next year with Crispian. The Kerry blue had become very aggressive after Margaret's death and was attacking other dogs. He also bit one man's leg and another's hand. Margaret's will stipulated that Roberta would inherit certain royalties if she agreed to care for Crispian, which Walter knew. After Margaret died, he asked Roberta if he could keep Crispian, and she agreed, unaware of the stipulation in Margaret's will. Having gained custody of Crispian, Walter filed a claim to receive the publication rights originally granted to Roberta. The court refused his request. Roberta and Bruce Bliven believed Walter to be the source of a rumor circulating that Margaret's copyrights would be contested, which was unfounded, but the damage had been done. Publishers thought it too risky to purchase Margaret's remaining work. As the probate of the will dragged on, even the pending contracts for manuscripts were canceled. Many of Margaret's publishers believed it impolite to edit her work without her consent. At a loss for what else to do, Roberta neatly packed the hundreds of onionskin manuscripts into a sturdy trunk and stored them away.

Cobble Court still stands today in Greenwich Village. In the late 1960s when the owner decided to demolish the house to build a nursing home, the current tenants couldn't bear to see it disappear, so they paid to have it relocated to a vacant lot on Charles Street. A flatbed truck transported the house to the quaint little street on the West Side of the city. The chimney of the fireplace that inspired the one in *Goodnight Moon* still crowns the quirky little house, and the same cobblestone dots the entry.

Jessica Dunham, Margaret's Bank Street colleague and friend, was inspired to gather evidence of the amazing mind that lay behind

Margaret's books before that brilliance was forgotten. With the assistance of Dot and Roberta, Jessica wrote to all of Margaret's publishers and collaborators, asking them to submit anything of Margaret's they had to the public library in Westerly, Rhode Island. Margaret and Jessica had spent time together picnicking around the picturesque little town, and Jessica thought Margaret would have liked the idea that her work had found a permanent home at the elegant Carnegie library. Editors, illustrators, and publishers willingly complied, turning over dummy books, manuscripts, and a smattering of letters to be housed at the library.

The collection of materials and a full set of Margaret's publications was dedicated at Westerly in 1957. Louise Seaman Bechtel, who had worked with Margaret at Bank Street, spoke on behalf of many of Margaret's colleagues, who had contributed letters, manuscripts, and their own memories of their beloved friend. In her remarks, Louise said she was not bringing a formal wreath of roses in honor of Margaret; such a thing would not have been representative of the woman she had known. For Margaret, only wild roses would do because although she had been cultured, she had also been a savage, untamed spirit.

Leonard Weisgard helped Roberta and Bruce with Margaret's mess of manuscripts. He also tried to get *The Green Wind* published, offering to illustrate the massive collection of over two hundred poems Margaret had written. Because some of the works in the collection were held by different publishers and music companies, the task of sorting the rights was declared to be too problematic for the possible financial return.

. . .

Pebble wanted a tattoo of a bunny on his shoulder and asked Leonard to design one. Leonard refused, but Pebble got the tattoo anyway.

Pebble did sail around the world and wrote a memoir of his journey, *Man on His Island*. In Norway, he met Liv Coucheron Torp, the former wife of *Kon-Tiki* author Thor Heyerdahl. He fell in love with Liv, who favored Margaret in appearance and spirit.

It is easy to see how Margaret fell for Pebble—his charm and easy laughter fill a room. He spent his life building boats, which was exactly the life he told Margaret he wanted to live. He is a regular visitor to the Only House, which remains in almost the same condition as when Margaret left it. Her pens, paintings, and chairs are scattered around the rooms where she spent her days writing. A visitor feels as if Margaret has merely stepped away—gone off to gather wildflowers or to dig for a bucket of clams on a neighboring island. It was years after Margaret's death before Pebble could return to this idyllic hideaway. When he did come back, he brought along his wife and their two children, Liv and Stillman. His children grew up hearing the magical stories Margaret had once told their father. They also looked for fairies in the forest.

As Margaret requested in her will, Pebble placed a stone marker in a forest clearing near the Only House and spread her ashes in the sea. Her chosen epitaph, "Writer of Songs and Nonsense," is carved into the stone. One might argue with her choice of words, for the nonsense she wrote has transported generations of children into the timeless world of stories. She has lifted children from their own little worries into the life of bear or bee or bunny, or into a bed surrounded by soothing green walls, saying good night to the moon. Margaret's simple wish, to make children laugh, or to jog them with the unexpected and then to comfort them with their own familiar world, has come true millions of times over.

The stone marker is now dotted with bright gold lichen. Pebble also added a quote from *The Little Island* to the marker and then his own words of gratitude: "You gave us all so much. A chance to love. A place to rest. A window into living." The marker sits in a small grassy spot surrounded by Margaret's beloved island forest and the sea just beyond. This was where she found inspiration as she gazed at the wonders of nature around her. A weathered wooden chair near the aging stone bearing her name awaits those who wish to do the same.

I will let the last words be Margaret's own. She wrote this in a diary she kept at the time she was falling in love with Michael and contemplating writing a biography of their lives together:

What is biography, what is there to tell beyond the endearing humanity of one on a scale more intense and larger than others? And the significance—aliveness and honesty in their own years. The Gods, the heroes, the man and his devils. All the long-range back and forth in the shuffle and shuttle of being alive. And the preservation of a few of the heights in all the years. For I believe that at five we reach a point not to be achieved again and from which ever after we at best keep and most often go down from. And so at 2 and 13, at 20 & 30 & 21 & 18—each year has the newness of its own awareness to one alive. Alive—and life.

That is the significance of this biography, one who has dared to be gloriously good and gloriously bad in one life. No Limbo for her. Rather let life itself grow living monuments out of trees and living words so that death can never take from our half-lives this radiant living that was lived among us.

Acknowledgments

I'm forever grateful to the exceptional team at Flatiron Books, especially Bob Miller, Whitney Frick, and Jasmine Faustino for their encouragement, creativity, and patience. I also wish to thank Don Fehr, my agent at Trident Media Group, for placing this book in their talented hands.

The people I interviewed for this biography often remarked that Margaret had the most beautiful eyes they had ever seen, but differed in their memory on their color. Some said they were blue, others green, but each thought she was the most fascinating person they had ever met. I am grateful to Roberta Rauch, Bruce Bliven, Montgomery Hare, Gratz Brown, and Dorothy Wagstaff Ripley for sharing their stories about Margaret. It was my first and last intention to capture the Margaret they knew and loved.

My deepest gratitude to Jim Rockefeller for sharing part of his life on these pages and for so generously giving me his time. I also want to thank his wife, Marilyn, for her hospitality and persuasiveness in convincing Jim to contribute his eloquent foreword to this book.

My journey with Margaret began when my business partner, Faith Nance, insisted I write Roberta and ask if we could publish one of Margaret's books. I am so glad she pushed me into Margaret's path. Thanks also to Marla Persky and Craig Heberton for keeping that little company we started going all these years. Additional thanks to all of the people who have worked with us on Margaret's manuscripts for the past twenty-five years, particularly Michele Gay, Angie Nash, Alison Payne, Sara Conn, Taryn Seale, Susan Evans, and Caroline Bon Temps.

The keepers of Margaret's papers were essential from beginning to end. I wish to thank Beth Harris at Hollins University and Beth Waller at Woods Rogers for being beside me on this journey through the maze of Margaret's papers. I also am grateful to Nina Wright at Westerly Public Library for carefully preserving the evidence of Margaret's brilliance entrusted there and lending your thorough knowledge of those papers to this project. Thanks also to Lindsey Wyckoff at Bank Street College; Beth Ziemacki, Emily Brenner, and Nancy Inteli at HarperCollins; Diane Muldrow at Golden Books; Meredith Mundy and Bill Luckey at Sterling Publishers; and Wendy Friedman at Parragon for their help with this book and their dedication to Margaret's legacy. The professional assistance of Doctors Karen and Bill Rhueban helped me understand Margaret's mind and body—thank you, dynamic duo.

I also am forever indebted to Laurel Ripley Galloway for sharing her own memories of Margaret and her mother's stories from the Birdbrain Club members. Although they didn't know Margaret, Liv Rockefeller and Stillman Rockefeller grew up in the ever-present shadow she cast on the Only House. I am grateful to them for allowing me access to that magical place. Many thanks to Liv's valiant husband, Ken Shure, for braving the elements to deliver me to that rocky coast whenever I asked. Thank you all for helping me unfold the Margaret documented on these pages and for your friendship.

Friends and family became more important to me than ever as I began to write this book. My husband, Nap Gary, passed away the day after I finished my first chapter. He was my toughest editor, but my greatest supporter. I want to thank my parents, brothers, and sisters from the Little Clan and Team Gary for buoying me during those darkest of days. Additional thanks to Daniele Lang, Colleen Murphy, and Linda Smigel for lending me your beautiful homes in which to write the book and rewrite my life. Hugs and heartfelt thanks also to Terry Finley, J. B. Hopkins, Katie Finley, Laura Juarez, Jeannie Bailey, Judy Ault, Beth Sahlie, Cyd Moore, Lucinda Wilson, and the Goddesses. You are my Birdbrain Club, and when I'm with you it feels like Christmas.

A round of applause to my children Emily, Britt, and David for patiently listening to Margaret's stories when they were young and my stories about her as I wrote this book. They remain my North, East, South, and West.

Sources

Prologue
1950

Baker, J. C. Journals of the Buckram Beagles. Archives & Manuscript Collections, MC 0015. 1936–1948. National Sporting Library.

Brown, M. W. Correspondence from Margaret Wise Brown. 1936–1952. Margaret Wise Brown Collection. Box 19, Folder 1. Special Collections. Westerly Library, Westerly, RI.

Brown, M. W. "Every Year." Margaret Wise Brown Collection. 1949. Box 14, Folder 5. Special Collections. Westerly Library, Westerly, RI.

Brown, M. W. Margaret Wise Brown Papers. 1938–1960. Archives, Q-4a. Wyndham Robertson Library, Hollins University.

Brown, M. W. Margaret Wise Brown papers. 1940–1952. James S. Rockefeller Jr. Personal collection.

Brown, M. W. "Running to Hounds." Margaret Wise Brown Collection. 1937. Box 13, Folder 9. Special Collections. Westerly Public Library, Westerly, RI.

Brown, M. W. *White Freesias.* Edited by A. Gary. Montevallo, AL: WaterMark, 1999.

Dycus, G. L. *The Sandanona Harehounds: Beagling and Basseting in Millbrook.* Hopewell Junction, NY: Liberty Hall Publications, 2004.

Paget, J. O. *Beagles and Beagling*. London: Hutchinson, 1923.

Rauch, R. Interview with author. 1987–1995.

Rauch, R. Letters. Margaret Wise Brown Papers. 1952–2002. Wyndham Robertson Library, Hollins University.

One
1910–1914

American Manufacturing Company. 2015. Saveindustrialbrooklyn.org.

Brown, G. Interview with author. 1990–1996.

Brown, M. W. Autobiographical notes. *Junior Book of Authors*. New York: H. W. Wilson, 1951.

Brown, M. W. Biographical material. Margaret Wise Brown Collection. ca. 1945. Box 19, Folder 1. MWB 01. Special Collections. Westerly Library, Westerly, RI.

Brown, M. W. Margaret Wise Brown Collection. 1910–1952. MB01. Special Collections. Westerly Library, Westerly, RI.

Brown, M. W. Margaret Wise Brown Papers. 1940–1952. James S. Rockefeller Jr. Personal collection.

Brown, M. W. Tim diary. Margaret Wise Brown. 1928–1933. Margaret Wise Brown Collection. Series II, Box 16. Special Collections. Westerly Library, Westerly, RI.

Brown, M. W. *The Unpublished Works of Margaret Wise Brown*. Edited by A. Gary. Montevallo, AL: WaterMark, 1992.

"The Comet Hidden, Its Glory Dimming." *New York Times,* May 23, 1910.

"Comet's Poisonous Tail." Special to the *Times*. *New York Times,* 1910.

Commelin, A. C. D. "Comet May Cause Aurora." *New York Times,* May 16, 1910.

"Halley in 1910." Planetary Data System. NASA. 2014. Retrieved from https://pds.jpl.nasa.gov/planets/captions/smallbod/hal1910.htm.

"Moon Eclipsed Tonight." *New York Times,* May 23, 1910.

Rauch, R. Interview with author. 1987–1995.

Two
1917–1923

Book of Knowledge, The. Edited by A. Mee. 1912. Vol. IV Collection. Grolier Society.

Breckenridge, D. "History Repeats Itself." *Lexington Leader,* 1911.

Brown, G. Interview with author. 1990–1996.

Brown, M. W. Green diary. 1947–1952. Margaret Wise Brown Papers. Unpublished. Wyndham Robertson Library, Hollins University.

Brown, M. W. *Goodnight Songs: A Celebration of the Seasons.* Edited by M. Mundy. New York: Sterling Children's Books, 2015.

Brown, M. W. Margaret Wise Brown Collection. 1910–1952. MB01. Special Collections. Westerly Library, Westerly, RI.

Brown, M. W. Margaret Wise Brown Papers. 1938–1960. MWB01. Wyndham Robertson Library, Hollins University.

Brown, M. W. Margaret Wise Brown Papers. 1940–1952. James S. Rockefeller Jr. Personal collection.

Brown, M. W. Red diary. Margaret Wise Brown Collection. 1940–1950. Series II, Box 16. Special Collections. Westerly Library, Westerly, RI.

Jefferson, T. *The Papers of Thomas Jefferson.* Charlottesville, VA: University of Virginia Press, 1797.

Rauch, R. Interview with author. 1987–1995.

Steinmeyer, J. *The Last Greatest Magician in the World.* New York: Tarcher, 2011.

Three
1924–1927

Blitz, T. "Les Temps des Cerises." Daily Motion. 2014. Retrieved from www .dailymotion.com/video/xqpawy_le-temps-de-cerises-various-artists -french-english-subtitles_music.

Breckenridge, D. "History Repeats Itself." *Lexington Leader,* 1911.

Brown, B. G. *Freedom for Missouri.* Saint Joseph, MO: The State Historical Society of Missouri, 1862.

Brown, B. G. *Universal Suffrage: An Address by Hon. B. Gratz Brown: Delivered at Turner Hall, St. Louis, Mo., September 22, 1865.* Saint Louis, MO: Democrat Office, 1865.

Brown, M. W. Diary from MWB's time at Dana Hall boarding school. 1926–1928. Margaret Wise Brown Collection. Folder 16, Box 20. Special Collections. Westerly Library, Westerly, RI.

Brown, M. W. Margaret Wise Brown Collection. MB01. Special Collections. Westerly Public Library, Westerly, RI.

Brown, M. W. Margaret Wise Brown Papers. 1940–1952. James S. Rockefeller Jr. Personal collection.

Brown, M. W. *Mouse of My Heart.* New York: Hyperion, 2001.

Clark, J. Interview with author. 2014.

Gooley, L. P. "History: Before Water-skiing, There Was Aquaplaning." Adirondack Almanack. 2012. Retrieved from www.adirondackalmanack.com /2012/07/history-before-water-skiing-there-was-aquaplaning.html.

Greeley and Brown. Presidential campaign poster. New York: H. H. Lloyd, 1872.

Jefferson, T. *The Papers of Thomas Jefferson.* Charlottesville: University of Virginia Press, 1797.

"Kentucky's First Sunday School." *Lexington Leader,* 1940.

"Liberty Hall." Liberty Hall. 2014. Retrieved from http://libertyhall.org.

Liberty Hall: An Old Kentucky Home. Louisville, KY: Liberty Hall, 1930.

Liberty Hall, Frankfort, Kentucky. Louisville, KY: Liberty Hall, 1943.

Morrissey, J. Interview with author. 2014.

O'Neill, D. Interview with author. 2014.

"Our Objectives." Brillantmont International School. 2014. Retrieved from http://www.brillantmont.ch.

Passenger List, Ship *Orduña.* 1925. Ancestry.com.

Passport Application: Margaret and Roberta Brown. 1923. National Archives and Records Administration (NARA).

Rauch, R. Interview with author. 1987–1995.

Rockefeller, J. S., Jr. "Margaret Wise Brown and Cumberland." Chapter 5. Unpublished manuscript. Personal collection.

Swann, M. *Promoting the Classroom and Playground of Europe: Swiss Private School Prospectuses and Education Focused Tourism Guides, 1890–1945.* Vancouver,

BC: University of British Columbia, 2007. Retrieved from www
.collectionscanada.gc.ca/obj/s4/f2/dsk3/BVAU/TC-BVAU-216.pdf.

Four
1928

Brown, M. W. Diary from MWB's time at Dana Hall boarding school. 1926–
1928. Margaret Wise Brown Collection. Folder 16, Box 20. Special Collections. Westerly Library, Westerly, RI.

Brown, M. W. Margaret Wise Brown Papers. 1938–1960. Archives, Q-4a.
Wyndham Robertson Library, Hollins University.

Clark, J. *Cumberland Island Saved: How the Carnegies Helped Preserve a National Treasure.* Lexington, KY: Gravesend, 2014.

Clark, J. Interview with author. 2014.

"Coffee Pot." RetroGalaxy. 2014. Retrieved from www.retrogalaxy.com/culture
/party/coffee-pot.asp.

Dana Hall. Catalog. 1991.

"Dies from Broken Heart." *New York Tribune,* February 10, 1907. Retrieved
from http://chroniclingamerica.loc.gov/lccn/sn83030214/1907-02-10
/ed-1/seq-7/.

Greeley and Brown. New York: H. H. Lloyd, 1872.

Hare, M. Memories of Margaret Wise Brown. 1991.

Liberty Hall: An Old Kentucky Home. Louisville, KY: Liberty Hall, 1930.

"Lucy Carnegie's Great Camp on Raquette Lake." Adirondack Almanack. 2014.
Retrieved from www.adirondackalmanack.com/2014/04/lucy-carnegies
-great-camp-raquette-lake.html.

Rauch, R. Interview with author. 1987–1995.

Rockefeller, J. S., Jr. Interview with author. 2014.

Rockefeller, L. Interview with author. 2013–2014.

Rockefeller, N. C. *The Carnegies & Cumberland Island.* Cumberland Island, Camden County, GA: 1993.

Schurz, C. *Letter from Senator Carl Schurz to B. Gratz Brown.* Washington, D.C.:
F. & J. Rives & G. A. Bailey, 1872.

Seabrook, C. *Cumberland Island: Strong Women, Wild Horses.* Winston-Salem, NC: John F. Blair, 2004.

"Seasonal snowfall totals for Boston, MA." National Oceanic and Atmospheric Administration. 2015. Retrieved from www.noaa.gov.

Shure, K. Interview with author. 2013–2014.

Five
1929–1932

"The Battle for Baltimore." National Park Service. 2015. Retrieved from www .nps.gov/stsp/learn/historyculture/battlebaltimore.htm.

Breckenridge, D. "History Repeats Itself." *Lexington Leader,* 1911.

Brown, M. W. Diary from MWB's time at Dana Hall boarding school. 1926–1928. Margaret Wise Brown Collection, Folder 16, Box 20. Special Collections. Westerly Library, Westerly, RI.

Brown, M. W. Green diary. Margaret Wise Brown Papers. 1938–1960. Archives, Q-4a. Special Collections. Wyndham Robertson Library, Hollins University.

Brown, M. W. Margaret Wise Brown Papers. 1938–1960. Archives, Q-4a. Wyndham Robertson Library, Hollins University.

Brown, M. W. Margaret Wise Brown Papers. 1940–1952. James S. Rockefeller Jr. Personal collection.

Brown, M. W. Tim diary. Margaret Wise Brown Collection. 1928–1933. Series II, Box 16. Special Collections. Westerly Library, Westerly, RI.

Brown, M. W. Unpublished manuscripts. 1936–1952. Margaret Wise Brown Papers. Acc 1-7/1993, Series 1. Wyndham Robertson Library, Hollins University.

"George Hueville Armistead." Ancestry.com. 2015. Retrieved from http:// person.ancestry.com/tree/18254598/person/18359026969/facts.

Hare, M. Personal letters to Dorothy Ripley, courtesy of Laurel Ripley Galloway.

Niederer, F. *Hollins: An Illustrated History.* Charlottesville, University of Virginia Press, 1973.

Peterson, N. Interview with author. 2015.

Rauch, R. Interview with author. 1987–1995.

Smith, W. R. L. *Charles Lewis Cocke: Founder of Hollins College.* Boston: Gorham Press, 1929.

The Spinster. Roanoke, VA: Hollins University, 1931.

The Spinster. Roanoke, VA: Hollins University, 1932.

Wheeler, J. P. J. "Before the Writing Program there was Margaret Wise Brown." Paper presented at the Hollins University Alumnae Reunion, Hollins University, Roanoke, VA, 2003.

Wheeler, J. P. J. Interview with author. 1993–2001.

Six
1934–1935

Antler, J. *Lucy Sprague Mitchell.* New Haven, CT: Yale University Press, 1987.

Brown, M. W. Biographical material. Margaret Wise Brown Collection. ca. 1945. Box 19, Folder 1. MWB 01. Special Collections. Westerly Library, Westerly, RI.

Brown, M. W. Letters. 1934–1942. University Archives, F-3a. Wyndam Robertson Library, Hollins University.

Brown, M. W. Margaret Wise Brown Collection. 1910–1952. MB01. Special Collections. Westerly Public Library, Westerly, RI.

Brown, M. W. Margaret Wise Brown Papers. 1940–1952. James S. Rockefeller Jr. Personal collection.

Brown, M. W. Outgoing correspondence. 1934–1952. Margaret Wise Brown Papers. Series 5. Wyndham Robertson Library, Hollins University.

Brown, M. W. *Bumble Bee.* New York: HarperCollins, 1999.

Galloway, L. R. Interview with author. 2014.

"Gertrude Stein Arrives and Baffles Reporters by Making Herself Clear." *New York Times,* October 25, 1934.

Hewlett, R. *Melody Sheet Music Lyrics Midi.* n.p.: Richard Hewlett, 2014.

Lundell, W. Radio interview with Gertrude Stein. NBC Radio, 1934. New York.

Mitchell, L. S. *Another Here and Now Storybook.* New York: E. P. Dutton, 1937.

Mitchell, L. S. "Margaret Wise Brown, 1910–1952." *Children Here and Now* 1, no. 1 (1953).

Niemeyer, John H. *Lucy Sprague Mitchell, 1878–1967.* New York: Bank Street College of Education, 1967.

Ripley, D. Interview with author. 1996.

Ripley, D. Memories of Margaret Wise Brown. 1954–1995. Laurel Ripley Galloway Collection.

Three Lectures by Gertrude Stein. Brooklyn, NY: Brooklyn Academy of Music, 1934.

Seven
1936–1937

Baker, J. C. Journals of the Buckram Beagles. 1936–1948. Archives & Manuscript Collections. MC 0015. National Sporting Library.

Bliven, Bruce, Jr. Interview with author. 1990–1995.

Brown, M. W. Composition book. Margaret Wise Brown Collection. Box 18, Folder 1. Special Collections. Westerly Library, Westerly, RI.

Brown, M. W. Green diary. Margaret Wise Brown Papers. 1938–1960. MWB01. Special Collections. Wyndham Robertson Library, Hollins University.

Brown, M. W. Letters. 1934–1942. University Archives, F-3a. Wyndham Robertson Library, Hollins University.

Brown, M. W. Margaret Wise Brown Papers. 1937–1952. DG1129. de Grummond Children's Literature Collection. McCain Library and Archives, Hattiesburg, MS.

Brown, M. W. Margaret Wise Brown Papers. 1940–1952. James S. Rockefeller Jr. Personal collection.

Brown, M. W. Outgoing correspondence. 1936–1952. Margaret Wise Brown Papers. Series 5. Wyndham Robertson Library, Hollins University.

Brown, M. W. *When the Wind Blew.* New York: Harper & Brothers, 1937.

Jackson, K. T., L. Keller, and N. Flood. *Encyclopedia of New York City.* 2nd edition. New Haven, CT: Yale University Press, 2010.

Paris International Exposition. 1937. Paris, France.

Phelps, M. "Lucy Sprague Mitchell." *Horn Book,* May 1937.

Pollak, M. "New York's Huckleberry Friend, Region." *New York Times,* August 26, 2010.

Press, U. "Rises to Paint Woes of Spain." *Corpus Christi Caller-Times,* August 27, 1937.

Rauch, R. Interview with author. 1987–1995.

Rauch, R. Letters. Margaret Wise Brown Papers. 1952–2002. Wyndham Robertson Library, Hollins University.

Various. Incoming correspondence. Margaret Wise Brown Papers. 1936–1952. Series 4. Wyndham Robertson Library, Hollins University.

Eight
1938

"Alumnae Updates." *Hollins Alumnae Quarterly,* 1938.

Bliven, Bruce, Jr. Interview with author. 1990–1995.

Books for Children. New York: 69 Bank Street Publications, 1938.

Brown, G. Interview with author. 1990–1996.

Brown, M. W. Composition book. Margaret Wise Brown Collection. 1937. Box 18, Folder 1. Special Collections. Westerly Library, Westerly, RI.

Brown, M. W. "Dress Rehearsal for a Book." *Bank Street Annual,* 1938.

Brown, M. W. *The Fish with the Deep Sea Smile.* New York: E. P. Dutton, 1938.

Brown, M. W. Green diary. Margaret Wise Brown Papers. 1938–1960. Vol. Archives, Q-4. Special Collections. Wyndham Robertson Library, Hollins University.

Brown, M. W. *Heart on a Rib.* Margaret Wise Brown Collection. 1939. Series IV. Special Collections. Westerly Library, Westerly, RI.

Brown, M. W. "How to Read to Children." *Story Parade,* 1938.

Brown, M. W. "Leonard Weisgard Wins the Caldecott Award." *Publishers Weekly,* July 5, 1947.

Brown, M. W. Margaret Wise Brown Papers. 1937–1952. DG1129. de Grummond Children's Literature Collection. McCain Library and Archives, Hattiesburg, MS.

Brown, M. W. Margaret Wise Brown Papers. 1940–1952. James S. Rockefeller Jr. Personal collection.

Brown, M. W. Outgoing correspondence. Margaret Wise Brown Papers. 1934–1952. Series 5. Special Collections. Wyndham Robertson Library, Hollins University.

"Girl New to Stage to Star in 'Miracle.'" *New York Times,* November 26, 1923.

Hurd, C. Letters and presentation. Margaret Wise Brown Papers. 1952–1955. Special Collections. Wyndham Robertson Library, Hollins University.

Hurd, C. "Remembering Margaret Wise Brown." *Horn Book,* October 1983.

Nolen, B. *Story Parade,* 1938.

Publication List. New York: W. R. S. Publisher, 1938.

Rauch, R. Interview with author. 1987–1995.

Rauch, R. Outgoing correspondence. Margaret Wise Brown Papers. 1952–1990. Series 8. Special Collections. Wyndham Robertson Library, Hollins University.

"Rosamond Pinchot Ends Life in Garage." *New York Times,* January 25, 1938.

"Social Register Drops Stage Folk." *New York Times,* November 24, 1934.

Walt Disney Story Books. Boston: D. C. Heath, 1938.

Weisgard, L. Letters. Margaret Wise Brown Papers. 1952–1985. Special Collections. Wyndham Robertson Library, Hollins University.

Weisgard, L. Letters to Dorothy Ripley. 1990–1994. Laurel Ripley Galloway Collection.

The Writers Laboratory. New York: 69 Bank Street Publications, 1938.

Young Books: Publication List. New York: William R. Scott, 1938.

Nine
1939

"America First Committee." NNDB. Retrieved from www.nndb.com/org/039/000057865/.

"Among Hollins Writers." *Hollins Alumnae Magazine,* Winter 1939.

Barrymore, D., and G. Frank. *Too Much, Too Soon.* New York: Henry Holt, 1957.

Brown, M. W. *The Fog Bound Saint.* 1939. Margaret Wise Brown Papers. Series 1. Special Collections. Wyndham Robertson Library, Hollins University.

Brown, M. W. Green diary. Margaret Wise Brown Papers. 1938–1960. MWB01. Special Collections. Wyndham Robertson Library, Hollins University.

Brown, M. W. Green diary. Margaret Wise Brown Papers. 1947–1952. Unpublished. Special Collections. Wyndham Robertson Library, Hollins University.

Brown, M. W. "Leonard Weisgard Wins the Caldecott Award." *Publishers Weekly,* July 5, 1947.

Brown, M. W. Letters. 1934–1942. University Archives, F-3a. Wyndham Robertson Library, Hollins University.

Brown, M. W. Margaret Wise Brown Collection. 1910–1952. MB01. Special Collections. Westerly Library, Westerly, RI.

Brown, M. W. Margaret Wise Brown Papers. 1937–1952. DG1129. de Grummond Children's Literature Collection. McCain Library and Archives, Hattiesburg, MS.

Brown, M. W. Margaret Wise Brown Papers. 1940–1952. James S. Rockefeller Jr. Personal collection.

Brown, M. W. Unpublished manuscripts. Margaret Wise Brown Papers. 1910–1952. Series 1. Special Collections. Wyndham Robertson Library, Hollins University.

Galloway, L. R. Interview with author. 2014.

Gaston, B. *The Loveliest Woman in America.* New York: William Morrow, 2008.

Hare, M. Memories of Margaret Wise Brown. 1991. Laurel Ripley Galloway Collection.

Rockefeller, J. S., Jr. Interview with author. 2014.

Paris International Exposition. 1937. Paris, France.

Rauch, R. Interview with author. 1987–1995.

Ripley, D. Memories of Margaret Wise Brown. 1954–1995. Laurel Ripley Galloway Collection.

Slobodkina, E. Esphyr Slobodkina Papers. 1938–1980. DG0905. de Grummond Collection. McCain Library and Archives, Hattiesburg, MS.

Strange, M. *Who Tells Me True*. New York: Charles Scribner's Sons, 1940.

Weisgard, L. Letters. Margaret Wise Brown Papers. 1952–1985. Special Collections. Wyndham Robertson Library, Hollins University.

Weisgard, L. Letters to Dorothy Ripley. 1990–1994.

Ten
1940

Barrymore, D., and G. Frank. *Too Much, Too Soon*. New York: Henry Holt, 1957.

Bechtel, L. S. "Margaret Wise Brown." Paper presented at the dedication of papers to Westerly Public Library, Westerly, RI. 1957.

Bechtel, L. S. "Margaret Wise Brown: Laureate of the Nursery." *Horn Book*, June 1958.

Brown, M. W. [Golden MacDonald, pseud.] *Big Dog, Little Dog*. Garden City, NY: Doubleday, Doran, 1943.

Brown, M. W. Brown diary. Margaret Wise Brown Collection. 1940–1950. Series III, Box 15. Special Collections. Westerly Library, Westerly, RI.

Brown, M. W. Green diary. Margaret Wise Brown Papers. 1938–1960. MWB01. Special Collections. Wyndham Robertson Library, Hollins University.

Brown, M. W. "Leonard Weisgard Wins the Caldecott Award." *Publishers Weekly*, July 5, 1947.

Brown, M. W. Lucy Sprague Mitchell Papers. 1935–1952. Rare Book and Manuscript Library, Columbia University.

Brown, M. W. Luncheon with Michael Strange. Margaret Wise Brown Papers. 1910–1952. Special Collections. Wyndham Robertson Library, Hollins University.

Brown, M. W. Margaret Wise Brown Papers. 1940–1952. James S. Rockefeller Jr. Personal collection.

Gaston, T. Interview with author. 2014.

"Hunt Followers at Buckram Ball." Special to the *Times*. *New York Times*, March 31, 1940.

Mitchell, L. S. Lucy Sprague Mitchell Papers. 1878–1967. Rare Book and Manuscript Library, Columbia University.

"Room for a Child, Aged Four." *Contemporary American Industrial Art: 15th Exhibition.* New York: Museum of Modern Art, 1940.

Rockefeller, J. S., Jr. Interview with author. 2014.

Strange, M. Letters. Margaret Wise Brown Collection. 1940–1950. Special Collections. Wyndham Robertson Library, Hollins University.

Strange, M. *Who Tells Me True.* New York: Charles Scribner's Sons, 1940.

"The Walt Disney Story Books." *New York Times,* December 10, 1940.

Weisgard, L. Letters to Dorothy Ripley. 1990–1994. Laurel Ripley Galloway Collection.

Whitney, E. B. "Social Economy Engrosses Michael Strange, Author, Poet, Playwright, Now in Maine." *Lewiston Journal,* August 24, 1940.

Who's Who in America. New York: Marquis Publications, 1941.

Eleven
1941

Bliven, Bruce, Jr. Interview with author. 1990–1995.

"Book Review: A Penguin's Education." *New York Times,* December 7, 1941.

Brown, M. W. Brown diary. Margaret Wise Brown Collection. 1940–1952. Series II, Box 16. Special Collections. Westerly Library, Westerly, RI.

Brown, M. W. Composition book. Margaret Wise Brown Collection. 1941. Box 18, Folder 2. Special Collections. Westerly Library, Westerly, RI.

Brown, M. W. Green diary. Margaret Wise Brown Papers. 1947–1952. Special Collections. Wyndham Robertson Library, Hollins University.

Brown, M. W. Margaret Wise Brown Collection. 1910–1952. MB01. Special Collections. Westerly Library, Westerly, RI.

Brown, M. W. Margaret Wise Brown Papers. 1940–1952. James S. Rockefeller Jr. Personal collection.

Brown, M. W. "Notes on a Ski Town." Margaret Wise Brown Papers. 1943. Box 17. Special Collections. Wyndham Robertson Library, Hollins University.

Brown, M. W. Red diary. Margaret Wise Brown Collection. 1940–1950. Series II, Box 16. Special Collections. Westerly Library, Westerly, RI.

Brown, M. W. *Runaway Bunny.* New York: Harper and Brothers, 1942.

Brown, M. W. Unpublished manuscripts. Margaret Wise Brown Papers. 1910–1952. Series 1. Special Collections. Wyndham Robertson Library, Hollins University.

Frandzen, T. "James Boswell." 2004. Retrieved from http://www.jamesboswell.info/aboutjb.

Hare, M. Memories of Margaret Wise Brown. 1991. Laurel Ripley Galloway Collection.

Johnson, S. J. "Book Review: Brer Rabbit." *Library Journal,* January 1, 1942.

Kahn, E. J., Jr. "A Reporter at Large: Tallyho!" *New Yorker,* March 8, 1941.

Mitchell, L. S. Lucy Sprague Mitchell papers. 1878–1967. Rare Book and Manuscript Library, Columbia University.

Mitchell, L. S. "Margaret Wise Brown, 1910–1952." *Children Here and Now* 1, no. 1 (1953).

"New Apartments Planned and Under Construction." *New York Times,* December 22, 1929.

Rhueban, D. W. Interview with author. 2014–2015.

Runners, T. S. "A History." Thunderbolt Ski Run. 2014. Retrieved from http://www.thunderboltskirun.com/history.html.

Strange, M. Letters. 1940–1950. Margaret Wise Brown Papers. Special Collections. Wyndham Robertson Library, Hollins University.

Weisgard, L. Letters to Dorothy Ripley. 1990–1994. Laurel Ripley Galloway Collection.

Twelve
1942

"300,000 Acclaim Navy Day Parade; 10,000 March Down 5th Ave. in 2-Hour Demonstration-British Seamen in Line." *New York Times,* October 25, 1942.

Barrymore, D., and G. Frank. *Too Much, Too Soon.* New York: Henry Holt, 1957.

Bliven, Bruce, Jr. Interview with author. 1990–1995.

Brown, M. W. Brown diary. Margaret Wise Brown Collection. 1940–1952. Series II, Box 16. Special Collections. Westerly Library, Westerly, RI.

Brown, M. W. *Don't Frighten the Lion!* New York: Harper & Brothers, 1942.

Brown, M. W. Green diary. Margaret Wise Brown Papers. 1938–1960. Vol. Archives, Q-4a. Special Collections. Wyndham Robertson Library, Hollins University.

Brown, M. W. Lucy Sprague Mitchell papers. 1935–1952.

Brown, M. W. Margaret Wise Brown Collection. 1910–1952. MB01. Special Collections. Westerly Library, Westerly, RI.

Brown, M. W. Margaret Wise Brown Papers. 1940–1952. James S. Rockefeller Jr. Personal collection.

Brown, M. W. Red diary. Margaret Wise Brown Collection. 1940–1950. Series II, Box 16. Special Collections. Westerly Library, Westerly, RI.

Brown, M. W. Unpublished manuscripts. Margaret Wise Brown Papers. 1910–1952. Series 1. Special Collections. Wyndham Robertson Library, Hollins University.

Brown, M. W. Unpublished manuscripts. Margaret Wise Brown Papers. 1936–1952. Acc# 1-7/1993, Series 1. Special Collections. Wyndham Robertson Library, Hollins University.

Brown, M. W. *White Freesias.* Edited by A. Gary. Montevallo, AL: WaterMark, 1999.

Gaston, B. Interview with author. 2014.

"Leonard Thomas Obituary." *New York Times,* 1937.

"LGBT Mental Health Syllabus." Association of LGBTQ Psychiatrists. 2014. Retrieved from http://aglp.org/gap/1_history/.

"Love Filled Her Poems but Looted Her Life." *Milwaukee Sentinel,* October 11, 1942.

"Michael Strange Is Sued." *New York Times,* September 30, 1942.

Mitchell, L. S. Lucy Sprague Mitchell papers. 1878–1967. Rare Book and Manuscript Library, Columbia University.

Mitchell, L. S., and M. W. Brown. *Farm and City.* Boston: D. C. Heath, 1944.

Mitchell, L. S., M. W. Brown, et. al. *Animals, Plants, and Machines.* Boston: D. C. Heath, 1945.

Mitchell, L. S., M. W. Brown, et. al. *Teachers Guide for Animals, Plants, and Machines.* Boston: D. C. Heath, 1945.

"New Apartments Planned and Under Construction." *New York Times,* December 22, 1929.

Nordstrom, U. Letters. Margaret Wise Brown Papers. 1942–1952. Special Collections. Wyndham Robertson Library, Hollins University.

O'Hagan, A. "A Beautiful Club for Women." *Century,* LXXXI, December 1910, 216–224.

Officers, Members, Constitution & By-laws of the Colony Club. New York: Colony Club, 1945.

Parsons, L. "Studios Are Already on the Job Creating Movies about Women in Uniform." *Fresno Bee,* July 22, 1942.

" 'Profile' Died Lonely, Broke." *The Spokesman-Review,* 1942.

Rauch, R. Interview with author. 1987–1995.

Rhueban, Dr. W. Interview with author. 2014–2015.

Riley, N. "The Barrymore Brat." *Collier's,* October 3, 1942.

Strange, M. Letters. Margaret Wise Brown Papers. 1940–1950. James Stillman Rockefeller Jr. Personal Collection.

Strange, M. Diary. Margaret Wise Brown papers. James Stillman Rockefeller Jr. papers. 1943–1948.

Strange, M. Will, dated 1950. Margaret Wise Brown Papers. Special Collections. Wyndham Robertson Library, Hollins University.

"Suit Worn by Michael Strange." Rhode Island School of Design Museum. 2013. Retrieved from http://risdmuseum.org/art_design/objects/1733_suit_worn_by_michael_strange_pseudonym_of_blanche_oelrichs.

"Summer Theaters." *Life Magazine,* July 31, 1939.

Tweed, B. Interview with author. 2014.

Warren, V. L. "The Colony Club: It's Still Exclusive, Conservative and Ladylike." *New York Times,* July 21, 1968.

Weisgard, L. Letters. Margaret Wise Brown Papers. 1952–1985. Special Collections. Wyndham Robertson Library, Hollins University.

Weisgard, L. Letters to Dorothy Ripley. 1990–1994. Laurel Ripley Galloway Collection.

Wheeler, J. P. J. "Before the Writing Program there was Margaret Wise Brown." Paper presented at the Hollins University Alumnae Reunion, Hollins University, Roanoke, VA, 2003.

Wheeler, J. P. J. Interview with author. 1993–2001.

Thirteen
1943

Bays, R. B. "Stringfellow Barr." Encyclopedia Virginia. 2014. Retrieved from http://www.encyclopediavirginia.org/Barr_Stringfellow_1897-1982#start _entry.

Bliven, Bruce, Jr. Interview with author. 1990–1995.

Brown, M. W. Brown diary. Margaret Wise Brown Collection. 1940–1952. Series II, Box 16. Special Collections. Westerly Library, Westerly, RI.

Brown, M. W. Green diary. Margaret Wise Brown Papers. 1938–1960. Vol. Archives, Q-4a. Special Collections. Wyndham Robertson Library, Hollins University.

Brown, M. W. Red diary. Margaret Wise Brown Collection. 1940–1950. Series II, Box 16. Special Collections. Westerly Library, Westerly, RI.

Galloway, L. R. Interview with author. 2014.

Palmer, L. "For Younger Readers." *New York Times,* November 28, 1943.

Rauch, R. Interview with author. 1987–1995.

Ripley, D. Interview with author. 1996.

Ripley, D. Memories of Margaret Wise Brown. 1954–1995. Laurel Ripley Galloway Collection.

Rockefeller, J. S., Jr. Interview with author. 2014.

Rockefeller, L. Interview with author. 2013–2014.

Shure, K. Interview with author. 2013–2014.

Strange, M. Diary. Margaret Wise Brown papers. 1943–1948. James Stillman Rockefeller Jr. Personal Collection.

Fourteen
1944

Barrymore, D., and G. Frank. *Too Much, Too Soon*. New York: Henry Holt, 1957.

Brown, M. W. Biographical material. Margaret Wise Brown Papers. ca. 1945. Box 19, Folder 1. MWB 01. Special Collections. Westerly Library, Westerly, RI.

Brown, M. W. Brown diary. Margaret Wise Brown Collection. 1940–1952. Series II, Box 16. Special Collections. Westerly Library, Westerly, RI.

Brown, M. W. Brown diary. Margaret Wise Brown Collection. 1940–1950. Series III, Box 15. Special Collections. Westerly Library, Westerly, RI.

Brown, M. W. Composition book. Margaret Wise Brown Collection. 1935–1952. Box 16, Folders 5–7. Special Collections. Westerly Library, Westerly, RI.

Brown, M. W. *Goodnight Moon* manuscript. 1945. Kerlan Collection. University of Minnesota, Minneapolis, MN.

Brown, M. W. *Goodnight Moon: A 50th Anniversary Edition*. New York: Harper-Collins, 1997.

Brown, M. W. Margaret Wise Brown Collection. 1910–1952. MB01. Special Collections. Westerly Library, Westerly, RI.

Brown, M. W. Margaret Wise Brown Papers. 1940–1952. James S. Rockefeller Jr. Personal collection.

Brown, M. W. Margaret Wise Brown Papers. 1942–1959. Kerlan Collection. University of Minnesota, Minneapolis, MN.

Brown, M. W. Outgoing correspondence. Margaret Wise Brown Papers. 1934–1952. Series 5. Special Collections. Wyndham Robertson Library, Hollins University.

Brown, M. W. Red diary. Margaret Wise Brown Collection. 1940–1950. Series II, Box 16. Special Collections. Westerly Library, Westerly, RI.

"Dies from Broken Heart." *New York Tribune,* February 10, 1907. Retrieved from http://chroniclingamerica.loc.gov/lccn/sn83030214/1907-02-10/ed-1/seq-7/.

"Ex-Sailor Dies in Leap from 86th Floor of Empire State, Quarter of a Mile Drop." *New York Times,* December 17, 1943.

Galloway, L. R. Interview with author. 2014.

Hurd, C. Clement Hurd papers. 1936–1952. Kerlan Collection. University of Minnesota, Minneapolis, MN.

Hurd, C. Letters and presentation. Margaret Wise Brown Papers. 1952–1955. Special Collections. Wyndham Robertson Library, Hollins University.

Hurd, C. "Remembering Margaret Wise Brown." *Horn Book,* October 1983.

Krebs, A. "Wayne Lonergan, 67, Killer of Heiress Wife." 1986. Retrieved from www.nytimes.com/1986/01/03/obituaries/wayne-lonergan-67-killer-of -heiress-wife.html.

Little Lost Lamb advertisement. Doubleday Jr. Books. New York: *Parents Magazine,* 1945.

Mitchell, L. S. Lucy Sprague Mitchell papers. 1878–1967. Rare Book and Manuscript Library, Columbia University.

Mitchell, L. S., M. W. Brown, et. al. *Animals, Plants, and Machines.* Boston: D. C. Heath, 1945.

Mitchell, L. S., M. W. Brown, et. al. *Teachers Guide for Animals, Plants, and Machines.* Boston: D. C. Heath, 1945.

Nordstrom, U. Letters. Margaret Wise Brown Papers. 1942–1952. Special Collections. Wyndham Robertson Library, Hollins University.

Ripley, D. Personal papers. 1954–1995. Laurel Ripley Galloway Collection.

Strange, M. Diary. Margaret Wise Brown Papers. James Stillman Rockefeller Jr. papers. 1943–1948.

Strange, M. Letters. Margaret Wise Brown Papers. 1940–1950. James Stillman Rockefeller Jr. Personal Collection.

Weisgard, L. Letters. Margaret Wise Brown Papers. 1952–1985. Special Collections. Wyndham Robertson Library, Hollins University.

Fifteen
1945–1946

Bliven, Bruce, Jr. "Child's Best Seller." *Life Magazine,* December 1946. Retrieved from http://books.google.com/books?id=nk0EAAAAMBAJ&printsec =frontcover&dq=December+1946+life+magazine&hl=en&sa=X&ei =ojWsU67qKsecyAShv4KQDg&ved=0CDsQ6AEwBA#v=onepage&q =December%201946%20life%20magazine&f=false.

Bliven, Bruce, Jr. Interview with author. 1990–1995.

Brown, M. W. Composition Book. Margaret Wise Brown Collection, (1935-1952). Box 16, Folder 5-7. Special Collections. Westerly Library, Westerly, RI.

Brown, M. W. Composition book. Margaret Wise Brown Collection. 1946. Box 18, Folder 3. Special Collections. Westerly Library, Westerly, RI.

Brown, M. W. *Goodnight Moon: A 50th Anniversary Edition.* L. Marcus edition. New York: HarperCollins, 1997.

Brown, M. W. *The Little Island.* Garden City, NY: Doubleday, Doran, 1946.

Brown, M. W. Margaret Wise Brown Papers. 1937–1952. DG1129. de Grummond Children's Literature Collection. McCain Library and Archives, Hattiesburg, MS.

Brown, M. W. Outgoing correspondence. Margaret Wise Brown Papers. 1936–1952. Series 5. Special Collections. Wyndham Robertson Library, Hollins University.

"Here's Your 1945 Knockout for the Nursery Trade." *Publishers Weekly,* 1945.

Hurd, C. Clement Hurd papers. 1936–1952. Kerlan Collection. University of Minnesota, Minneapolis, MN.

Hurd, C. Letters and presentation. Margaret Wise Brown Papers. 1952–1955. Special Collections. Wyndham Robertson Library, Hollins University.

Hurd, C. "Remembering Margaret Wise Brown." *Horn Book,* October 1983.

Little Lost Lamb advertisement. Doubleday Jr. Books. *Parents Magazine,* 1945.

Nordstrom, U. Reviews of *Red Light, Green Light.* Margaret Wise Brown Papers. 1944. Special Collections. Wyndham Robertson Library, Hollins University.

"The Perfect Easter Book!: *The Runaway Bunny*." F. A. O. Schwarz postcard advertisement. New York: Harper & Brothers, 1938.

"Philippe Halsman." 2014. Retrieved from http://philippehalsman.com.

Publication catalog. New York: Harper & Brothers, 1946.

Strange, M. *Diary*. Margaret Wise Brown Papers. James Stillman Rockefeller Jr. papers. 1943–1948.

Strange, M. Brochure for Great Words with Great Music. Margaret Wise Brown Collection. Special Collection. Westerly Library, Westerly, RI.

Strange, M. Letters. Margaret Wise Brown papers. 1940–1950. James Stillman Rockefeller Jr. Personal Collection.

Various. Incoming correspondence. Margaret Wise Brown Papers. 1936–1952. Series 4. Special Collections. Wyndham Robertson Library, Hollins University.

Williams, G. *Little Fur Family* advertisement. New York: Harper & Brother, 1946.

Sixteen
1947

Bader, B. *American Picturebooks from Noah's Ark to the Beast Within*. New York: Macmillan, 1976.

Bader, B. "Only the Best: The Hits and Misses of Anne Carroll Moore." *Horn Book,* September/October 1997.

Barrymore, D., and G. Frank. *Too Much, Too Soon*. New York: Henry Holt, 1957.

Brown, M. W. Esphyr Slobodkina papers. 1938–1952. de Grummond Collection. McCain Library and Archives, Hattiesburg, MS.

Brown, M. W. *The Golden Egg Book*. New York: Simon & Schuster, 1947.

Brown, M. W. Green diary. Margaret Wise Brown Papers. 1947–1952. Unpublished. Special Collections. Wyndham Robertson Library, Hollins University.

Brown, M. W. "Leonard Weisgard Wins the Caldecott Award." *Publishers Weekly,* July 5, 1947.

Brown, M. W. *The Little Island*. Garden City, NY: Doubleday, Doran, 1946.

Brown, M. W. Margaret Wise Brown Collection. 1910–1952. MB01. Special Collections. Westerly Library, Westerly, RI.

Brown, M. W. Margaret Wise Brown Papers. 1940–1952. James S. Rockefeller Jr. Personal collection.

Brown, M. W. Outgoing correspondence. Margaret Wise Brown Papers. 1934–1952. Series 5. Special Collections. Wyndham Robertson Library, Hollins University.

Brown, M. W. Red diary. Margaret Wise Brown Collection. 1940–1950. Series II, Box 16. Special Collections. Westerly Library, Westerly, RI.

Clary, P. "Movie Colony in Free-For-All at Decker's Party." *United Press,* 1946. Retrieved from www.newspapers.com/image/56373311/?terms =diana+barrymore.

"Deaths." Obituary of Maude Johnson Brown. *New York Times,* January 12, 1947.

Dingle Benners Hotel. 2014. Retrieved from www.dinglebenners.com/index .html.

Galloway, L. R. Interview with author. 2014.

Gaston, W. Letters to the Editor. *Life,* 1949.

Hare, M. Memories of Margaret Wise Brown. 1991. Laurel Ripley Galloway Collection.

Kelly, B. "A Writer, an Illustrator, and a Peaceable Kingdom." *Christian Science Monitor,* December 10, 1984. Retrieved from www.csmonitor.com/1984 /1210/121024.html.

"*Life* visits Rector's for a Gay Nineties Party." *Life,* March 10, 1947.

McCormick, E. "Librarians Hate Us, but the Public Loves Golden Books." *American Libraries,* May 1981.

Pilpel, H. Letters. Margaret Wise Brown Papers. 1948–1952. Special Collections. Wyndham Robertson Library, Hollins University.

Pilpel, H. Legal papers. Margaret Wise Brown Papers. 1949–1952. Series 9. Special Collections, Wyndham Robertson Library, Hollins University.

Ripley, D. Memories of Margaret Wise Brown. 1954–1995. Laurel Ripley Galloway Collection.

Slobodkina, E. Esphyr Slobodkina papers. 1938–1952. Special Collections. Wyndham Robertson Library, Hollins University.

Slobodkina, E. Esphyr Slobodkina papers. 1938–1980. DG0905. de Grummond Collection. McCain Library and Archives, Hattiesburg, MS.

Strange, M. Diary. Margaret Wise Brown Papers. 1943–1948. James Stillman Rockefeller Jr. Personal Collection.

Strange, M. Letters. Margaret Wise Brown Papers. James Stillman Rockefeller Jr. papers. 1940–1950.

Various. Incoming correspondence—other organizations. Margaret Wise Brown Papers. 1948–1952. Folder 1. Special Collections. Wyndham Robertson Library, Hollins University.

Weisgard, L. Letters to Dorothy Ripley. 1990–1994. Laurel Ripley Galloway Collection.

Seventeen
1948

Brown, M. W. Correspondence from Margaret Wise Brown. Margaret Wise Brown Collection. 1936–1952. Box 19, Folder 1. Special Collections. Westerly Library, Westerly, RI.

Brown, M. W. Correspondence with Katharine Colie of the Grolier Society. Margaret Wise Brown Collection. 1949–1951. Box 19, Folder 5. Special Collections. Westerly Library, Westerly, RI.

Brown, M. W. *Creative Writing for Very Young Children*. New York: Grolier Society, 1951.

Brown, M. W. Green diary. Margaret Wise Brown Papers. 1947–1952. Unpublished. Special Collections. Wyndham Robertson Library, Hollins University.

Brown, M. W. Ideas for plays, records, television and radio. Margaret Wise Brown Collection. 1952. Box 15, Folder 9. Special Collections. Westerly Library, Westerly, RI.

Brown, M. W. Margaret Wise Brown Collection. 1910–1952. MB01. Special Collections. Westerly Library, Westerly, RI.

Brown, M. W. Outgoing correspondence. Margaret Wise Brown Papers. 1934–1952. Series 5. Special Collections. Wyndham Robertson Library, Hollins University.

Brown, M. W. Red diary. Margaret Wise Brown Collection. 1940–1950. Series II, Box 16. Special Collections. Westerly Library, Westerly, RI.

Brown, M. W. "Writing for Children." *Hollins Alumnae Magazine,* Winter 1949.

Campbell, J. Letter. 1949. Margaret Wise Brown papers. 1940–1952. James S. Rockefeller Jr. Personal collection.

Duplaix, G. Personal correspondence. Margaret Wise Brown Papers. 1945–1952. Folders 5a and 5b. Special Collections. Wyndham Robertson Library, Hollins University.

Ogle, L. Incoming correspondence—publishers. Margaret Wise Brown Papers. 1948–1952. Folders 5c and 5d. Special Collections. Wyndham Robertson Library, Hollins University.

Pilpel, H. F. Incoming correspondence—Greenbaum, Wolff & Ernst. Margaret Wise Brown Papers. 1950–1952. Folder 7. Special Collections. Wyndham Robertson Library, Hollins University.

Pilpel, H. Letters. Margaret Wise Brown Papers. 1948–1952. Special Collections. Wyndham Robertson Library, Hollins University.

Pilpel, H. Legal papers. Margaret Wise Brown Papers. 1949–1952. Series 9. Special Collections. Wyndham Robertson Library, Hollins University.

Strange, M. Diary. Margaret Wise Brown Papers. 1943–1948. James Stillman Rockefeller Jr. Personal Collection.

Strange, M. *Great Words with Great Music.* New York: 1945.

Strange, M. Letters. Margaret Wise Brown Papers. James Stillman Rockefeller Jr. Papers. 1940–1950.

Trager, H. G. "The Story of Ten Years of Young Scott Books." *Publishers Weekly,* April 24, 1948.

Various. Correspondence to Margaret Wise Brown. Margaret Wise Brown Collection. 1936–1952. Box 19, Folder 2. Special Collections. Westerly Library, Westerly, RI.

Various. Incoming correspondence. Margaret Wise Brown Papers. 1936–1952. Series 4. Special Collections. Wyndham Robertson Library, Hollins University.

Various. Incoming correspondence. Margaret Wise Brown Papers. 1952–1990. Series 8. Special Collections. Wyndham Robertson Library, Hollins University.

Various. Incoming correspondence—other organizations. Margaret Wise Brown Papers. 1948–1952. Folder 1. Special Collections. Wyndham Robertson Library, Hollins University.

Eighteen
1949

Bader, B. *American Picturebooks from Noah's Ark to the Beast Within*. New York: Macmillan, 1976.

Barrymore, D., and G. Frank. *Too Much, Too Soon*. New York: Henry Holt, 1957.

Brown, M. W. Correspondence with Katharine Colie of the Grolier Society. Margaret Wise Brown 1949–1951. Box 19, Folder 5. Special Collections. Westerly Library, Westerly, RI.

Brown, M. W. *Creative Writing for Very Young Children*. New York: Grolier Society, 1951.

Brown, M. W. Margaret Wise Brown papers. 1940–1952. James S. Rockefeller Jr. Personal collection.

Brown, M. W. "Stories to Be Sung and Songs to Be Told." *The Book of Knowledge 1952 Annual*. Edited by E. V. McLoughlin. New York: Grolier Society, 1952.

Brown, M. W. "Writing for Children." *Hollins Alumnae Magazine,* Winter 1949.

Cousins, M. Children's Page. *Good Housekeeping,* April 1948.

Dunne, I. L. *The American Hostess Cookbook*. Garden City, NY: Halcyon House, 1949.

Duplaix, G. Personal correspondence. Margaret Wise Brown Papers. 1945–1952. Folders 5a and 5b. Special Collections. Wyndham Robertson Library, Hollins University.

"Elementary Concerts." *New York Times,* October 7, 1949.

Galloway, L. R. Interview with author. 2014.

Hare, M. Memories of Margaret Wise Brown. 1991. Laurel Ripley Galloway Collection.

"Helen Hayes Theatre Celebrates 100th Birthday." Theatre Historical Society of America. 2012. Retrieved from www.historictheatres.org.

Hurd, C. Letters and presentation. Margaret Wise Brown Papers. 1952–1955. Special Collections. Wyndham Robertson Library, Hollins University.

Hurd, C. "Remembering Margaret Wise Brown." *Horn Book,* October 1983.

Ingram, E. D. "So Again Children's Books Are the Most Beautiful." *Kansas City Star,* December 3, 1949.

Ives, B. Letter. 1950–1951. Margaret Wise Brown Collection. Box 19, Folder 4. Special Collections. Westerly Library, Westerly, RI.

Kilgallen, D. Gossip in Gotham. *Pittsburgh Post-Gazette,* April 26, 1949.

Kilgallen, D. Jottings in Pencil. *Pottstown Mercury,* 1949.

McCormick, E. "Librarians Hate Us, but the Public Loves Golden Books." *American Libraries,* May 1981.

"Obituary for Yvonne Thomas." *Aspen Times,* September 4, 2009. Retrieved from http://www.aspentimes.com/article/20090904/OBITUARIES/9090 49988.

"Old Mother Hippletoe: Rural and Urban Children's Songs." *Anthology of American Music,* 2002. Retrieved from www.newworldrecords.org/liner_notes/80291 .pdf.

Pilpel, H. Legal papers. Margaret Wise Brown Papers. 1949–1952. Series 9. Special Collections. Wyndham Robertson Library, Hollins University.

Ripley, D. Interview with author. 1996.

Ripley, D. Personal papers. 1954–1995. Laurel Ripley Galloway Collection.

Simont, M. Memories of Margaret Wise Brown. 1991. Laurel Ripley Galloway Collection.

Strange, M. Letters. Margaret Wise Brown Papers. James Stillman Rockefeller Jr. Papers. 1940–1950.

Tynes, T. "At the Helen Hayes Theatre, A New Act for Second Stage." Walking Off the Big Apple. 2014. Retrieved from www.walkingoffthebigapple.com /2012/05/at-helen-hayes-theatre-new-act-for.html.

Young People's Record Time. New York: Young People's Record Club, 1949.

Zerbe, J. "The Newest Michael Strange Career." *Sunday Mirror Magazine,* February 1949.

Nineteen
1950

Brown, M. W. Brown diary. Margaret Wise Brown Collection. 1940–1952. Series II, Box 16. Special Collections. Westerly Library, Westerly, RI.

Brown, M. W. Correspondence from Margaret Wise Brown. Margaret Wise Brown Collection. 1936–1952. Box 19, Folder 1. Westerly Library, Westerly, RI.

Brown, M. W. *The Dark Wood of the Golden Birds.* New York: Harper & Brothers, 1950.

Brown, M. W. Green diary. Margaret Wise Brown Papers. 1947–1952. Unpublished. Wyndham Robertson Library, Hollins University.

Brown, M. W. Margaret Wise Brown Papers. 1940–1952. James S. Rockefeller Jr. Personal collection.

Brown, M. W. Outgoing correspondence. Margaret Wise Brown Papers. 1936–1952. Series 5. Wyndham Robertson Library, Hollins University.

Brown, M. W. *White Freesias.* Edited by A. Gary. Montevallo, AL: WaterMark, 1999.

"Dies from Broken Heart." *New York Tribune,* February 10, 1907. Retrieved from http://chroniclingamerica.loc.gov/lccn/sn83030214/1907-02-10/ed-1/seq-7/.

Gaston, T. Interview with author. 2014.

Kilgallen, D. Voice of Broadway. *Pittsburgh Post-Gazette*, April 26, 1949.

Lieberson, G. Incoming correspondence. Margaret Wise Brown Papers. 1950. Folder 1. Special Collections. Wyndham Robertson Library, Hollins University.

"Michael Strange Dies in Boston." *Newport Daily News,* November 6, 1950.

"Michael Strange in Hospital." *New York Times,* May 8, 1950.

Ogle, L. Incoming correspondence—Publishers. Margaret Wise Brown Papers. 1948–1952. Folders 5c and 5d. Special Collections. Wyndham Robertson Library, Hollins University.

Pilpel, H. Legal papers. Margaret Wise Brown Papers. 1949–1952. Series 9. Special Collections. Wyndham Robertson Library, Hollins University.

Rauch, R. Interview with author. 1987–1995.

Strange, M. Diary. Margaret Wise Brown papers. James Stillman Rockefeller Jr. Papers. 1943–1948.

Strange, M. Letters. Margaret Wise Brown papers. James Stillman Rockefeller Jr. Papers. 1940–1950.

Various. Incoming correspondence—other organizations. Margaret Wise Brown Papers. 1948–1952. Folder 1. Special Collections. Wyndham Robertson Library, Hollins University.

Weisgard, L. Letters. Margaret Wise Brown Papers. 1952–1994. Special Collections. Wyndham Robertson Library, Hollins University.

Weisgard, L. Letters to Dorothy Ripley. 1990–1994. Laurel Ripley Galloway Collection.

Twenty
1951

Brown, M. W. Correspondence with John McCullough. 1950. Margaret Wise Brown Collection. Box 19, Folder 3. Special Collections. Westerly Library, Westerly, RI.

Brown, M. W. Green diary. Margaret Wise Brown Papers. 1947–1952. Unpublished. Special Collections. Wyndham Robertson Library, Hollins University.

Brown, M. W. Lucy Sprague Mitchell Papers. 1935–1952. Rare Book and Manuscript Library, Columbia University.

Brown, M. W. Margaret Wise Brown Papers. 1940–1952. James S. Rockefeller Jr. Personal collection.

Brown, M. W. *Mister Dog: The Dog Who Belonged to Himself*. New York: Simon & Schuster, 1952.

Brown, M. W. *North, East, South, West*. Margaret Wise Brown Collection. 1936-1952. Box 7, Folder 1. Special Collections. Westerly Library, Westerly, RI.

Brown, M. W. *Willie the Whistling Giraffe*. Montevallo, AL: WaterMark, 1999.

Duplaix, G. Personal correspondence. Margaret Wise Brown Papers. 1945–1952. Folders 5a and 5b. Special Collections. Wyndham Robertson Library, Hollins University.

Galloway, L. R. Interview with author. 2014.

Hare, M. Memories of Margaret Wise Brown. 1991. Laurel Ripley Galloway Collection.

"History of the Barter Theatre." Barter Theatre. 2014. Retrieved from www
.bartertheatre.com/#historyalumni.

Krasnow, H. Incoming correspondence. Margaret Wise Brown Papers. 1951.
Folder 1. Special Collections. Wyndham Robertson Library, Hollins University.

Lustig, L. Incoming correspondence. Margaret Wise Brown Papers. 1948–
1951. Folder 4. Special Collections. Wyndham Robertson Library, Hollins
University.

Mitchell, L. S. Lucy Sprague Mitchell Papers. 1878–1967. Rare Book and
Manuscript Library, Columbia University.

Nordstrom, U. Incoming Correspondence. Margaret Wise Brown Papers.
1950–1952. Folder 3. Special Collections. Wyndham Robertson Library,
Hollins University.

Nordstrom, U. Letters. Margaret Wise Brown Papers. 1942–1952. Special
Collections. Wyndham Robertson Library, Hollins University.

Pilpel, H. F. Incoming correspondence—Greenbaum, Wolff & Ernst. Margaret
Wise Brown Papers. 1950–1952. Folder 7. Special Collections. Wyndham
Robertson Library, Hollins University.

Pilpel, H. Legal papers. Margaret Wise Brown Papers. 1949–1952. Series 9.
Special Collections. Wyndham Robertson Library, Hollins University.

Pilpel, H. Letters. Margaret Wise Brown Papers. 1948–1952. Special Collections. Wyndham Robertson Library, Hollins University.

Rauch, R. Interview with author. 1987–1995.

Ripley, D. Memories of Margaret Wise Brown. 1954–1995. Laurel Ripley
Galloway Collection.

Slobodkina, E. Esphyr Slobodkina Papers. 1938–1980. DG0905. de Grummond Collection. McCain Library and Archives, Hattiesburg, MS.

Strange, M. *Letters*. Margaret Wise Brown Papers. 1940–1950. James Stillman
Rockefeller Jr. Personal Collection.

Strange, M. Will, dated 1950. Margaret Wise Brown Papers. Special Collections. Wyndham Robertson Library, Hollins University.

Various. Incoming correspondence. Margaret Wise Brown Papers. 1936–
1952. Series 4. Special Collections. Wyndham Robertson Library, Hollins
University.

Various. Incoming correspondence. Margaret Wise Brown Papers. 1952–1990. Series 8. Special Collections. Wyndham Robertson Library, Hollins University.

Twenty-one
1952

AMB Cote D'Azur Èze. 2013. Retrieved from www.amb-cotedazur.com/eze-stunning-hilltop-village/.

Bliven, Bruce, Jr. Interview with author. 1990–1995.

Brown, M. W. *Goodnight Songs: A Celebration of the Seasons.* Edited by M. Mundy. New York: Sterling Children's Books, 2015.

Brown, M. W. Green diary. Margaret Wise Brown Papers. 1947–1952. Special Collections. Wyndham Robertson Library, Hollins University.

Brown, M. W. Margaret Wise Brown Papers. 1938–1960. Vol. Archives, Q-4a. Special Collections. Wyndham Robertson Library, Hollins University.

Brown, M. W. Margaret Wise Brown Papers. 1940–1952. James S. Rockefeller Jr. Personal collection.

Brown, M. W. Red diary. Margaret Wise Brown Collection. 1940–1950. Series II, Box 16. Special Collections. Westerly Library, Westerly, RI.

Brown, M. W. *The Sailor Dog.* New York: Golden Books, 1953.

Chèvre d'Or Èze. 2014. Retrieved from www.chevredor.com/uk/Château-chevre-d-or-eze-official-site.php.

Clark, J. *Cumberland Island Saved: How the Carnegies Helped Preserve a National Treasure.* Lexington, KY: Gravesend, 2014.

Dickinson, S. "Former Virginia College Student Leads in Children's Book Writing." *News Leader,* April 1, 1952.

Duplaix, G. Personal correspondence. Margaret Wise Brown Papers. 1945–1952. Folders 5a and 5b. Special Collections. Wyndham Robertson Library, Hollins University.

Feature of *Le Petit Lion.* 2014. Retrieved from http://www.amazon.com/Petit-Lion-Jacques-Photographs-Prevert/dp/B001GIY1F0/ref=sr_1_1?s

=books&ie=UTF8&qid=1440790409&sr=1-1&refinements=p
_27%3APrevert+Jacques%2F+Ylla.

Galloway, L. R. Interview with author. 2014.

Hare, M. Memories of Margaret Wise Brown. 1991. Laurel Ripley Galloway Collection.

Kirkus, V. "The House of a Hundred Windows." *Publishers Weekly,* April 1, 1945.

Martin, D. "Bruce Bliven Jr., 85, Author Who Brought Verve to an Assortment of Subjects." *New York Times,* January 14, 2002.

Nordstrom, U. Incoming correspondence. Margaret Wise Brown Papers. 1950–1952. Folder 3. Special Collections. Wyndham Robertson Library, Hollins University.

Nordstrom, U. Letters. Margaret Wise Brown Papers. 1942–1952. Special Collections. Wyndham Robertson Library, Hollins University.

Ogle, L. Incoming correspondence—publishers. Margaret Wise Brown Papers. 1948–1952. Folders 5c and 5d. Special Collections. Wyndham Robertson Library, Hollins University.

Pilpel, H. F. Incoming correspondence—Greenbaum, Wolff & Ernst. Margaret Wise Brown Papers. 1950–1952. Folder 7. Special Collections. Wyndham Robertson Library, Hollins University.

Pilpel, H. Legal papers. Margaret Wise Brown Papers. 1949–1952. Series 9. Special Collections. Wyndham Robertson Library, Hollins University.

Pilpel, H. Letters. Margaret Wise Brown Papers. 1948–1952. Special Collections. Wyndham Robertson Library, Hollins University.

Rauch, R. Interview with author. 1987–1995.

Rauch, R. Outgoing correspondence. Margaret Wise Brown Papers. 1952–1990. Series 8. Special Collections. Wyndham Robertson Library, Hollins University.

Rhueban, D. K. Interview with author. 2014–2015.

Ripley, D. Memories of Margaret Wise Brown. 1954–1995. Laurel Ripley Galloway Collection.

Rockefeller, J. S., Jr. Interview with author. 2014–2015.

Rockefeller, J. S., Jr. "Margaret Wise Brown and Cumberland." Chapter 5. Unpublished manuscript. Personal collection.

Rockefeller, J. S., Jr. "A Writer of Songs and Nonsense." Holding Ground. *The Island Journal,* 1994.

Rockefeller, L. Interview with author. 2013–2014.

Rockefeller, N. C. *The Carnegies & Cumberland Island.* Cumberland Island, GA, 1993.

Various. Incoming correspondence. Margaret Wise Brown Papers. 1936–1952. Series 4. Special Collections. Wyndham Robertson Library, Hollins University.

Various. Incoming correspondence. Margaret Wise Brown Papers. 1952–1990. Series 8. Special Collections. Wyndham Robertson Library, Hollins University.

Various. Papers relating to Margaret Wise Brown's death. Margaret Wise Brown Papers. 1952. Series 7. Special Collections. Wyndham Robertson Library, Hollins University.

Weisgard, L. Letters. Margaret Wise Brown Papers. 1952–1985. Special Collections. Wyndham Robertson Library, Hollins University.

Weisgard, L. Letters to Dorothy Ripley. 1990–1994. Laurel Ripley Galloway Collection.

Epilogue

Audet, L., and T. M. Rivicnus. "The Psychological Genius of Margaret Wise Brown." *Children's Literature in Education* 23, no. 1 (1990).

"Autopsy Fails to Show Cause of Diana Barrymore's Death." *Lodi News-Sentinel,* January 27, 1960.

Bechtel, L. S. "Margaret Wise Brown." Paper presented at the dedication of papers to Westerly Public Library, Westerly, RI. November 1956.

Bechtel, L. S. "Margaret Wise Brown: Laureate of the Nursery." *Horn Book,* June 1958.

Gussow, M. "Garth Williams, Book Illustrator, Dies at 84." *New York Times,* May 10, 1996.

"Leonard Weisgard." 2015. Retrieved from http://leonardweisgard.com.

Marcus, L. *Margaret Wise Brown: Awakened by the Moon.* Boston: Beacon Press, 1992.

Martin, D. "Bruce Bliven Jr., 85, Author Who Brought Verve to an Assortment of Subjects." *New York Times,* January 14, 2002.

Patterson, R. C., and M. W. Brown. "I Like People." New York: Golden Records, 1952.

Rockefeller, J. S., Jr. Interview with author. 2014.

Rockefeller, J. S., Jr. *Man on His Island*. New York: W. W. Norton, 1957.

Rockefeller, J. S., Jr. "A Writer of Songs and Nonsense." Holding Ground. *The Island Journal,* 1994.

Rockefeller, L. Interview with author. 2013–2014.

Saxon, W. "Edith Hurd, 86, Who Introduced the Planet to Young Readers, Obituary." *New York Times,* January 28, 1997.

Scout. "Will This 200-Year-Old Farmhouse Be Torn Down for Condos?" ScoutingNY.com, July 8, 2014.

"Thacher Hurd." 2011. Retrieved from http://thacherhurd.com.

Winters, E., and A. Pommer. *Exploring the Original West Village*. New York: History Press, 2011.

Index